UNVEILING

SHACKLES

A JOURNEY FROM DISCOVERY TO
EMPOWERMENT

Sun-Diya Kumar

Published by Hemingway Publishers

Cover design by Hemingway Publishers

ISBN: Printed in the United States

Dedication

I am grateful to my ancestors, whose struggles have paved the way for my freedom to live and write my thoughts. In recognition of the enduring relationships that shape our lives every day, I dedicate this book to my children, Dev and Cea, who have stood by me and supported me on this journey. I extend my heartfelt appreciation to my children's spouses, who listened and read my stories and were very supportive. And to my spouse, who encouraged me and has been my guiding light. This book is a testament to love, family, and community that has nurtured me throughout this journey.

Sun-Diya Kumar 2024

Table of Contents

Chapter 1

Slavery and Heritage

My family history starts in the 1920s on the shores of India, where the British enslaved people from India. Many Indians were coerced into boarding the awaiting ships and held against their will. Throughout generations, my family members have handed down the stories of their journey and enslavement. My ancestors on my father's and Mother's side told everyone that the Fiji "Girmit" era was known as a very difficult period for our people. My ancestors witnessed the torture and deaths of many during the journey to Fiji. It took my ancestors decades to talk about and fully disclose the harrowing stories of their plight.

The world at large referred to this period as the Indian indenture system, implemented by the British. The Indian indenture system was banned in 1917. It was not profitable anymore, and pressure from the Indian government eventually led to the termination of laborer contracts. Some colonies in the 1930s still received Indian migrants through different programs. The British migrated Indians from 1920 to 1938 using a new system referred to as assisted immigration. The end of the "Girmit" era, or as others called it, the indenture system, was an ongoing procedure that involved many colonies and countries. In my book, I will refer to it as the Girmit era to honor my ancestors.

My ancestors' fates were sealed to be slaves, to tend to the sugar cane fields. The British played on the naïve people's emotional well-being, enticing them that they would make lots of money or could have a better life in another country. A majority were taken against their will. Some, like my ancestors, were lured by touring the ships and then not letting them leave. *There are a lot of detailed accounts of the journeys of the enslaved Indians, and I would recommend searching under Fiji Girmit and reading it.* Our ancestors might have felt embarrassed about their enslavement, but I do not believe they have anything to be embarrassed about, as situations like this existed in many countries.

The only thing that made me sad was the entire history of enslavement, and the deaths of so many just broke my heart. The lack of accountability from the British government toward the enslaved people is deeply troubling, the inhumane treatment and exploitation of my ancestors and other enslaved individuals. The lack of recognition and accountability for their suffering is a dark era in the history of the British that cannot be erased. The British government should be responsible for the incident. To acknowledge the turmoil and suffering endured by the enslaved individuals would be a good start towards healing.

I watched an Indian Diplomat talking to Congress about the enslavement of Indians. He was seeking acknowledgment and accountability for all the enslaved individuals. My reaction was that this guy was amazing going up against the British. I wished I was seated there to see the reaction. This history cannot be denied as there is too much proof out there, and it is hard to hide something that has affected many different countries. It was good to get our ancestor's plight out in the open and demand justice. However, I feel that the British will never accept accountability and their role in the events that led to traumatic experiences for many individuals and the deaths of many.

The Ganges ship was the ship that brought my ancestors to Fiji, along with many other individuals during this time, embarked on journeys from India to the colonies that were long and perilous. These voyages often resulted in numerous deaths and diseases among the passengers, reflecting the harsh realities of migration. The mortality rate was very high, with an average of one out of six migrants perishing during the crossing. Onboard the ships; the Indians endured hardships like overcrowded living spaces, limited supplies, and insufficient sanitation. These factors, combined with violence, torture by whipping, and malnutrition, contributed to many deaths. Despite these hardships, the migrants aboard the Ganges ship and others remained vigilant. They endured these arduous journeys, clinging to the belief that their resilience and determination would eventually lead to freedom from their captors.

However, those who managed to survive formed strong bonds with one another due to their shared fate. They were stripped of their Indian identities and developed a new identity. The migrants, now known as Indo-Fijians, are part of the larger global Indian diaspora, which has displaced millions of people worldwide. Indo-Fijians made significant changes in Fiji, and these changes started with small rebellions. The Indo-Fijians helped with the economic, social, and cultural development of their new homeland while also preserving their Indian heritage.

Upon arrival in Fiji, the enslaved individuals were subjected to demeaning treatment, being processed and inspected like cattle. They went through examinations, with their height and weight recorded, and were checked for any physical defects. Each person was assigned a specific work detail and given a job title, thus giving more control to the British over every aspect of the enslaved people. Both the men and women toiled from early morning to late night. In the colonies, the imprisoned individuals began to resist and rebel against their British oppressors. One major aspect of the resistance was the significantly high birth rates. They recognized the strength of unity and stood together, regardless of their religion or background. And further realized they had a better chance of being successful in their rebellion.

For my ancestors and others in Fiji, resistance was an essential step in regaining their independence and identity. This resistance aimed to challenge the repressive and exploitative practices enforced by the colonizers. And revive their traditional Indian culture, which had been suppressed under British rule, by empowering Indo-Fijians and fighting for self-determination. Their journey was not without challenges. My ancestors had to contend with existing land ownership laws that favored the privileged class, making land ownership incredibly difficult.

Additionally, farming also came with its own set of hurdles, including environmental changes, disease epidemics, and, among others, which threatened their livelihoods. None the less, they persevered by gathering financial support through their communities and developing partnerships. With collective efforts, they not only gained access to land but also implemented new farming techniques, contributing to Fiji's rapidly increasing agriculture sector.

As I reflect on these memories, I am filled with a sense of gratitude and pride. The struggles and triumphs of my ancestors are a part of who I am, shaping my identity and guiding my path forward. I carry their legacy with me, a reminder of the strength and determination that runs through my blood. I honor their sacrifices by living a life of purpose and meaning and by never forgetting the journey that brought me here. *Their story is my story, a testament to the power of resilience and the enduring spirit of the human soul.*

I investigated my family's past and uncovered my grand-father's "Sanjappan" immigration pass, which revealed the specific region in southern India where our family originated. Upon sharing this discovery with my father and watching as he held the pass in his hand, he was moved to tears. Expressing gratitude for my efforts, he questioned what inspired me to seek out this information. I clarified that my curiosity and longing to comprehend our family heritage were the main driving forces behind my research. He then expressed his disappointment that none of my siblings seemed interested in exploring our roots or history, as they remained fully immersed in Western lifestyles, seemingly forgetting our Indian roots.

I provided reassurance to my father that I would continue to treasure and preserve our family's history, carrying forward the traditions and stories handed down by our ancestors. I hope to motivate our family to reconnect with their roots while taking pride in our cultural heritage and the traditions of our ancestors. It holds immense importance to me that future generations understand and value our ancestry, acknowledging the sacrifices and hardships faced by them. Preserving our roots and heritage is important, as it has a vital role in shaping our identity and steering our future path.

By delving into our family history, we have a deeper understanding of who we are and where we came from. Passing on this knowledge to younger generations enables them to respect and honor the sacrifices made by their ancestors, instilling a sense of belonging and pride in our cultural heritage. Embracing our past not only enriches our present but also ensures that the legacy of our ancestors endures for generations ahead.

My grandfather (Ajja) on my father's side was a well-known figure in Fiji, with tremendous wealth and influence within the Hindu community. He had acquired a significant amount of land through his smart business deals and was also known for his humanitarian pursuits. The unwavering commitment he had to his religious and personal ideals often caused conflicts within his family and social groups. Despite the challenges, he remained devoted to his three wives, a common practice in Indian culture but disapproved by some of his peers.

His determination earned him admiration from many, but it also led certain members of the community to pass judgment on his unconventional lifestyle, creating divisions within his social circles. In addition to his successful business and charitable endeavors within the Hindu community, he paved the way for success for many individuals in Fiji. However, his polygamous lifestyle and uncompromising beliefs did draw negative attention, causing further rifts within his family. My grandfather was a demanding and stern man who sometimes caused friction with his large family, especially his children.

My grandfather's impact on Fiji's history of supporting temples and my family's legacy has been undeniable. He was influenced by his era's cultural norms, life experiences, and upbringing. The interaction between cultural traditions, economic opportunities, and personal experiences influenced my grandfather's values and beliefs and defined him as a distinctive and intricate figure in our family history. For example, his commitment to traditional values despite changing economic circumstances highlights the complexity of his character.

His legacy continues to thrive through the preservation of our family's cultural heritage, showcasing the lasting impact of his decisions on future generations. His children and grandchildren actively uphold his values, traditions, and beliefs, ensuring that his influence remains strong in our family for generations to come.

As far as my grandfather's plural marriage, I think managing the psychological requirements and demands of multiple spouses can be overwhelming and difficult. Individuals cannot effectively divide their time and attention between multiple wives, especially when it comes to both quality and quantity. Managing each of the wives' feelings, as well as their interactions, is challenging, and it may result in a significant impact on the family's overall harmony and stability. Conflicts and strained interactions between the wives can hurt the children, causing emotional distress and turbulence as they witness the family's discord.

Living with many people under one roof can create friction and complicate matters. Issues like disagreements and discord about personal space can cause conflicts and also arguments. Plural bonds and extended families may not be healthy for everyone. Characteristics like possessiveness, trust issues, and envy can create complexities and strains in relationships. These marriages can reveal important aspects of a person's personality, such as highlighting negative or positive traits; it is crucial to understand that they involve significant issues and can deeply impact people's lives.

In polygamous marriages, favoritism was a significant issue based on personal experiences and family anecdotes. There was a tendency to favor one child or a specific wife in these marriages. The favoritism of certain family members, who cook meals based on preferences and do not eat together, causes tension and leads to resentment within the household. Accordingly, these actions led to feelings of exclusion and jealousy among family members, ultimately resulting in a breakdown of trust and communication within the family dynamics.

These experiences vividly highlight the challenging and distressing nature of life within a polygamous marriage in Fiji. The lack of equal treatment among family members also extended to other aspects of daily life, such as the allocation of resources and attention from the husband. This unequal distribution of love and resources created a toxic environment where competition and animosity thrived. Over time, the strained relationships and unresolved conflicts within the family became too much to bear, leading to a breakdown in unity and harmony. The stories of exclusion and jealousy within these marriages serve as cautionary tales about the complexities and pitfalls of navigating multiple relationships within a single household.

I often find myself contemplating the actions that could have been taken to avert the tragic suicide of my grandmother. Offering more support and understanding for her mental health struggles could have potentially made a difference. Had the family come together and openly discussed their feelings and needs, they might have found a better path forward. Regardless of the specifics, it is evident that seeing suicide as a solution is never the right choice, given the profound impact on everyone involved.

Suicide leaves a permanent scar on those left behind, causing a ripple effect of pain and questions that may never be fully answered. It is a stark reminder of the importance of mental health awareness and the need for open communication within families. Moving forward, I vow to prioritize these values in my own life and never underestimate the power of support and understanding in times of crisis. My grandmother's memory will always serve as a poignant reminder of the devastating consequences of not addressing mental health issues openly and honestly.

In my family's history of polygamous marriage, my father's presence served as a stark reminder of the intricate relationships and challenges involved. As my grandfather participated in multiple marriages, it resulted in challenges within the family. These complex relationships frequently lead to emotional and physical abuse, leading to traumatic experiences for certain individuals. Addressing and overcoming these challenges is crucial for ensuring the well-being and harmony of all individuals in polygamous marriages.

In polygamous relationships, open communication is a fundamental tool that can assist in addressing emerging issues, resolving conflicts, and ultimately strengthening the bond among family members. Building a foundation of trust and understanding is essential for the success and longevity of polygamous marriages. Regular assessments, conducted with the head of the household or a trusted individual, play a crucial role in proactively identifying and addressing issues, thereby ensuring the stability and health of relationships within polygamous families. Creating a nurturing and supportive environment is vital for fostering the growth and longevity of multiple marriages. Recognizing and acknowledging individual needs and emotions is crucial. In cultivating a harmonious and fulfilling relationship, family members must show compassion and understanding, especially in addressing mental health crises, to promote overall well-being and stability.

My grandmother felt burdened with isolation and hardship as a young, unmarried woman in Fiji. Despite facing societal constraints and a lack of resources, she found solace and optimism for a brighter future by marrying my grandfather. In a patriarchal society where men held authority and societal norms hindered a woman's progress toward independence, marriage often brought stability and a sense of security. For Grandmother, at age 13, marrying grandfather provided numerous opportunities, such as having a family, but also a sense of belonging and hope for a brighter future. Their union was not without challenges, as they faced financial struggles and societal judgment for their polygamous marriage at such a young age. However, Grandparents worked together as a team, supporting each other through thick and thin. Grandmother's decision to marry Grandfather ultimately proved to be a turning point.

My grandparents worked diligently in farming to ensure their family's well-being. In addition to working hard, they invested in farmland, laying the foundation for a brighter future by buying fertile land and making wise financial decisions. Despite enduring financial hardships and societal barriers, my grandmother's unwavering commitment to providing for her future children remained steadfast. Her decision to marry showcased her strength, perseverance, and determination. She demonstrated her foresight by proactively securing a better future for her loved ones. Their challenges became more overwhelming when my grandmother welcomed a baby boy in December 1937, significantly increasing the responsibility of caring for a baby.

My grandmother's life journey illustrates how societal norms, economic pressures, and personal aspirations can influence familial decisions. In Fijian society, there were strict expectations for women that were shaped by religious and traditional beliefs. Women had limited scope for personal aspirations. Therefore, it is important to create support systems, encourage good health, and promote understanding within families. Having honest and open conversations, seeking external support, and practicing self-care is important when navigating the challenges of plural marriages with kindness. Recognizing the unique paths of individuals and empowering them can lead to a more inclusive society that embraces everyone.

Governments should provide education and opportunities that can enhance autonomy and break cycles of dependency. By embracing agency and resilience, we aim to foster a culture of respect for diverse family dynamics. With understanding and empathy, we navigate familial relationships with solidarity, honoring diverse paths toward a better future. While government intervention can provide resources and support, it may also unintentionally perpetuate dependency by not encouraging individuals to take full responsibility for their growth and development. It is crucial to achieve a compromise between offering assistance and empowering individuals to navigate their paths toward autonomy.

Chapter 2

Inter-faith Love

When my father was only five years old, his mother tragically committed suicide. Due to her inability to deal with the difficult living conditions and the favoritism shown by her husband towards his other wives, the abusive behavior of the other wives towards her and her son. Grandmother's death left a deep wound in the family, especially for my father, who struggled to come to terms with the sudden loss of his mother. He grew up without a mother's love and support, which was a significant source of pain and trauma for him.

My father became vulnerable and defenseless. The stepmother's mistreatment of him inflicted abuse upon him. The stepmothers, driven by jealousy and insecurity, transformed his life into a relentless battlefield, harming his emotional well-being. Even though multiple marriages were culturally accepted and consensual, my father still met adversity and emotional turmoil. After the traumatic events, my grandfather's emotional wounds worsened, leading him to distance himself from those around him, including his own family.

The aftermath of his mother's death strained his relationship with his father and stepmother, making home life tumultuous. Despite his determination and resilience, the difficulties he faced were immense. This conflict within the home created a hostile environment, leaving my father vulnerable and deeply affected. He took on a significant amount of responsibility for his siblings' well-being at an early age as his father struggled to provide the necessary care and support.

As my father matured, he became increasingly dissatisfied with his father's strict rules. Feeling restricted by his family's traditional values, he longed for freedom and adventure. At fourteen, he boldly chose to leave home and carve his path. Although he wanted independence, it is important to remember that leaving home might not solve family or personal problems permanently and could be risky. It is important to stress that seeking help and talking openly with family members can offer practical alternatives to explore.

During a challenging period in his life, alone and isolated, my father refused to surrender and remained steadfastly focused on his aspirations. He learned to cultivate mental and physical resilience from a tender age as he tried to shape his path in life.

Engaging in diverse roles, such as serving as a tour guide and conductor for the Fiji Railroad, my father undertook arduous endeavors to earn a livelihood and sustain himself. Despite the hardships entailed by his work, it provided him with a consistent source of income, enabling him to fend for himself. Throughout his lifespan, my father kept an intense sense of independence. While he harbored enduring memories of the pain and resentment he held toward his father, refusing to allow these emotions to dictate his existence.

This inner strength and resilience became his source of guidance as he navigated the difficulties of life. He faced each obstacle with determination and a strong belief in his abilities. Despite the challenges he met, he always remained focused on his dreams and aspirations. His experiences shaped him into a strong, independent individual who was unafraid to take risks and pursue what truly mattered to him. Through it all, he remained a source of strength and inspiration, showing those around him the power of perseverance and self-belief.

Growing up and running away from home had a lasting impact on my father. It influenced his character and values. He learned to rely on himself and become self-sufficient, which is a valuable trait to have in life. His determination and resilience in challenging times were admirable. He was a fighter who never gave up. Despite experiencing a dysfunctional family, he did not let it define him. Instead, he used his experience as a source of strength. My dad's life story shows how strong he is. He's been through a lot, and the most defining quality he has is that he never gives up. He developed into a stronger individual, leaving his descendants a legacy of inspiration and perseverance. It is clear from the valuable lessons he learned and shared with our family. Despite facing adversity, my father showed us that transforming challenges into opportunities for growth and strength is reachable. He proved that, with utmost determination and a positive outlook, we can successfully navigate life's challenges and appear resilient and capable.

His steadfast belief in resilience acts as a guiding light for us, shaping our approach to challenges with courage and hopeful fortitude. His ability to remain optimistic in the face of adversity continues to inspire us to push through tough times with grace and strength. Through his example, he instilled in us the importance of perseverance and a positive mindset in overcoming obstacles. By setting a powerful example, he showed that anything is achievable. His life story serves as a constant reminder that our struggles can inspire and motivate others. It highlights how our experiences, both positive and negative, have the power to mold us into more robust, more resilient individuals.

When my mother, Nisha, was only 13 years old, she met my father at a local coffee shop. She was a slender, light-skinned

Muslim girl, while my father, towering at six feet, exuded a commanding presence with his broad build. Despite their physical differences, they developed a profound emotional connection that eventually led to love. After five years of facing challenges, my mother asked my father if he would eventually get married. While contemplating my mother's words, my father finally gathered the courage to propose to her.

In December 1966, they decided to elope, going against their families' expectations and traditions, which resulted in considerable backlash from various sources. Labeled as outcasts and faced with disapproval from their relatives, they met more challenges from rumors and malicious gossip that aimed to destabilize their relationship. Amid the turmoil, my parents courageously chose to sever ties with their families to safeguard their relationship. While it was a difficult decision for them, they understood the importance of their choice for their future. Despite facing financial and social obstacles as a newlywed couple, their commitment to each other remained unwavering. Their marriage had highs and lows like any other marriage except this one, which had challenges due to cultural expectations and pressures. Despite these difficulties, my father was determined to show that love knows no boundaries and that interfaith marriages can thrive amidst challenges. Despite the obstacles, my parents' love for each other never wavered.

My father always spoke highly of my mother, for she was more than just a supporting pillar to him; she was his best friend, the person he could openly confide in without fear of judgment. Together, they shared their deepest secrets, dreams, and fears, forming a bond that defied societal norms and stereotypes. Breaking barriers and cultural norms, they stood hand in hand, celebrating each other's achievements, facing challenges head-on, and cherishing moments of pure joy and laughter in defiance of societal expectations.

The essence of their family life was a beautiful tapestry woven with love and unity. They were engaging in activities, such as going on trips and playing games, that strengthened their bond and created lasting memories. They displayed mutual support and respect for each other. Through their interactions, our parents taught us the importance of kindness by volunteering, showed empathy toward each other, and fostered understanding through open discussions. Their home was a haven, with cozy nooks perfect for reading, walls adorned with cherished pictures of each child, and a backyard echoing with the joyful sounds of laughter, creating a sanctuary for personal growth and self-expression. Throughout his life, my father remained steadfast in his values and principles, never compromising his integrity despite facing obstacles and enjoying many victories. He held traditional beliefs about Hindu gender roles and always stood up for what he believed was fair and just as the head of our household. Together, they faced their challenges and grew stronger with each day. Whether it was financial or emotional struggles, they were there for each other. Even in tough times, their love supported them, guiding them through challenges and filling their lives with warmth and resilience.

The impact of a loving relationship on emotional healing and personal growth is remarkable. Mutually, they supported each other by facing their inner struggles and conquering fears and insecurities. Their connection created a safe space for self-discovery and vulnerability. Their bond empowered them to confront past traumas, embrace love and understanding, and support each other. Their love fostered personal growth and transformation. Despite the challenges my father faced within his family, he overcame them and created a new family filled with love and possibilities. My parents overcame every obstacle and remained devoted to each other. They had been married for 55 years. Empathy and affection for others can help overcome any obstacle and achieve success. My father exemplifies resilience, and his strength serves as a guide for overcoming challenges. I am also grateful for my mother and her love and support for him. Together, they have shown me the healing power of love, even in the face of deep wounds.

The shift in our family dynamics left Rani and me feeling like outsiders due to unfair treatment, which made us feel excluded and marginalized. I will clarify the theme of our family dynamics in future chapters to provide a deeper understanding of the challenges. As I entered a new phase of my life, my parents, with different religions (my father was Hindu, and my mother was Muslim), faced challenges in their relationship and marriage. Intrusions from family members and disputes about their union led my parents to elope, which meant they ran away to get married in secret. To understand the hostility in our family life and the mindset of our extended families, we must delve into the key discussions on the tensions between Hindus and Muslims.

Let us talk about the friction between Hindus and Muslims, which has been a long-standing issue in India with roots that go back generations. The animosity between the two religions often stemmed from their different religious beliefs. For example, Hindus worship multiple deities, while Muslims believe in the oneness of Allah. Conflicts and tensions between Hindus and Muslims have flared up at various times in history, and unfortunately, they continue to this day.

During the Indian independence movement, prominent figures like Mahatma Gandhi and Maulana Abul Kalam Azad led efforts to unite people from both Hindu and Muslim communities in the fight for independence. The goal was to create a secular nation that could support multiple religious and ethnic groups. Religious differences caused violence and conflicts throughout the world. The partition of India in 1947, which sought to divide the country into a

Muslim-majority Pakistan and a Hindu-majority India, was a traumatic event for many families and communities, leading to widespread displacement and loss. Despite efforts to bridge the gap between Hindus and Muslims and foster greater understanding and tolerance between the two groups, there is still work to be done. Prejudice and discrimination persist on both sides, perpetuating a cycle of fear and mistrust.

There are also many voices of reason and compassion in India who work tirelessly to bridge divides and promote unity and understanding among people of all faiths. After independence, the issue of communalism resurfaced, and tensions between the two communities remained. Unfortunately, the resentment was and still is directed towards individuals, blaming them for the decisions of the masses. This animosity also existed in colonialism because of the hatred that was passed down through generations. It can also be traced back to historical events such as the Mughal Empire's rule, which saw the emergence of Islamic culture and practices in India. The introduction of British rule further worsened the issue, as they employed a divide-and-rule policy that pitted different communities against each other to maintain their absolute control over India. This resulted in communal clashes and violence that continued even after India gained independence in 1947. The partition of India and the creation of Pakistan were defining moments in the history of the subcontinent. It was a result of decades of political and social unrest, with the Muslim elite demanding a separate state for themselves.

However, the partition led to the displacement of millions of people, with Hindus and Muslims alike forced to migrate across the newly formed borders. The violence that followed resulted in the deaths of hundreds of thousands of people, leaving a lasting impact on the population, with widespread injuries and trauma reported. The partition also had long-lasting effects on the relationship between India and Pakistan, leading to ongoing tensions and conflicts between the two nations. The scars of partition continue to shape the political landscape of the subcontinent to this day. Resentment and distrust between Hindus and Muslims continue to exist in India and other former colonies. Occasional acts of violence and bigotry keep the flame of hatred burning. The legacy of communal violence and the partition of India has left a deep and lasting impact on the subcontinent. The ongoing dispute over Kashmir, the Babri Masjid-Ram Janmabhoomi issue, and other events have further sown the seeds of discord and tension. The effects of communalism run deep, affecting social cohesion, economic development, and political stability in profound ways.

However, historical events have also fueled hatred and communal tensions. The demolition of Babri Masjid in 1992 sparked widespread violence and communal riots across India. The Indian Supreme Court later delivered a landmark Judgment in 2019, ordering the construction of a new mosque at a different site while rejecting the claim of restoration of the original site. The dispute over the Ayodhya site involves not just Hindus and Muslims but also other religious groups. While cultural exchange programs and interfaith dialogues are important initiatives, addressing underlying social and economic inequalities and power imbalances is crucial in promoting understanding and harmony between communities.

Government policies, the implementation of discriminatory laws, and the handling of religious conflicts have contributed to higher tensions between the two communities. Some argue that Hindu nationalist policies have led to the marginalization of Muslims and the promotion of Hindu supremacy; others argue that appeasement policies toward Muslims have resulted in a sense of entitlement and division between the two communities.

The hostility between Hindus and Muslims is a multifaceted issue. Various intricate factors have influenced people's beliefs. A comprehensive understanding of the historical, social, economic, and political circumstances contributed to the divide. Furthermore, fostering unity and understanding between these two communities requires a steadfast commitment.

It is often a perplexing question: *why should matters that do not directly affect an individual's life decide the course of action for so many?* These matters hold symbolic and cultural significance, shaping identities and influencing collective behaviors. However, the underlying motivation lies in a desire to naturally align themselves with larger entities and groups, seeking validation and purpose, thereby contributing to the success of their goals.

Exploring the complexities of hatred or dislike towards interfaith children proves to be challenging due to the emotional sensitivities involved. While the principle of equality among individuals is foundational, some prioritize their religious beliefs to the extent that they distort their faith with personal biases, fostering a toxic belief in their superiority. This distorted perspective may lead to the view that interfaith children are impure or inferior to those from a singular religious background. Moreover, the presence of interfaith children challenges established norms, inciting fear and resistance from those hesitant to embrace change.

It is important to note that these reasons for hatred or dislike towards interfaith children are not universal and do not apply to everyone. Many individuals embrace diversity and celebrate the richness that comes from different religious backgrounds. It is undeniable that there are segments of society where interfaith children face prejudice and discrimination. To address these issues, education and increased exposure to diverse perspectives are crucial. Promoting acceptance, understanding, and respect for all religions can help eradicate hatred and prejudice towards interfaith children. Encouraging dialogue and fostering environments where individuals can learn from one another's experiences and beliefs can also contribute to a more inclusive and harmonious society.

Our experiences have perplexed us even though we are siblings born to the same loving parents from different religious backgrounds. The way we are viewed and treated has evolved because of our society's advancement and modernity. Though it brings to light the injustices that Rani and I endured in the past because of our religious differences, this change in perspective might feel bittersweet.

Our family bond was overshadowed by societal animosity. Nevertheless, as society slowly embraces acceptance and tolerance, there is a glimmer of hope for a brighter future. We were denied acceptance simply because we belonged to two different faiths. Despite our parents' efforts to shield us from these conflicts, we could not escape the consequences entirely. As a result, we missed the valuable connections that typically develop within extended families, including relationships with grandparents, aunts, uncles, and cousins.

The complete rejection by our extended family to engage with us as children deprived us of the chance to challenge or alter their perspectives. The disappointment of being judged without a fair opportunity to display our inherent goodness lingers. The intricate interplay of emotions and biases in human behavior complicates the outcome, bespeaking the multifaceted nature of our feelings towards religious diversity. Through this lens, I have come to appreciate the richness and complexity of diverse religious practices, rejecting notions of one faith's superiority over another.

Being raised in an interfaith family has taught me the importance of open-mindedness and embracing differences. It has instilled in me the belief that diversity should be celebrated rather than feared and that there is much more to be gained from engaging with individuals from different religious backgrounds. However, I am aware that not everyone shares my perspective and that some individuals or communities still hold prejudices and biases against interfaith children. We need to advocate for education and dialogue to challenge misconceptions and promote inclusivity.

In conclusion, the dislike or hatred towards interfaith children arises from a range of factors, such as personal beliefs, societal pressures, and ignorance. Overcoming these biases requires promoting understanding, acceptance, and respect for all religious beliefs. Engaging in dialogue, education, and exposure to diverse perspectives can lead to a more tolerant and inclusive society.

From my own experience growing up in an interfaith family, I have learned the importance of respecting and appreciating different beliefs. This has not only strengthened my faith but also fostered understanding and unity with those from different religious backgrounds. It has instilled empathy, kindness, and acceptance in our diverse society. I realize that respecting other beliefs enriches my faith and deepens my understanding of spirituality. Experiencing multiple religions has broadened my perspective and emphasized that we all share common values.

To foster understanding and unity, we should cultivate empathy and celebrate our differences, regardless of religious affiliations. By offering support and breaking down religious barriers, we can create a space where differences become opportunities for growth and connection. Open-mindedness and human connection should take precedence over rigid religious boundaries. Through dialogue and mutual respect, we can strive for a society where religion becomes less relevant, allowing us to appreciate our shared humanity.

Embracing and celebrating mixed-faith families requires empathy, education, dialogue, and inclusive policies. Governments play a crucial role in promoting peace and understanding by supporting interfaith programs, providing resources, and enforcing laws that protect religious freedom. Together, we can create a more inclusive and harmonious world that values and respects diverse religious identities.

India and Pakistan might experience peace, harmony, and understanding if the Kashmir dispute is resolved. It might provide youngsters with diverse religious origins growing up in conflict-ridden areas that need more security and stability while also lessening their mental load. By fostering a more welcoming atmosphere where they can learn about and value the many different religious backgrounds, we have the chance to close the cultural divide that these children experience as they traverse their parents varied religious associations.

It would also pave the way for comprehensive religious education programs that emphasize tolerance and respect, allowing these children to understand their religious identities better. Additionally, resolving the conflict would contribute to an inclusive and accepting environment for interfaith children, reducing prejudice and discrimination based on religious differences. Overall, the resolution of the Kashmir conflict has the potential to foster unity, acceptance, and equality in the region and beyond.

Education plays a crucial role in promoting unity and understanding among individuals from diverse backgrounds, including interfaith children. Schools provide a platform for children to interact and learn from one another, fostering mutual respect and tolerance from an early age. By implementing interfaith education programs and promoting cultural exchange, schools can help break down barriers and prejudices, creating a more inclusive and harmonious society.

Teaching children about the contributions of diverse -
cultures and celebrating diversity in the curriculum helps them
develop important social skills such as empathy, communication,
and problem solving. This enables them to navigate conflicts
constructively and fosters positive relationships with individuals of
differing faiths.

The media also plays a significant role in shaping public
opinion and promoting positive narratives about interfaith harmony.
By portraying diverse religious communities in a respectful and
unbiased manner, the media can contribute to building bridges of
understanding and acceptance. Highlighting stories of cooperation
and shared values among different faiths can help create a more
inclusive society. Through positive representation and storytelling,
the media can play a vital role in promoting interfaith harmony and
fostering a culture of mutual respect and appreciation for diversity.
From an early age, the values of acceptance and respect for all
religions were instilled in me, as my family consisted of individuals
from various faiths, including Hinduism, Islam, and Christianity.
My father emphasized the importance of treating every individual
with respect, regardless of their religious beliefs, and encouraged me
to keep an open mind towards differing viewpoints.

As I matured, I saw firsthand the significance of respect for
and acceptance of other religions. Observing people from diverse
faith backgrounds come together and collaborate towards common

goals, irrespective of their beliefs, underscored the idea that mutual respect and understanding transcend religious differences. It became clear that a person's religion should not dictate how they are treated and that kindness and empathy should form the basis of all interactions.

Looking back at the mid-eighties, I draw upon firsthand experiences with my Muslim extended family. Their unwavering respect and love for me, like that for their very own, shines through brightly. Conversations flowed freely, devoid of constraints, allowing for openness and understanding. Beyond these foundational pillars of respect and love, their consistent support and acts of generosity stand out prominently. Whenever I found myself in need of a listening ear or comforting presence, I always found solace in their constant support. In moments when I sought a reprieve from my parents, they graciously offered the warmth of their home as a refuge. Their son, embodying selflessness, went the extra mile by offering his room, ensuring my comfort during my stay. These gestures of care and willingness to provide unwavering support left me not just accepted but truly cherished and embraced.

Amidst the backdrop of rampant religious conflicts and intolerance in our world, it becomes crucial to navigate through the complexities by embracing cultural diversity and religious pluralism. Engaging in meaningful interfaith dialogues and accepting the beliefs of others can serve as catalysts for enriching not only our lives but also our communities. Diversity ought to be seen as an asset that fosters harmony and mutual respect among individuals of diverse faith backgrounds.

By actively learning and appreciating the different religious perspectives, I can forge strong connections with individuals from diverse backgrounds and contribute to the creation of a more peaceful and cohesive society. Embracing religious diversity and promoting acceptance is a crucial step towards fostering a world where differences are celebrated and unity prevails.

When I started high school, I met a guy named Zayn. He was quite a character with his long, curly locks and outlandish attire. His bold array of colors made his shirt so vibrant that it dimmed the sun, and his tight pants, featuring the famous bell bottoms, made me and my friends think they would rip if he sat down. Our paths crossed at Queen Elizabeth Park, where I used to hang out and watch friends drag race. We were all drag racing enthusiasts in grades 8, 9, and 10. Our friendship bloomed, and we connected because we were both rebellious teenagers. It turned out that both of our families were also rigid and conservative.

Zayn came from a unique religious background, with a Muslim father and a Hindu mother. It was a different mix from my own family, where my dad was Hindu, and my mom was Muslim. This blending of practices and beliefs provided an intriguing dimension to our friendship. As we got closer, Zayn talked about his curiosity to explore his mother's religion; he felt that his father's faith was restricting his personal growth. Initially, I struggled to fully understand Zayn's desire to delve into his mother's faith. To me, his actions seemed bold and unconventional, challenging societal norms that dictate following the religion of one's father in Muslim and Hindu cultures.

However, as time passed, I began to understand the depth of his search for identity and a sense of belonging, just like myself. It was then that I realized the significance of our journeys. Zayn would always say, 'You and I should get married because you are half, and I am half; together, we can become whole.' However, I would laugh at him and say, 'You are crazy.' Though we stayed just friends throughout high school, our bond grew stronger with each passing day. Zayn became more than just a friend; he became my older brother figure, offering guidance and support whenever I needed it.

Reflecting, Zayn's friendship spanned from drag racing adventures to profound conversations about religion and identity during our high school years, shaping our connection and fostering our personal growth. Even though our paths diverged after the tenth grade, the memories of our bond are indelibly etched in my mind, serving as a testament to the depth of our friendship. Looking back on this phase when Zayn was an integral part of my life, I am filled with a blend of nostalgia, gratitude, and introspection. Our friendship, rooted in our shared backgrounds and divergent beliefs, was a voyage of mutual understanding and growth. The merger of our parents' religious backgrounds and the different paths we chose to tread added layers of complexity and richness to our relationship.

As Zayn explored the two religions and his quest for identity, I, too, embarked on a parallel journey of self-discovery. His words about us completing each other, despite my first amusement, resonated with me on a deeper level as the years passed. Our shared experiences shaped us in ways we could not have imagined. While life took us down separate paths after high school, the memories of our time together remain vivid and cherished.

Looking back on that chapter of my life, I am grateful for the meaningful friendship we shared and the profound impact it had on my personal growth and understanding of the world. Reflecting on the influence Zayn had on my life, I often find myself pondering the hypothetical scenario of him being my real brother. Would he have stood idly by as my father subjected me to abuse as a victim of deeply entrenched gender biases?

Would his progressive and contemporary views on societal norms have sparked a different response—a stance of unwavering support and advocacy for equality? These questions linger in my mind, prompting me to explore the complexities of family dynamics, cultural influences, and the transformative power of empathy and understanding. As my narrative unfolds, the impact of Zayn's friendship on my beliefs, soul searching for my identity, relationships, and societal expectations will be further explored and dissected, revealing layers of introspection and revelation yet to be unveiled.

Chapter 3

Life Changes

In the heart of a bustling household in Fiji, where my mother tirelessly managed the family and home, a significant event unfolded in 1967: the arrival of a new princess, Rani; unknown to them, their lives were about to embark on a rollercoaster of drama. The next year, in July 1968, heralded the arrival of another bundle of joy, Sundi (me), into the expanding clan. A baby girl later became known for her goody-two-shoes attitude, always striving to go by the book.

Meanwhile, my father's unrelenting dedication to the vibrant tourism industry and bustling railway industry never wavered as he diligently saved money for his expected journey to Canada. His aspirations remained steadfast despite the challenges he faced. To provide his family with a better life, shielded from the strife and discord that had plagued their household, remained at the forefront of his efforts.

The departure of Father in 1969 marked a significant juncture in the family's narrative. As he ventured to Canada in pursuit of opportunities that promised an escape from the turmoil that once engulfed our lives, my father navigated the realms of Canadian life; the stark contrasts between his accustomed cultural norms and the newfound freedoms and cultural nuances in Canada discernibly shaped his outlook. His observations of a society that had a lack of personal involvement stood in stark contrast to the closely-knit familial bonds and cultural impositions he had known.

While my father's migration tale illuminates a distinct perspective on adaptation and cultural assimilation, it is essential to acknowledge that individuals may traverse varied paths and harbor diverse viewpoints based on their unique backgrounds and life circumstances. My father's venture to Canada was a formidable - test, unveiling the struggles of starting anew in a foreign land. Despite his ability in English, the adjustment proved arduous. Recounting his immigration experience, my father often shared - how officials altered his name from "Sanjappa" to "Sanjappan" due to pronunciation difficulties. His primary goal was migration, so he agreed without dispute. This narrative casts light on the challenges faced by individuals who do not align with dominant cultural standards, underscoring the importance of fostering greater understanding and inclusivity in immigration processes.

Through perseverance and determination, my father overcame the hurdles, eventually securing his place as a proud citizen of his adopted homeland. Grateful for the opportunity to embark on a fresh chapter in Canada, he toiled diligently to forge a more promising future for himself and his loved ones. My father's odyssey epitomizes resilience and determination in looking to set up roots in an unfamiliar land. While in Fiji, my mother, Rani, and I faced significant challenges. My mother struggled to support us, relying on my father's half-siblings for help.

When my father initially arrived in Canada, he met hardships as the family he stayed with took advantage of him, claiming his entire paycheck. This left him in a difficult financial situation, affecting his ability to support his family. My father had to adjust to his new life in Canada while fulfilling his obligations to his loved ones. His journey to Canada was successful; he was able to overcome these obstacles and succeed in creating a new life in Canada. Immigration is a complicated and alienating process that can challenge even resilient individuals. He was focused on trying to build a better life for himself and his family without realizing the repercussions of his actions for those he left behind.

The emotional toll of immigration is significant and cannot be overstated. We must provide support and understanding to those undergoing this challenging journey. Additionally, immigration is a complex issue encompassing legal and social dimensions. Legal barriers, like restrictive immigration policies and visa requirements, can hinder family reunions and prevent individuals from achieving their aspirations. Immigrants face challenges such as social barriers, discrimination, and limited access to vital services. Other factors, like financial instability, make it challenging for them to assimilate.

A welcoming environment can help immigrants overcome obstacles and thrive in their new communities. Providing resources is being done right now, but more needs to be done. Possibly creating a better immigrant support group, like a life coach, that focuses on individual families and on the steps needed to assimilate might help ease the burden. This support group could offer practical guidance, emotional support, and a sense of community for immigrants.

Additionally, reducing high application fees and providing access to affordable legal representation can alleviate the financial pressures faced by immigrants striving to create a better future in a new country. Regular immigration appointments can add to the anxiety and pressure experienced by immigrants, intensifying the challenges they meet on their journey. By creating a more welcoming and supportive environment, immigrants can receive the help they need to integrate into their new communities successfully.

These systemic barriers perpetuate inequality and injustice in the immigration process, highlighting the need for comprehensive reform to ensure fair and accessible pathways for all individuals looking to build a new life in a foreign land. We must strive to create an inclusive and welcoming environment for immigrants. In which they feel safe, valued, and empowered to contribute to their communities. This involves providing language training, education, healthcare, and other essential services to help newcomers adjust to their unfamiliar environment.

My father eventually found tranquility and community through the Hare Krishna movement. Participating in cultural events and forming friendships with like-minded individuals strengthened his feeling of belonging. As he became more involved in the community, he realized how much he missed all of us. Father worked even harder to bring us to Canada, where we could reunite and begin our family life together. Throughout his journey, he recognized the importance of keeping ties to his heritage while embracing the possibility of a fresh start.

My father's perseverance and determination to overcome the challenges of the immigration process serve as a reminder of the resilience and strength that immigrants often show in pursuit of a better life. His narrative illustrates the sacrifices, challenges, and victories met by immigrants, highlighting the necessity of compassion, aid, and empathy from the wider community. By sharing his experiences, the goal is to shed light on the realities of immigration and inspire empathy toward those embarking on similar paths.

My uncle played a vital role in helping us with the migration process, helping us organize documents, and booking our flights. This was especially important as my mother, who did not speak English, faced more challenges throughout these tasks. With heavy hearts, my mother, Rani, and I bid farewell to our families in Fiji, preparing to embark on a new journey to Canada. The farewell evoked a mix of sorrow and anxiety as we left to reunite with our father in a distant land. Although the joy of reuniting with him after two years was exhilarating, my mother could not shake off the uncertainties about our future in this new chapter of our lives.

As we boarded the flight, Rani and I quickly dozed off, oblivious to the distance we were flying. Meanwhile, my mother's mind raced with thoughts of what awaited us at our destination. Eager to see our father again, she could not shake off the worry that he might not be there to welcome us. The journey was a mix of anticipation and anxiety, with my mother contemplating the possibilities and outcomes of our reunion. Upon arriving in Canada in 1971, our father and his friends warmly welcomed us, providing a temporary place to stay. This section of our migration was based on my mother's perspective and recollection.

My father shared the difficulties that immigrants often meet and stressed the significance of being cautious of those who could exploit us. He stressed this concern, advising my mother against disclosing too many details about our personal lives to strangers, as our matters were private and did not require sharing. This time constituted a period of transition and adaptation for Mother, Rani, and me. My father tried to protect Mother from being taken advantage of like he was when he first came to Canada.

I remember Praveen, the daughter of my father's cousin, who was older than Rani and me. Once, she sneaked downstairs to share leftovers from her dinner with us. Sadly, her mother caught her and prohibited any further sharing. Although Praveen cherished our family and respected her parents' rules, which Father understood but found disappointing, he made it clear to his cousin that, had he been present, such incidents of sharing leftovers would not have occurred.

When I ran into Praveen during high school, she apologized for not standing up to her parents' rules all those years ago. I reassured her that she did not have to carry that guilt, explaining that parents often wield significant influence over their children, regardless of their parenting style. Whether they are warm and nurturing or cold and controlling, parents can shape our decisions and values during our formative years. I recalled my struggles with my parents' expectations and how it is natural for children to feel torn between pleasing their parents and staying true to themselves.

By acknowledging this common struggle, I hoped to help Praveen let go of her regret and move forward.

Nevertheless, I am grateful that this incident influenced my father's mindset and commitment to ensuring that others would not have to endure the same hardships around lack of food as our family did. Father held a deep conviction, ensuring no one went hungry. With time, as my father matured, he took it upon himself to help feed homeless individuals in need. Witnessing his efforts, I learned the importance of lending a hand to those who are less fortunate. Reflecting on that childhood memory, I understand that the core issue was children seeking access to food and essential help. It is heartbreaking to see individuals who solely prioritize their interests and ignore the needs of those in hardship.

The absence of empathy and self-centered behavior shown by some adults profoundly saddens me. How could anyone ignore the plight of innocent, hungry children in such dire circumstances? This situation further prompts me to contemplate values and morals. This realization fueled my passion for helping others and being an advocate for those who are marginalized or in need. I recognized the power of empathy and how it can influence someone's life.

It was about being present, showing compassion, and offering a listening ear. To stand up for what is right and use my voice, it is critical to act and not ignore those who are suffering. To make a constructive impact on the world at large and inspire others to do the same. It is crucial to show by our actions and not simply turn away from those who suffer.

As we started our new life in Canada, my family faced incredibly challenging circumstances, grappling with extreme poverty and a lack of necessities such as beds, clothing, and food. My parents went without meals for several nights so my sister Rani and I could have enough to eat. During the night, as we lay on the cold floor, my mother's saree was our only source of warmth and comfort. Despite these harsh conditions, my father always exuded a sense of positivity and hope, assuring us that things would improve with time.

Even in the face of poverty and sacrifice, my father's unwavering optimism changed our mentality. Gathered around us, he shared stories of individuals who had turned their lives around despite battling similar hardships. These tales served as beacons of hope, reminding us that our circumstances did not have to define us. My father was a person of action, tirelessly toiling long hours at multiple jobs to make ends meet. Despite coming home exhausted, he always managed to keep a smile on his face, assuring us that his efforts would not go in vain and that each day brought us closer to financial security.

Alongside his hard work, my father's resourcefulness and creativity shone through. He took on odd jobs for neighbors, repaired things, and found ways to cut costs without compromising our well-being. He never gave up and always found a way, no matter how tough things got. Beyond his actions, it was his unwavering belief in us that kept our spirits high. He often reminded us of our strengths, inspiring us to dream big and pursue our aspirations. His teachings showed us that setbacks were transient obstacles and that we held the power to overcome them. After enduring several difficult living situations, my father finally secured a rental place - in 1972. My mother stayed at home to care for us. Unlike many - other families in the neighborhood, we did not own a television and spent much of our time playing outdoors. As newcomers to the community, we found ourselves isolated at times, lacking familiarity with anyone in the area.

I vividly remember the arguments our parents had about money and the sacrifices they made to keep our family afloat. Both expressed frustration and anger about their situation, often forgetting that my sibling, Rani, and I were caught in the middle. These heated moments made it seem like our parents were fighting with each other, but we eventually realized that they were fighting for us. The sense of belonging, friends, and family was lost, and starting over in a new land created uncertainty and discord between our parents.

I believe that any family who migrates goes through similar challenges. I am amazed by the strength and resilience my father displayed during these tough times. His unwavering optimism encouraged us to keep going, even when things seemed dire. His reassurances gave us hope and taught us that with demanding work and a positive mindset, we could overcome any obstacle.

As the years passed, we became a close-knit family with a solid foundation built on love, gratitude, and hope. We knew that tough times might come again, but we also knew that we had the power to face them head-on, just like our father did. And for that, I am forever grateful for his wisdom, perseverance, and belief in a brighter future for our family. Through his example, he taught us the importance of staying unified and supporting one another through thick and thin. He showed us that no matter how difficult the circumstances might be, love and hope can conquer all.

As we experienced various milestones together, including high school and college graduations, weddings, and the birth of children, our family bond deepened. My father's unwavering presence and constant encouragement instilled in us the belief that we could overcome any challenges that came our way. During moments of stress or uncertainty, my father always reminded us to focus on the blessings in our lives and find gratitude in even the smallest things. His gratitude had a ripple effect within our family, creating a positive and uplifting atmosphere.

Most importantly, he instilled in all of us a sense of hope and optimism for a better future. He stayed steadfast in his vision of success and happiness for our family, even during the toughest times. His belief in our potential gave us the determination and drive to persevere through any hardships. Reflecting on the passage of time, I am overwhelmed with gratitude for the invaluable teachings that my father bestowed upon us. His lessons in love, gratitude, and hope have served as a solid foundation for our family, guiding us through life's trials.

While our father passed away, his spirit lives on within each of us, prompting us to embrace each new day with a full heart and a hopeful outlook. His influence is still a driving force within us, encouraging us to face challenges with love and resilience. As we confront the uncertainties that lie ahead, we find solace in the enduring of our father. His wisdom continues to resonate within us, urging us to strive for personal growth and embody the values he holds dear. Armed with his teachings and the constant support of our family, we are prepared to confront any obstacle that comes our way. For this steadfast legacy, I am forever grateful.

Father often expressed his frustration to our mother that she was not trying to adapt to their new life in Canada. He would worry about her struggling to communicate in English and how it was affecting her relationship with everyone. Rani and I would help her practice writing every evening after dinner. It was a slow process, but eventually, she began to pick up bits of English. I remember being so proud when she finally learned to write her name and recognize it - it was a small victory but a significant one. As she started working at the UBC cafeteria, she would come home each day exhausted but exhilarated, recount her day with us and stories about the food they served like macaroni and cheese, and the people she met. It was amazing to see her confidence grow as she navigated this new world. But despite her progress, I remember feeling a twinge of sadness when she told us she did not see the point of learning how to read or write - it was as if she was giving up on a part of herself.

Our parents worked tirelessly to support our family. Rani and I spent most of our time under the care of a babysitter. Sadly, the elderly sitter from India was not the most attentive; she preferred gossiping with friends and taking long naps during the day. The situation deteriorated when she began mistreating Rani, even resorting to twisting her ear as a form of discipline. Courageously, Rani spoke up about the abuse to our parents, resulting in the immediate dismissal of the babysitter. With no relatives nearby to offer support or share our burdens, those early years posed undeniable difficulties for us.

Adjusting to life in Canada was initially challenging for our mother. She expressed feelings of homesickness for her family and friends, as well as the familiar customs and culture she was accustomed to in Fiji. She often longed to return to her homeland, where family values and traditions were more prominent. Further more, she saw the differences in attire and body coverings in Canada compared to Fiji, noting the absence of sarees and traditional clothing. Despite her struggles, our father continuously encouraged her that learning to adapt to the new environment was crucial for building a life in Canada.

After months of working at the UBC cafeteria, our mother finished her shift one evening and headed to the bus stop to make her way home. As she walked, she noticed a car trailing her. Suddenly, a male driver pulled up and tried to pull her into his vehicle forcibly. In a courageous act, she fought back against the man, drawing attention from nearby students who rushed to her aid, causing the assailant to flee the scene in haste. Unfortunately, our mother's inability to write in English prevented her from noting down the vehicle's license plate. She was taken back to UBC, where the authorities were called to handle the situation. The police contacted our father, and we hurriedly drove to pick up our mother.

Upon our arrival, we were met with the sight of our distressed and tearful Mother, which also caused us to break down in tears. Our father, seething with anger towards the perpetrator, drove around with us in search of the man, while our mother, in her anxious state, questioned him about his intentions if he were to catch the culprit. Despite her turmoil, our mother wisely suggested leaving the matter to the police. Sadly, a few weeks later, the authorities informed our father that the man had not been apprehended.

This harrowing incident left our family on high alert and vigilant in the days that followed. After the terrifying incident, our mother no longer felt safe walking alone, and we made sure to go with her whenever possible. She decided to stop working at UBC and stay home, as the event had significantly affected her mental well-being, causing her to struggle with anxiety and fear. Our family provided all the support for our mother during this challenging time, creating a safe space for her to express her emotions.

Although the perpetrator was never apprehended, we took comfort in the fact that our mother managed to fight back and escape unharmed, serving as a stark reminder of the importance of staying vigilant in potentially dangerous situations. This traumatic event brought our family closer together. We became more supportive of one another and prioritized each other's safety. It also instilled in us a greater appreciation for the small joys in life and reminded us not to take anything for granted.

Recalling the incident involving our mother, it was a terrifying experience that taught us valuable lessons about resilience, unity, and the significance of personal safety. Throughout her healing journey, we continued to support her and ensure she felt safe and loved. As she aged, we remained vigilant, always watching over her and recommending that she not go anywhere alone. Our father's insistence on keeping the incident from extended family members aimed to shield our mother from harm and judgment.

However, our family's reputation and dignity carried such profound weight, especially given our limited connections in the foreign country we lived in, which raises questions about the value placed on these aspects. A Canadian immigration official changed our family name, but our father remained steadfast in prioritizing the preservation of our family's reputation and dignity. The irony is clear in the fact that rectifying the immigration officer's mistake about our name was not a concern. At the same time, the elopement and marriage decisions made by our parents posed a potential - threat to our family's image. It is conceivable that, for our father, safeguarding the honor and prestige of our family was a deeply embedded value.

While changing the family name due to external circumstances might have been seen as a temporary setback, the maintenance of the family's image and dignity continued to be of utmost importance despite the alteration in our name. Alternatively, it is possible that our father harbored a nostalgic attachment to our original family name and the heritage that it symbolized, even within a foreign landscape with minimal relatives. Upholding the family's honor may have served as a means for him to stay connected to our roots and keep a sense of identity amidst the changes. Our father's ability to keep our family's reputation intact could have been preserving a link to our past and ensuring that external influences or alterations did not overshadow our heritage.

It was a truly frightening experience that deeply affected - our mother and the entire family, serving as a stark reminder of the dangers in the world and underscoring the importance of vigilance and mutual support. Our mother's bravery in combating her attacker was admirable, highlighting her fortitude and resilience. In addition to the physical attack, this incident brought to light the vulnerabilities and obstacles immigrants encounter when assimilating into a new country. It exposed the challenges she faced in adapting to Canadian culture, along with feelings of nostalgia and the absence of familiar traditions.

Looking back, while it was a horrifying experience, this incident taught us valuable lessons. It taught everyone to appreciate the trivial things in life and to cherish the safety and security we often take for granted. It also reinforced the values of resilience and perseverance as we witnessed our mother's determination to overcome the trauma and rebuild her life. Additionally, our own beliefs merged with our father's strong convictions on family duty and honor.

However, this amalgamation does not mean sacrificing ourselves or abandoning our aspirations. As we navigate life's complexities and grapple with the weight of our enduring traditions, I have made a personal commitment to shield my future children from the constraints of this rigid culture and remain resolute in my stance. It became evident to me that if my partner did not share my values, I would firmly decide not to have children.

They say that when life gives you lemons, you always get more than one. Our parents were busy working, so we had various babysitters from the neighborhood. One day, the babysitter told Rani and me to take a nap since we were preschoolers. However, we were not the type to nap, and we wanted to play outside in front of our rented house. Rani decided to sneak out of the house to play with her friends across the street. I saw her leaving and started to follow her, but when I got to the front yard, she yelled for me to leave. I found myself frozen in confusion when a car struck me, sending me flying across the pavement and onto the grass.

My parents were immediately notified and rushed home while the neighbors came to my aid and transported me to the hospital as I remained unconscious. The car that hit me quickly fled the scene, leaving no clues behind. This incident took place during a simpler time in history when the focus was on day-to-day survival; there were no dashboard cameras or red-light cameras to assist in locating the vehicle. As newcomers to the country, my parents struggled with a lack of knowledge and resources to navigate the complexities of government, healthcare, and other essential aspects of life.

During my time in the hospital, I remained unconscious following my accident. This news deeply worried my parents, and they spent time praying for my recovery. When I finally regained consciousness, I was acutely aware of my surroundings, longing for the comfort of my own home. The damage caused by the accident was healing. The doctor shared with my parents that I had been incredibly fortunate. Given the severity of the accident, it almost felt like a guardian angel had been watching over me.

Unfortunately, during adulthood, I started to experience occasional leg cramps and spasms because of the accident. These discomforts served as a subtle reminder of the fragility of life and the importance of cherishing each day. Despite these challenges, I remain grateful that the outcome of the accident was not more dire. It is through such near-death experiences that we recognize the precious gift of life and the strength within us to persevere. It taught me to appreciate the gift of life and never take it for granted. My being young helped me recover, but more so, my grandmother was watching over me, and ultimately, it was God's divine intervention.

It taught my parents to appreciate the importance of keeping a watchful eye on the two of us, especially when we were under the care of strangers. They made sure only to leave us with trusted individuals and always check on us, even when we were sleeping. In a way, this incident brought our family closer together, and we started to look out for each other.

As I grew older, I also learned the value of forgiveness. I forgave Rani for telling me to leave and understood that she was just trying to protect me because she did not want me to get hurt. I also forgave the driver who hit me, knowing that it was an accident and that holding on to the anger and resentment would only hurt me overall. Instead, I chose to focus on my recovery and my appreciation for my life.

Chapter 4

A Loving Family?

Despite the challenges in Canada, our family made sure to spend quality time together on the weekends. Saturdays were reserved for exploring local parks and enjoying the outdoors. In the evenings, we would attend the local temple and reflect on our blessings, as our Father often called them. On Sundays, Rani and I attended a Christian church, as our father believed in the power of divine intervention to help us become better people. These spiritual experiences taught us to be humble and kind, values that have stayed with us.

In retrospect, this incident may have served as a catalyst for future rebellions by Rani and me. It was not a result of any negative association with the church. Still, rather, it provided us with an opportunity to engage with other children and view life from their perspective. We began to socialize in church with different families, which heightened our awareness of the disparities in our up bringings as well as in our traditions and cultures. These differences prompted us to question the reasons behind them, but our parents never offered us any explanations.

Growing up, I fondly recall bonding with my father over our shared love for music. Our time together was filled with the enchanting melodies of renowned artists like Jagjit Singh, singing along to classics such as "Ek Pyar Ka Nagma." We would spend hours lost in the tunes, courtesy of his cherished new record player. The sound of the needle touching the vinyl, the crackling before the music began—these details heightened our joy. It was a special time of laughter and music, with my father's attempts at dancing bringing a unique charm to our moments. Over time, I learned the songs well enough to join in, cherishing those memories of music-filled bliss.

After all these years, I am still captivated by the timeless beauty of classical Indian music, particularly by artists like Jagjit Singh. The intricate compositions and soulful vocals transport me back in time, connecting me to my roots and evoking a sense of nostalgia. Whether I am listening on a record player, streaming on my phone, or attending a live performance, the melodies have a magical quality that transcends time and space. Each note takes me on a melodic journey, weaving a path of memories and connecting me to the cherished moments I shared with my father. It is remarkable how a simple song can evoke such powerful emotions and leave a lasting impact.

Much like the harmonious moments shared with my father, being enveloped in the soul-stirring tunes of classical Indian music now brings me solace and elation. The enduring legacy of artists like Jagjit Singh serves as a beacon, illuminating the splendor of this musical tradition and underscoring the significance of embracing my cultural heritage. As I delve deeper into the realms of classical Indian music, I am profoundly grateful for the profound impact it has had on my life, providing a nostalgic backdrop to cherished memories and an avenue to explore the depths of human emotions. These timeless melodies not only transport me back to the innocence of childhood but also bridge the gap, connecting me with my father in a way that transcends mere words.

In 1973, my father purchased a black-and-white television with a manual antenna that required constant adjustment for good reception. The task of adjusting the antenna often fell on my shoulders, and after some trial and error, I managed to find the right spot. While the picture quality improved significantly, there were still occasional signal disruptions. The television had a limited number of channels, typically between three and five, and switching channels was a manual task assigned to me. One of our favorite father-daughter activities was watching cartoons together. Shows like Scooby-Doo, The Flintstones, and Tom and Jerry brought us immense joy and created a special bond between us. Watching these series not only entertained us but also formed lasting memories that uniquely connected us. My father cherished the opportunity to experience these cartoons, as he had missed them during his childhood.

The church that Rani and I attended sent a notice home that all kids were invited to go camping for the week, with fees being paid for those who could not afford it. Rani asked our parents if she could go, and while my father was hesitant, my mother convinced him to let her attend. Camping was a way for kids like Rani to escape from their parents and household chores. However, I never had any interest in camping and consistently chose to stay home instead. Being a homebody, I found comfort and joy in the presence of my family and the familiarity of home.

The idea of venturing into the wilderness never appealed to me as much as it did to many other kids. The thought of cold showers, outdoor toilets, and the overall inconvenience of camping just did not seem worth it to me. I preferred the coziness of my bed and the convenience of having everything I needed at home. Even though I love being outdoors, I enjoy activities like building tree forts, biking, participating in water sports, and swimming. But Camping just was not for me.

Our father went shopping for a backpack, sleeping bag, and warm clothes. Rani was excited about the camping trip. She packed her bags and gear the night before, ensuring she had everything. The next morning, we all drove her to the church, where the kids were gathering and preparing to leave for the campsite. As we dropped off Rani, I felt a pang of reluctance. I hoped she would be safe and enjoy her adventure. After saying our goodbyes, we drove back home.

The week passed quickly, with me spending my days reading books, helping my father with yard work, or helping neighbors with outdoor tasks. Finally, the day arrived for Rani's return. My parents and I waited for her at church. Spotting us, Rani rushed over and embraced our mother. Though tired, she appeared content. Rani enthusiastically shared details of her camping experience during the drive back home. I offered a smile and expressed my happiness that she enjoyed her time away. Secretly, I acknowledged that I derived pleasure from the coziness of home. Camping did not resonate with me, and I was content to let Rani indulge in that adventurous pursuit.

On occasions like my birthday or Christmas, my father's friends would give me gifts. This couple could not have children of their own, and they appreciated my honesty and hard work often; they would give me money or a large box of cookies. Upon receiving the money, I recalled a saying my parents instilled in us as children: *'That money does not grow on trees.'* Intrigued, I decided to evaluate this theory by burying the money in the backyard. Weeks later, Rani and I went to check on it, only to find no tree or money remaining. We both shook our heads, conceding that our parents were correct.

As for the cookies, I had quite the reputation as a cookie monster and a good kid, so the cookies were a reward for being kind and hardworking. While initially reluctant to share them, I recalled my father's words, 'God wants us to share, as this is a quality he looks for in people.' Reluctantly, I shared the cookies with everyone, and I found solace in knowing that I had done something that would make God happy. This lesson of kindness and sharing stayed with me throughout my life.

While I may not have a secret stash of buried money or a large box of cookies hidden away, I make it a priority to approach all my interactions with kindness and honesty. These qualities are what truly matter in the grand scheme of things. I feel profoundly grateful for the kind and generous individuals who have been a part of my life. The gifts they bestowed upon me not only brought joy but also imparted valuable lessons. Although the physical gifts may no longer be present, the memories and lessons will forever remain etched in my mind. The true treasure lies in the relationships that have been nurtured over time, founded on trust, empathy, and kindness.

By spreading positivity and kindness, I hope to create a ripple effect of goodwill—The generosity shown to me by my father's friend. I want to be an individual who is trustworthy, honest, and dependable. The gifts I received taught me valuable lessons about honesty and accountability, as well as the importance of building relationships and the immense power of kindness. These memories will always stay with me, motivating me to pass on that same kindness to others.

The wounds on my father's side of the family had not - healed, even with time. Grandfather harbored bitterness and anger, maintaining a strict stance against any form of communication with my dad. He neither initiated contact nor acknowledged our attempts to reconnect. The root of this enmity lay in my father's decision to marry outside his religion and run away, a choice Grandfather could never reconcile with.

This lingering discord cast a heavy cloud of sorrow and longing over our family, yearning for a semblance of reconciliation. On the other hand, my mother's decision to marry my father did not sit well with her own family. Their resistance to her marrying outside of their faith stirred up a storm of anger and disapproval. My maternal family chose to disown her, severing all bonds for years.

However, as is often the case, time worked its magic, fostering chances for change and transformation. After years of silence, my mother's brother suddenly reached out to us, expressing a desire to immigrate to Canada. Welcoming him and his family with open arms, my parents granted us the presence of relatives who were related to us after ages. They resided in the basement suite of our home, and though they harbored different religions and beliefs, it eventually felt as if a lost piece of our family was restored. Spending quality time together, we exchanged stories and shared meals, fostering a newfound bond.

Guided by my parents' assistance in navigating job searches, healthcare registrations, and school enrollments for their kids, they acclimatized to the unfamiliar environment. Overcoming cultural and language barriers was not without its challenges, yet collectively, we endeavored to create a welcoming atmosphere and help them feel at home. Over time, our relationship with our newly reconnected relatives grew stronger. We started celebrating holidays together, taking trips to Alberta and local parks, and helping each other out when needed. It was like we had always been close despite the years of separation. Since my cousins came to stay with us, our home was buzzing with excitement and activity.

I have treasured memories of getting together with my cousins around the kitchen table and enjoying meals despite our financial challenges. Our lunches often revolved around a humble yet satisfying combination: a plate of rice accompanied either by a heap of butter or a slather of ketchup; these moments held special significance for me, as they symbolized our ability to find joy and contentment even in the face of limited resources. It was thrilling to have family around to share these little moments with and play games together. For me, it was the first time I did not feel glued to my father's side. My cousins and I looked out for each other on the playground, making sure we all had someone to play with at school.

While reflecting on this experience, I came to appreciate that family transcends mere genetic connections; it encompasses love, support, and shared bonds. The unexpected reunion with my long-lost uncle and his family filled me with gratitude, teaching me the importance of embracing family, regardless of past disconnects. This encounter underscored the power of forgiveness, illuminating that the reasons behind prolonged silence pale in comparison to the joy of reunion. Over time, I discovered commonalities, honored diverse beliefs, and celebrated each unique tradition.

Though the journey was not always smooth, and there were challenges along the way, the love and acceptance we had for each other outweighed any differences. It was a testament to the power of family and the bond that can be rebuilt. As we continued to walk this newfound path together, I could not help but feel immense gratitude for my parents' willingness to embrace our relatives. Through their example, I learned the importance of compassion, understanding, and giving second chances.

I recalled all the friction and dislike I had toward Rani for the way she treated me. Rani's taunts had a hold on me and affected my eating habits. I skipped meals, including breakfast and lunch, and often cried to sleep. Later, my mother began openly calling me 'fatty' Moti. She always asked me why I was not trying to lose weight. I did not understand why my weight had such an effect on her. However, I realized that she idealized a woman as slim, light-skinned, and smart to fit into the Muslim community and also Canadian society.

I tried to lose weight by eating less and exercising, but it never was enough for my mother. Her nagging only made me feel worse about myself, and I began to develop an unhealthy relationship with food and my body. Years later, I learned to love and accept myself, regardless of my size or shape. Although her idealization of beauty still affects me, I am slowly letting go of her expectations and focusing on my happiness and well-being. It was not easy to break free from those expectations, but I am proud of the progress I have made.

While I still struggle with body image at times, I remind myself that my worth is not tied to my appearance. I am no longer confined by my mother's or anyone else's expectations, including those of Rani. My Aunt Baby, who had become my biggest support system, shared valuable insights with me. She reminded me that physical appearances change as we age and that we should not dwell on them. When I was young, I misunderstood the meaning of being referred to as 'Moti' fatty by Rani. It seemed like she was influenced by adult interactions.

The act of name-calling can have a significant impact on a child's self-esteem, which is something that I experienced firsthand. Surprisingly, even now, Rani continues to address me with that demeaning name. As adults or even as parents, our attitudes should evolve. As I have grown older, I have learned not to let the opinions of my family define my self-worth. It takes a great deal of strength to reach this point, especially when our minds are conditioned to react negatively to criticism.

In retrospect, I acknowledge that my aunt provided me with genuine support, transcending our differences in religion and culture. She emerged as my primary source of inspiration, embodying qualities of empathy, kindness, and unwavering support. Through our bond, I learned that attitudes are not predetermined by heritage and that cultural and religious disparities do not need to define our interactions. It falls upon individuals to choose their treatment of others and break free from detrimental behavioral cycles. Surrounding ourselves with individuals who uplift and empower us to be our authentic selves is paramount.

Always try to stay away from those who inflict harm through hurtful words and actions. I appreciate the valuable lessons from my interactions with Rani and my mother despite the pain they may have caused. These experiences underscore the significance of self-love and self-acceptance, emphasizing the imperative of not letting external judgments dictate our self-worth or control our being. Each of us inherently deserves love and respect, irrespective of our physical attributes, ethnicity, or upbringing. It is time to shed toxic behaviors and perspectives and embrace a more constructive and compassionate way of life.

I remember the time my father bought me a doll. It was not a fancy Barbie doll, but a similar one that I was extremely excited to have. However, Rani was consumed by jealousy. She forcefully snatched the doll from me, insisting it was meant for her and that our father had made a mistake. Tears streamed down my face, prompting my parents to rush over to see what had happened. Father stepped in, instructing Rani to return the doll to me. Reluctantly, she threw it back at me, accidentally hitting me in the face. It was a painful blow, both physically and emotionally.

Later, when I searched for my doll, I was horrified to find it spray-painted black. I was in disbelief and tears as I held onto my vandalized doll until my father came across me. He questioned why I had painted the new doll black, but I explained that I found it like that when I woke up in the morning. He grew suspicious and confronted Rani, who eventually admitted to painting my doll black to make it look like me. I was devastated. How could Rani, my sister, whom I should trust blindly, do something so mean? I expressed my deep sadness to my father, swearing that I never wanted another doll again.

Rani faced consequences for her actions, or at least she should have. However, as always, Mother stepped in to save the day. She claimed that they were just little kids and that these things happened between siblings. However, I could not help but feel like this incident was the beginning of Rani's aggressive behavior, which would only worsen over time. It is challenging to see that moment as the catalyst for her escalating behavior, but it certainly marked a turning point. As the years went by, her behavior only became more hostile and hurtful.

Looking back on that day brings a mix of sadness, anger, and confusion. It serves as a reminder of the broken bond and the lingering pain. After having a daughter of my own, I found myself immersed in the world of acquiring every Barbie doll that had captivated my childhood imagination. The impulse to purchase stemmed from a traumatic experience in my past, leading to my daughter having a vast collection of Barbies that she did not open or play with all of them.

This reality remains unchanged to this day, as I observe them still neatly preserved in their original boxes. When my daughter tried to return them to me as a sentimental keepsake, I insisted that she hold onto them and eventually pass them on to her daughter. I had collected these dolls specifically for her enjoyment. I hope that no child goes through this type of situation.

As preteens, even though we were sisters, our relationship was doomed from an early age. It started with hurtful antics, which turned into biases and body shaming, and then she failed her rebellions. Rani wanted to get back at our parents, but the outcome impacted me as I severed the punishment. This led to my dislike for Rani and further complicated our relationship. The fact that our parents in the future ordered Rani and me not to talk to each other caused a divide that was impossible to heal. We will explore these situations in future chapters.

As we started kindergarten, our mother would walk with Rani and me to school and pick us up afterward. I cherished these walks because they gave me extra time to chat in English and share stories. Despite my enthusiastic chatter, our non-English-speaking mother often struggled to keep up, leading her to shake her head and hilariously tell my father about my fast talking. Even from an early age, I had a love for talking and found it hard to keep secrets. My parents playfully teased me, predicting that my honesty would never allow me to lie or withhold information.

As I grew older, my passion for communication only intensified, coupled with a strong commitment to honesty. I took pride in my integrity, always striving to share knowledge in the most truthful manner possible. There were always repercussions from family or friends. I felt it was a benefit rather than a disadvantage. Rani did not appreciate this value of mine, as I learned from my mother that you did not need to change to fit in.

Despite facing difficulties at school due to other kids making fun of my mother's choice to wear sarees, I always looked forward to our walks and appreciated the quality time we spent together. Those walks became a sanctuary for us, a place where we could escape the judgments and prejudices of others. With each step, we created a bond that no amount of teasing or criticism could break. My mother's resilience in staying true to herself, even in the face of adversity, taught me the importance of embracing and celebrating our cultural heritage. I learned to value authenticity and the courage to be different, and I carried those lessons with me throughout my life.

My mother was already struggling to adjust to our new home away from her family, and the taunting at school only made things worse. Her sarees were the only clothing she was used to wearing, and she refused to change her wardrobe just to fit in. Instead, she persevered and did her best to ignore the teasing. Her focus remained on our family and our daily routine. Despite the difficulties she faced, she continued to wear her sarees with pride, refusing to let the negativity of others affect her sense of self.

Over time, Mother began to embrace Canadian culture and the way of life. She started making friends with people from diverse cultural backgrounds in our new community, gradually appreciating the warm clothing styles and incorporating them into her wardrobe. As a family, we embraced and celebrated both our Indian heritage and Canadian traditions. While we still enjoyed traditional Indian dishes for dinner, my father adamantly stuck to his preference for Indian food, refusing to try turkey, pasta, or pizza.

We also embraced new traditions like Easter, Thanksgiving, and Christmas feasts. We learned to blend and balance both cultures, creating a unique experience that was truly our own. Embracing the new Canadian culture while still honoring our roots, we have woven a tapestry of diverse experiences that define our unique identity. Through this process, we have come to understand that cultural exchange is not about erasing a person's identity but about celebrating the beauty of diversity and finding connections amidst differences. Our journey has taught us valuable lessons on the importance of embracing change while remaining true to ourselves.

My father's dedication to helping others was not limited to our family's cultural transition. He extended his support to families from Ghana, the Philippines, and India who had recently migrated to Canada. In one remarkable instance, a man reached out to my father after finding his name in the phone book, recognizing it as

South Indian. My father generously offered him a place to stay with our family until he could be independent.

Another notable incident occurred when my father went above and beyond to assist a newly arrived family that was struggling with employment due to language barriers. Being fluent in both English and Tamil, he helped them navigate job applications and even set up job interviews through his network. Additionally, he connected them to organizations that helped them in settling down. My father drew inspiration from his own experiences facing challenges during migration and dealing with exploitation. Father's actions not only provided stability to these families but also influenced me, instilling within me the values of community engagement and volunteer work. I remember accompanying my father on these visits to the newcomers' homes. Seeing the relief on their faces and witnessing their gratitude towards my father was truly heartwarming. It made me realize the impact one person's kindness and support can have on someone's life.

However, my mother sometimes felt ignored or left out during these times. She would express her frustration, jokingly saying, "Like father, like daughter" (jaise Baap waise Beti). She was not against helping others, but she felt that my father and I were always preoccupied with our volunteer work and neglected spending time with the family. My mother was upset that my father and I always spent time together without anyone else. Reflecting on those moments, I understood her perspective. While it was inspiring to witness my father's dedication and commitment to helping others, it is crucial to strike a balance and ensure that our loved ones also feel included and valued.

When I volunteer and support various causes, I try to keep my mother's feelings in mind. I try to include her in my activities and incorporate her unique skills and experiences. Reflecting on my childhood experiences, I have learned the importance of empathy, compassion, and the impact of small acts of kindness. Through my journey, I am learning to balance my commitments, ensuring that my loved ones feel like a part of them rather than excluded.

One person who stands out as a beacon of inspiration in my life is my father. His actions exemplified the transformative power of helping others and motivated me to follow suit, leading me to engage in community work as an adult passionately. For three years, I dedicated myself to volunteering at the local community police station, where I contributed to enhancing safety and providing office support. I attribute this drive to my father, who ingrained in me the vital significance of empathy, compassion, and extending aid to those in need. Whether it was through small acts of kindness or large philanthropic endeavors, he consistently exemplified compassion and generosity. Witnessing firsthand the positive impact he had on the lives of those around him left an incredible mark on my values and beliefs. My father taught me that serving our community and volunteering our time and efforts should be a fundamental aspect of life.

During my elementary years, I began actively tutoring children of newcomers, and I always felt a deep sense of fulfillment. These experiences reinforced the valuable teachings my father had imparted to me, and I understood the transformative power of lending a helping hand. I strive to make a positive impact on the lives of others, just as he did. His teachings have shaped my values and instilled in me a sense of purpose. I passionately believe that together, we can create a more compassionate and supportive society. In conclusion, my father's actions exemplified human-itarianism, and his valuable teachings have nurtured within me a deep understanding of the importance of lending a helping hand.

As a result, my commitment to community involvement - and volunteer work stems from his inspiration, and I strive to continue making a positive impact on the lives of others. With my father's selfless volunteer work at the temple, whether assisting in renovations or aiding newcomers, he left an enduring impression on me. His dedication to enhancing lives ignited a passion in me to create a meaningful difference.

I began contributing to causes close to my heart, such as providing food for underprivileged children and recognizing the significant impact nutrition can have on their education and well-being. I also support organizations like World Vision, which prioritizes assistance for children in underdeveloped countries. I am determined to continue his legacy of selfless service and generosity, striving to make a tangible and lasting difference in the lives of those in need.

As I navigate my journey with retinopathy, I have realized that it is not just about the physical challenges but also an emotional and mental one for me. Along with these obstacles, my family has been my rock, offering me support and encouragement every step of the way. My husband and I have gained valuable lessons from our own experiences as immigrants, and we are passionate about helping others who are facing similar challenges. Through our shared experiences, we have developed a deep understanding of the importance of community and resourcefulness. We have seen firsthand how language barriers and limited resource access can hinder progress. This is why we are committed to empowering others to overcome these obstacles. As a family, we have stepped up to assist a cause close to my heart by offering advice on job searches, providing addresses for new employment opportunities, and having informal conversations with our new immigrant friends. We are dedicated to empowering individuals to overcome obstacles and realize their aspirations, regardless of their background or circumstances. Our family is driven by a sense of empathy and a desire to make a meaningful difference. We hope that by sharing our own experiences, we can help others find their path forward and achieve their goals.

Chapter 5

Differences and Lessons

I vividly remember the time when my cousin and I got into trouble for indulging in buckets of ice cream that my mother and Aunt Baby had in their freezers. The amusing part was that we devoured the vanilla and chocolate ice cream but left the strawberry untouched. We were mischievous kids, always sneaking around and engaging in activities we knew we should not be doing. Despite understanding the consequences of being caught, the allure of the cool, creamy treat was irresistible.

One afternoon, my aunt caught us red-handed with our spoons in the bucket of delicious ice cream. We froze, unsure of what to say. She looked at us sternly and inquired, "How much of the ice cream have you kids eaten?" She then asked me to leave, mentioning that if my mother found out, she would not be able to help. We looked at each other, trying to produce an excuse. But then my cousin spoke to his mother and said, "We only ate the chocolate and vanilla flavors. We did not touch the strawberry ice cream. We promise." My aunt let out a sigh of relief and could not help but laugh at our honesty.

Afterward, my aunt started telling us stories about her life in Fiji, where she never got to indulge in treats as her family could not afford them. The two of us were in shock at how a kid could go through life without ice cream or treats of any kind. Here, we were eating buckets of ice cream to ourselves. After hearing my aunt's story, we felt sad, but our love for ice cream grew even stronger. We were punished for our misbehavior, but we felt proud of ourselves for not touching the strawberry ice cream that we saved for my father.

Looking back, we never understood why my father loved the strawberry flavor. The punishment was not so bad; we both had to eat a whole bucket of ice cream by ourselves, including the strawberry flavor. Still, I'm not too fond of strawberry ice cream, but those were the days. We may have been naughty, but we had a lot of fun. Those sweet memories will always bring a smile to my face. Even though we got into trouble, we solved it with honesty. It made us realize how lucky we were to have the privilege of enjoying ice cream whenever we wanted.

It is a small but important lesson that has stayed with me throughout my life: to be grateful for the trivial things in life and never take them for granted. As for my aunt, she became our hero for introducing us to a new perspective and helping us realize how blessed we truly were. And those moments spent with my cousin and aunt over a bucket of ice cream will always hold a special place in my heart, reminding me of the beauty of honesty and the power of gratitude.

However, as life often goes, circumstances change, and my uncle's family moved. Suddenly, our summer gatherings became less frequent, and the distance between us grew vast. I found myself yearning for the company of my cousins and the wisdom of my aunt, who always had a story or lesson to share. The shared experiences and the bonds we had formed remained etched in my heart.

Every summer, we would travel to Alberta to visit my uncle and his family. These visits were always something I eagerly looked forward to. My heart would leap with excitement. It was a time of laughter, games, and the purest form of sibling companionship. In our culture, cousins were treated as siblings. As soon as we arrived at my uncle's house, the familiar sounds of joyful chatter and laughter enveloped the air.

My cousins, each with their distinct personalities and quirks, represented a melting pot of diverse cultures and beliefs. Through them, I learned about diverse traditions and practices that existed beyond my little world. We spent hours sharing stories about our lives, exploring our differences, and celebrating our similarities. It was during these conversations that I realized the true beauty of our mixed family and the unique upbringing it provided.

One of the most unforgettable memories I have of my cousins is the time we spent flying kites in Edmonton. It was a beautiful sunny day, with a gentle breeze that created the perfect conditions for kite flying. We raced up and down the hill, shouting with delight as our kites soared higher and higher. The colorful strings danced in the sky, forming intricate patterns against the backdrop of breathtaking scenery. At that moment, all our differences seemed inconsequential, and the sheer joy of the experience united us.

Another cherished memory is running around aimlessly with my cousins. We would explore the sprawling fields surrounding my uncle's house, feeling the grass beneath our feet and indulging in the freedom of endless play. We would laugh until tears streamed down our faces, not caring about the dirt on our clothes or the scrapes on our knees. Those moments of carefree abandonment brought us closer together despite our divergent backgrounds.

Growing up with my cousins was more than just a part of my childhood; it was an enriching experience that shaped me as a person. Our differences in religion and upbringing were a testament to the diversity and acceptance that exist within our extended family.

It taught me the importance of celebrating our individuality while cherishing the strong bonds that tie us together. Despite the distance that now separates us, the memories of flying kites in Edmonton and running aimlessly will forever hold a special place in my heart.

However, I also recall some minor conflicts that arose from our divergent cultural practices. I remember my cousins playing cards, a harmless game that was forbidden in my family due to religious beliefs. The beliefs passed down through generations in our family dictated that playing cards caused negative influences, potentially leading to bad behaviors. Rani and I got into trouble when we were caught playing cards.

As I reflect on my childhood experiences with my cousins, uncle, and aunt, I realize how fortunate I was to have grown up in such a unique and accepting family. They taught me that love, respect, and understanding transcend the boundaries of culture, religion, and race. They taught me that what truly matters in life are the connections we make with each other and the memories we create together. And for that, I will always be grateful. It was a chance to embrace our differences while sharing the childhood joys we all craved.

My family treated my uncle's family with mutual respect and understanding, creating a harmonious blend of culture and diversity. We embraced each other's traditions and celebrated different holidays, from Christmas to Eid and Diwali. This intermixing of customs allowed us to eagerly learn about the unique rituals and practices that shaped our respective backgrounds. Through this cultural exchange, I developed a profound appreciation for the rich diversity that exists in our world.

Cherishing moments of joy and camaraderie with my cousins, we gathered, laughed, and recounted tales of childhood escapades. For what seemed like an endless period, we immersed ourselves in games, ventured into the great outdoors, and crafted whimsical realms of imagination. In those moments, our diverse backgrounds held no significance; far more crucial was the warmth and bond that united us as a family.

I am grateful for the valuable lessons I learned from my cousins, uncles, and aunts. They instilled in me the importance of embracing diversity and the power of love and understanding. Through their guidance, I discovered the significance of treating others with kindness and respect, regardless of their backgrounds or beliefs. Exposure to diverse perspectives and beliefs from an early age molded my values and worldview. I learned the vital nature of approaching every person and situation with an open mind, seeking commonalities rather than differences.

These experiences cultivated my appreciation for the beauty of diversity and the enriching contributions it brings to our lives.

Moreover, I need to pass on the values of diversity and inclusion to future generations. By imparting the teachings I received from my cousins, uncle, and aunt, I will ensure that they understand the significance of embracing differences and nurturing a sense of belonging for all. Through this, I aim to contribute to a more understanding and tolerant world where people can unite and celebrate the beauty of our collective diversity. By promoting love, acceptance, and understanding, we can lay the foundation for a brighter future for all.

As a child, I have fond memories of constructing a tree fort at the end of our block next to our elementary school. Together with my friends John and Henry, we carried the wood up the side of the tree, hammer and nails in hand. I was grateful to have learned basic woodworking skills from my father, and it was exhilarating to pass on that knowledge to my friends. However, as often happens with newbies using hammers, both John and Henry hit their fingers, which I immediately regretted not warning them about. Despite the setback, we persisted in our building efforts until, eventually, we had a sturdy and defensible fortress up in the branches.

Unfortunately, our fun was cut short when my father received a call from the school instructing him to dismantle the structure. We solemnly took down the fort and carried the wood and tools back down the tree. We could not resist the temptation to rebuild, and to our joy, we never heard from the school again. We spent many happy hours in the fort, spying on people through our toy binoculars and reading our favorite Archie comics. Those childhood memories of John and Henry stand out as times of camaraderie and adventure, where the world was full of possibility and promise.

Rani and I did not play well together, so as time went by, the two of us started to disassociate; we started to find friends that aligned with our personalities. This upset our parents as they wanted the two of us to be closer. As the older sibling, Rani often felt a sense of jealousy and did not enjoy sharing her belongings or attention. At an early age, I learned that being family did not mean that everyone loved you unconditionally. I never fully grasped why some families did not get along, but as a child, that prospect did not exist in my mind.

On one memorable birthday, my father surprised me with a shiny new tricycle. I was filled with excitement and gratitude as I now had my bike, independent of Rani's possessions. I cherished the tricycle and rode it with immense joy for an entire day. However, the next morning, my heart sank as I discovered my beloved bike had been smashed and painted black. Without a doubt, he immediately knew Rani was behind this act of destruction. It was a disappointing and disheartening moment, as the bond between siblings should be one of support and care, not manipulation and cruelty. As expected, my mother intervened, defending her and downplaying her actions. The frustration and confusion I felt intensified. It was difficult to understand why she harbored such animosity toward me, her sibling. My father, wanting to make it right, offered to replace the tricycle with a new one.

Despite this, I decided to hold on to the broken, black-painted bike. I realized that obtaining a new tricycle would not automatically lead to a change in Rani's behavior or attitude. Keeping the damaged bike served as a reminder of my resilience and determination to shield myself from future disappointments and harm. It became a symbol of the independence and strength I had gained in navigating the complexities of my relationship with Rani. Consequently, I approached my interactions with Rani cautiously, always mindful of the possibility of deceit and cruelty. As I grew older, I found ways to establish my own identity, separate from her influence. Though our bond may have been strained, I learned to prioritize my well-being and forge my path, guided by the lessons learned from that fateful birthday and the broken tricycle. As a young child, our world was not confined by the boundaries of can or cannot but rather fueled by curiosity and the thirst for knowledge. Our parents bestowed upon us the precious gift of freedom—to explore, to discover, and to immerse ourselves in new experiences. They encouraged us to embrace the unknown with open arms and to learn from every twist and turn along the way.

However, as we transitioned into sixth grade, contrasting with the previous freedom we knew, our parents began to place certain restrictions on us. Suddenly, we found ourselves navigating a world of limitations and rules that we had never known. While this change may have initially felt stifling, it also presented us with new challenges to overcome and lessons to learn. With each restriction, we were forced to find creative solutions and alternative paths, teaching us resilience and adaptability. Although our journey took a different turn, those years of unbridled exploration in our early childhood laid a foundation of curiosity and growth that continued to shape us.

As the temperature continued to drop, our mother became fascinated by the snowfall, spending hours staring out the window. I have a vivid memory of her standing by the window with a cup of coffee in hand. One of the Canadian traditions she adopted was her love for coffee. I always wondered what she was thinking, looking out the window. I thought our mother was always lost in her world. I often wondered why she rarely joined us in outdoor activities.

One day, Rani and I decided to take our mother out to play in the snow. We bundled her up in layers of warm clothing and went outside. It was a joyous sight to see her giggling and throwing snowballs at us. She even attempted to make a snowman in the yard, but it turned out to be more of a snow pile than a snowman. Our mother kept slipping on the snow, and it was a challenge for her to walk. We tried to help her walk in the snow, but we all ended up falling into a pile of snow. The weather was so cold for our mother; her face turned red, especially her nose. She started to shiver and went inside. Rani and I were having too much fun to think about going inside. Winter brought us closer as a family as we spent more time indoors, with our mother cooking warm meals and all of us watching cartoons. As the season came to an end, we all agreed that we had grown to love winter. Although it was cold and sometimes tedious, it brought us together and created new memories that we would cherish forever. I loved playing in the snow. We would build snowmen and have snowball fights with the neighborhood kids. My favorite thing, though, was sledding down the hill by Knight Street. I was flying down the hill with the wind in my face and snow flying everywhere.

I have fond memories of engaging in fun-spirited street hockey matches with the boys in our neighborhood. Those street hockey matches were an absolute blast, with the energy and laughter from my friends and me filling the air. The adrenaline rush of chasing the ball, trying to outmaneuver my opponents, and scoring goals brought me pure joy. It was a physical activity that left me feeling alive and energized. My father's unwavering support and enthusiasm made the event more remarkable as he watched from the sidelines, cheering us on with a beaming smile. His dedication to nurturing my love for hockey was evident not only in the new hockey sticks he would buy for me but also in the homemade hockey net that he crafted from wood and a fishing net. It was a truly personalized creation that added an extra layer of joy and authenticity to our games. Those memories of us playing street hockey with the homemade net and my father's cheers will forever hold a special place in my heart.

Going back to childhood, I remember when our mother came to see Rani and me ice skating; she did not understand the concept of ice skating. The sport did not exist in Fiji, as it was a hot country, unlike Canada, which has freezing winters. She kept asking what kind of sport this was. Walking on ice is hard enough, but doing it with a knife on the bottom of your shoes? How could this be exciting?" She watched us fall with a look of shock on her face. Later, she told our father that she did not like this sport for the girls because they could get seriously hurt. Our father laughed and said, "It is fun; the girls like it; let them enjoy it."

Sometimes, our family would embark on thrilling ice-skating adventures at Trout Lake. Despite the lake being frozen solid, our mother never quite warmed up to the idea. Nevertheless, our father, the rule-maker of the house, made the ultimate decision, and so our mother went along with it. At first, stepping onto that icy surface filled me with an overwhelming sense of fear. But as I learned to find my balance and glide across the frozen expanse, a rush of exhilaration replaced the initial trepidation.

I recall those winter days with absolute fondness, for they hold some of the most cherished memories. The crisp, frigid air brushed gently against my face as I cut through it, each stroke propelling me further. Laughter echoed in the stillness as Rani and I chased each other across the glistening ice, leaving faint tracks of joy in our wake. It was as if time stood still, and we were caught in a whimsical dance of freedom. I hold onto those moments dearly, etching them into the deepest crevices of my heart. The memories of our ice-skating escapades at Trout Lake serve as a constant reminder of the boundless love and warmth that surrounded us. Each time I close my eyes, I can still feel the adrenaline coursing through my veins and hear the echoes of our laughter, forever etched in my soul.

Looking back on those days, I realized how important it was to have my parents' support and encouragement. Although they did not understand the sport at first, they were always there for us, sharing our triumphs and comforting us in our defeats, and that is all that matters in the end—having people who believe in you and stand by you through thick and thin. Their love and support gave us the confidence to pursue our passions, even when we faced obstacles or setbacks. It taught us that it is not about being the best or winning but about enjoying the journey and giving it your best try.

It reminds me to support and encourage those around me, especially when they are pursuing their dreams and passions. To be a cheerleader, a listening ear, and a shoulder to lean on when needed. Because that is what family is for—to be there for each other, no matter what. In the future, this will not be true. My parents, especially my father, believed that family was the key to having a fulfilling life, and he kept the family together. Unfortunately, due to his death, the family dynamics changed. We will delve into the changes in future chapters.

My father would often share stories with me about his upbringing in Fiji during the 1940s and his journey to Canada. He always included a moral lesson in each one. One story that stood out to me was about a man who wanted to ride two boats at the same time. He attempted to place one foot in each boat, which caused him to fall into the water, and he became the laughingstock of the town. The moral of the story was to remind us that sometimes there is only one path to success.

Rani never took an interest in any stories about our parents. I have always wanted to learn where our family originated from and how we got to Fiji and then Canada. But Rani was more interested in the latest fashion trends and school. Our father often teased her, saying she was like the man in the story, trying to balance her outdoor activities and school. Rani would roll her eyes and tell him that she had it all under control.

As I got older, the story about the man trying to ride two boats at once stuck with me. I realized that there were times in my own life when I tried to do too much and ended up falling short of everything. It reminded me to focus on one thing at a time and give it my all. My father was always full of wisdom and stories that continue to resonate with me to this day. I miss those days and wish we could go back to them. But even though we are all grown up now and have our own lives, we make new memories and continue the traditions that our parents have taught us.

My father was often frustrated with my mother because she did not share the same enthusiasm for outdoor activities as the rest of the family. While the rest of us enjoyed going out and exploring, she seemed content to stay at home. At times, I found myself wondering why she had this preference. Perhaps, deep down, she felt safer and more comfortable within the walls of her home. It is possible that the outside world presented unknown elements or potential risks that made her apprehensive.

I genuinely believed that if she learned English to read and write, it would have given her the confidence and encouragement she needed. Though my father's frustration was evident, it is important to understand and respect my mother's perspective, even if it differs from our own. Both viewpoints contribute to the complexity and dynamics of our family, reminding us of the importance of empathy and understanding within our relationships.

I found immense joy in embracing a more adventurous, active, and sporting lifestyle. While Rani spent hours perfecting her appearance and carefully selecting her outfits, I preferred to venture out into the neighborhood, get my hands dirty, and explore the great outdoors. As I indulged in this active lifestyle, I developed a curiosity about what was happening in the neighborhood and kept a close eye on everything. Meeting new people and learning their stories became a captivating hobby for me, to the point that my father affectionately referred to me as 'Sher ka Mantri,' the neighborhood ambassador.

Another passion was building tree forts, which became my specialty. Something was fulfilling about constructing a secret hideout up in the branches, away from the world below. But my interests extended beyond fort-building. I loved spending my afternoons painting fences for neighbors, adding a splash of color to our surroundings. It was a creative outlet that allowed me to express myself differently and not be compared to Rani. Helping neighbors was something that came naturally to me. If someone needed assistance with yard work or any odd jobs, I was always ready and willing to lend a hand. It felt good to contribute to our neighborhood and create connections with those around me.

Lastly, riding my bike, which was elegantly named "Street King" on the front bar, was my ultimate source of freedom. Exploring new paths, mastering new tricks, and feeling the wind against my face as I whizzed by—it was a sensation that never failed to fill me with happiness. My parents did not need to go far to look for me, as I was always within the neighborhood, checking on my elderly friends and lending a hand. One specific incident stands out in my memory: the day I lost control of my bike while riding down a steep hill on the road. As I approached the intersection, adrenaline rushed through my veins, and I could not believe my luck as there were no cars in sight. But in an unfortunate twist of fate, a police car suddenly appeared, blocking my path. It was too late to brake, and I collided with the police vehicle, tumbling off my bike and onto the unforgiving pavement. In that moment of chaos, the officer rushed to my aid, helping me up with concern etched on his face as blood dripped from my injured arm and scraped knees. Amid the pain and confusion, a fleeting thought crossed my mind: *my mother would be furious.* I knew my father would unleash his fury once he saw the sorry state of my beloved bike. To my surprise, Rani appeared on the scene, witnessing the aftermath of my collision.

The police officer, displaying unexpected kindness, decided to drive both my damaged bike and me home. I could sense Rani's disapproval as we left her to make her way home, but there was no time to dwell on that as we arrived home. As anticipated, our mother's anger erupted as soon as she saw Rani out on her own. Accepting the consequences of my recklessness, our father took charge and swiftly took me to the doctor. It turned out that I had dislocated my arm, resulting in the confinement of a sling. That bike accident will forever be etched in my memory, serving as a painful reminder of the consequences of misplaced excitement and the importance of being cautious on the road. I was grateful for the kind and empathetic people that have helped me in my life.

Anyhow, my mother shared her childhood stories with us to give a sense of her upbringing. Rani was not interested in sitting and listening. She told me that in the 1950s, she had to walk a mile to the river to get water. Filling up her water jugs, she then placed the filled jugs on top of her head and carried them back home. She and her sisters would take the family laundry to the same river to wash the clothes, which took hours, unlike the modern countries that had washers and dryers.

Despite the challenges, she always had a sense of community and belonging. Her family would often have salaah together and share meals. For my mother, it was a time when people depended on each other and formed strong bonds. As she grew older, my mother began to make friends of different faiths and discovered that her religion was just one of many in the world. She embraced charity and kindness as a way of life and learned that even the smallest acts of generosity and compassion can make a significant difference.

As a mother herself, she tried to instill these values in her children. She reminded them of the importance of helping others and being grateful for what they have. She shared stories of her youth, hoping to teach us the lessons that she has learned along the way. Through her stories, she showed us the beauty of a life lived with purpose and intention, one that is grounded in faith, community, and service.

Her stories are about working hard and taking pride in your work. She hopes we, her children, will become productive and assist society in future endeavors. My mother's experiences have taught her that we are all connected and that our actions have an impact on those around us. As I continue to grow and learn, I will carry these lessons with me and strive to live a life filled with compassion, generosity, and purpose. Her stories inspired me to give back to my community and to be a source of light to those around me.

I am grateful for her guidance and wisdom. I realize that my mother's expectations were rooted in cultural traditions that valued modesty and respect. But at the time, I struggled to reconcile these expectations with my own identity. I vividly remember feeling self-conscious and awkward when I had to wear a saree, and I longed to be able to wear comfortable, casual clothes instead. Over time, I have come to appreciate the beauty and elegance of ethnic clothing and sarees, and I now see them as an important connection to my cultural heritage.

Despite these differences, Rani and I remained vigilant, trying to bond over different interests like music and movies. It seemed like whenever we tried to bond, things always separated us, whether it was our different interests or just fate. Over time, we truly disconnected, and the sad part was that we were family but truly not there for each other as we should have been. We will delve into the incidents and situations that greatly separated us. The bond of trust was shattered, as were the differences in our perspectives on morals, culture, and traditions.

As we reflect on our failed attempts to connect, we must realize that sometimes, despite our best efforts, relationships cannot be salvaged. It is a painful realization to acknowledge that the bond we once held dear has now dissipated. Moving forward, we must accept that sometimes, despite our shared bloodline, some relationships are not meant to be. We must learn to let go of the past and move on, knowing that some bonds are not meant to last a lifetime.

Rani had a knack for throwing tantrums to get her way, and our parents always gave in to her demands. This behavior earned her the title of "Rani," which means queen in Hindi, and it seemed quite suited to her personality. However, this sense of entitlement had its drawbacks. Growing up, Rani became used to the idea that the world revolved around her, and she never learned how to cope with disappointment or do the challenging work needed to achieve her goals. As she got older, she struggled to manage criticism or setbacks.

Our parents always indulged her, buying the things she wanted but did not necessarily need whenever her tantrums ensued. They just wanted her to stop causing a scene and drawing attention to them. Parents need to set boundaries and teach children that they cannot get everything they want. This helps them develop resilience and the skills to cope with life's challenges. While it may be tempting to give in to a child's demands to avoid a tantrum, it is important to think about the long-term consequences and prioritize their emotional and social development.

Chapter 6

Religion: Diwali or Christmas

G rowing up and learning about our religion and culture was exhausting. Our religion had so many gods. Our father sat down with Rani and me to talk about each god and what they represented. I thought to myself, "What a complicated religion!" When I asked him why we pray to each of them, he answered, "You can choose one God if you wish, but to be fair, you should pay your respects to each." He went on to name the gods, such as Lord Krishna and Lord Shiva. There were many more, and I thought the list would never end.

As I grew older, I started reading the Bhagavad Gita and found solace in the passages about detachment and selflessness. However, I knew our religion was not just about devotion to a particular god. It was about understanding the interconnectedness of all things and living a balanced life. He always taught us to stay grounded in our values and principles.

My spiritual journey began with my parents' encouragement. They introduced me to temples, such as the Hari Krishna Temple. I found comfort and clarity in my understanding of Hinduism. Learning Sanskrit and singing devotional songs opened my eyes to the idea that spirituality encompasses more than just rituals and prayers; it is also about personal transformation and development. As an adult, I appreciated the intricate beauty of our religion's complexity.

It is our responsibility to discover a religion that deeply resonates with us and to follow that path. Personally, this journey has brought me peace and purpose. I have come to recognize the significance of serving others and giving back. I am constantly motivated to become a better individual and to contribute to the well-being of those around me. The teachings I have encountered have become a fundamental part of me, guiding my decisions and actions. I vividly recall my father's wise words: Being a good person requires hard work and dedication. I strive to uphold these values, endeavoring to exhibit kindness and understanding. Only by collectively embracing these principles can we, as a society, achieve true greatness.

In every interaction, I remind myself that every individual I meet faces their own set of challenges. Through striving to better myself and showing kindness and empathy towards others, I aim to impact their lives, no matter how small, positively. I appreciate the life lessons I have learned and eagerly look forward to continuous personal growth. Notably, my parents no longer practice Hinduism, marking a notable change in our family dynamics.

Growing up, my parents embarked on a spiritual journey that led them to Christianity, diverging from our Hindu roots. Despite this shift in beliefs, I am grateful for the values and foundation Hinduism has instilled in me. I have come to appreciate the common values of compassion, kindness, and love shared by various religions. My father never pressured me to change my beliefs or my religion, in contrast to my mother, who gave lengthy speeches and continually tried to sway my beliefs. I refused to choose between my husband and my parents, who follow different faiths. I did not want a divided family due to differing religious beliefs.

As I navigated my own beliefs, I dedicated myself to creating an environment of acceptance and freedom for my adult children to choose their spiritual path, free from pressure or conflict. This came about due to my children having long-term relationships with non-Indians. So, I had to adjust my thoughts and beliefs to change with the modern times we are living in.

Despite Rani and Elizabeth having embarked on their religious journey as Hindus, this did not prevent them from being critical of my faith. Their infrequent attendance at church and lack of adherence to biblical teachings contrasted with their judgmental attitudes. A genuine follower of any religion should align their lifestyle with its principles. It is important not to judge others based on their faith, gender, or social status, as acceptance and respect should be paramount.

We must acknowledge the interdependence between environmental protection and human well-being. Our choices and behaviors affect other people as well as the environment. We can foster understanding and encourage the community to be empathetic and kind to individuals close to us. Furthermore, we can contribute to ensuring a better and more peaceful world. By preserving the environment and making ethical choices, we can save it for future generations, as it is our collective responsibility.

From my perspective, I believe in the importance of embracing a global citizenship mindset and advocating for harmony in our interconnected world. I prioritize aligning my actions and attitudes with my core values and beliefs, striving to live authentically rather than simply voicing those values. Drawing upon the common principles of compassion, kindness, and love as foundations in various religions, I am dedicated to pursuing knowledge, fostering understanding, and contributing to a meaningful existence for myself and others. With faith as a guiding force, I am committed to embodying the highest version of myself.

My mother did not know much about Hinduism, but she was trying to learn it like us. I asked her, "Can you offer anything to God?" She was surprised by my question and said, "You can if it is sweet, but not meat." I improvised my offerings and started to offer chocolate bars. My father noticed and said, "I hope you know you have to share." So, I decided to split the chocolate and save half for myself. I placed the other half on the offering plate.

In the evening, my father asked who was going to clean the prayer area and re-set everything. Rani said, "No," but I knew I was the only one left to answer. It did not matter; I would still have to do it. My father then said, "Whoever cleans gets the prasad." I knew the chocolate was still there, so I asked him if no one had helped and if I could have all the prasad. He said, "Sure." I knew I had won again and did not have to share. I worked hard to cut grass for the neighbors to get my chocolate.

However, learning about Hinduism and our culture requires time and effort. It allowed us to understand our traditions and values better, fostering a deep appreciation for the diverse tapestry of India. Moreover, this exploration brought our family closer together, strengthening our identity and sense of belonging. Witnessing my parents and grandparents' selfless acts of kindness showed me the importance of sharing blessings and resources with others to make the world a better place. Their lives were a testament to the values and teachings we held dear—always ready to lend a helping hand

and give back to the community. By embracing these principles, unity and empathy flourished within our family, leaving a lasting impact that transcended generations.

I believe one does not need to attend a temple or church to find God or anywhere else. One can say or find solace in knowing that God is everywhere and nowhere at the same time. I learned that our religion and culture are not just limited to specific practices or beliefs; they are a way of life. They guide us to live a meaningful and fulfilling life and contribute to society's greater good. If you take religion out of the equation, you are left with fundamental principles of love, kindness, empathy, and understanding core values everyone is familiar with.

Hinduism embodies more than merely attending temples or engaging in rituals; it involves embracing the values of love, compassion, and service and endeavoring to impact our world positively. In Hinduism, we navigate life's challenges with the fundamental principles of compassion, respect, empathy, and understanding that are present in various religions and cultural traditions. These core values guide our interactions with others, shaping our perspectives and actions toward the world. By integrating these foundational components into our daily lives, we aim to cultivate love, kindness, and harmony in all our endeavors.

As our world continues to change and evolve at an unprecedented pace, it is more important than ever to adapt and evolve our traditions and cultures while still cherishing and preserving the core values they represent. Each person's spiritual journey is unique and personal. Regardless of the religion or belief system, the most important thing is that it leads us to be better individuals and brings us closer to the divine. Through my ongoing education and exploration of diverse religions, I have come to appreciate the similarities more than the differences. I see the common teachings of love, compassion, and respect for all beings woven throughout many faiths.

I view religion as a way of life that encourages learning and growth, both spiritually and intellectually. We were taught to respect and honor our ancestors, valuing the wisdom they passed down to us. I am grateful for my upbringing, which has shaped me into the person I am today. It has helped me develop a sense of identity and values that I hold dear. I have learned that it is possible to hold a nuanced view of one's faith, embracing its core principles while also questioning or disagreeing with certain aspects. This approach has allowed me to deepen my understanding of my faith while also staying true to my critical thinking and values.

In my recollection of religion, there is one incident that stands out vividly in my mind. It involves my father's prized possession—a rare record featuring George Harrison singing devotional Hindi songs. This record held a special place in my father's heart, as his faith and admiration for George Harrison were intertwined. Coincidentally, during the 1970s, he visited the Hare Krishna Temple in Vancouver, a small house that was the first temple in Vancouver, Canada.

My father had the opportunity to meet George Harrison. It was a surreal and unforgettable experience for him as he expressed his gratitude for the music's impact on his spiritual journey. However, tragedy struck the devotional record. The prized record was plundered, much to his dismay. It was later discovered that the thief responsible for this shocking act was none other than Rani, an 8-year-old who not only stole the record but also sold it. The revelation devastated my father.

The sentimental value attached to that specific record, combined with the spiritual connection he felt through the devotional Hindi songs, made it a deeply traumatic loss for him. He was upset and betrayed by Rani's actions. Something so precious and personal had been callously taken away, serving as a reminder of the fragile nature of material possessions and the transient nature of our attachment to them. Although physically gone, the spiritual significance of the record will forever remain in his heart and memories.

Father, are we celebrating Diwali or Christmas? I am so confused. He stated that we were celebrating both and gave me a definition of Diwali; he said it is also known as the Festival of Lights, a Hindu festival celebrated in India and other countries with a significant Hindu population. It marks the return of Lord Rama, his wife Sita, and his brother Lakshmana from their 14-year exile and their victory over the demon king Ravan. The people of Ayodhya welcomed them by lighting diyas and decorating the city with lights. Diwali is also associated with the goddess Lakshmi, and people believe that by lighting diyas and performing puja to her, they will be blessed with wealth and prosperity for the upcoming year.

The festival lasts for five days and involves decorating homes, exchanging gifts, enjoying festive food, and lighting fireworks. It is a time for families to come together and celebrate the triumph of light over darkness, good over evil, and knowledge over ignorance. With bated breath, we eagerly anticipated the arrival of Diwali. It was a magnificent time when we would be dressed in vibrant new clothes that were stunning in their bright hues.

As the sun danced its way up to the sky, my mother would rise like an Indian culinary queen. Her nimble hand conjures up exquisite vegetarian Indian dishes and Indian sweets like barfi and ladoo. Her food would tease our taste buds, each morsel she crafted with love and sweetness. Nothing compares to the flavor and the excitement for our senses. Under the canopy of darkness, my mother, Rani, and I embarked on our mission to light the diya's (candles) throughout the house and patio. The diya's lit the home; every nook and cranny in the home was full of beautiful lights and aroma from the sandalwood incense.

The environment left a feeling of peace and serenity within our home. As evening set in, we started our prayers and offerings of prasad to our God. In the embrace of this enchanting celebration, our senses were tantalized by the air full of beautiful scents and - soul stirring melodies. Diwali, a kaleidoscope of emotions and sensations, left an indelible imprint on our hearts, rekindling the fire of devotion and binding our spirits in eternal joy. We eagerly embraced a beautiful new tradition, immersing ourselves in the captivating allure of Christmas year after year. As a child, my heart would burst with anticipation for the joyous season.

During Christmas events in kindergarten, I started to understand the true meaning of Christmas. It was about celebrating the birth of Jesus Christ and spreading love, kindness, and generosity. I realized that the gifts we received were just a symbol of love and appreciation and that giving was more meaningful than receiving. I remained stubborn and tried to share my new-found understanding with my family, but Rani remained stubborn and materialistic. She continued to throw temper tantrums over gifts and refused to participate in charity events at church.

My father often emphasized that giving should not be confined to the holiday season; it can be practiced year-round. Inspired by his words, we extended our acts of kindness beyond Christmas, volunteering our time at the temple and church. These experiences have taught me invaluable lessons, and I am grateful for the opportunities to impact the world through each act of kindness positively. It became clear that spreading love and kindness was not just a part of the holiday season but a meaningful aspect of our daily lives.

As I continue to volunteer, give back, and spread kindness wherever I go, I hope to inspire others to do the same. The holiday season ceased to revolve around material possessions; instead, it transformed into a time dedicated to spreading love, kindness, and generosity to those most in need. This shift in perspective became the greatest gift of all. The holiday season transitioned into a reflection on how we could contribute to our community and assist others, intertwining with our daily lives. Giving and nurturing a culture of kindness beyond the holiday season became a lifestyle rich with meaning and beauty.

I initiated the Operation Shoebox collection, filling shoeboxes with essentials like pencils, pens, notebooks, paper, and small toys for children in third-world countries. Additionally, I launched a food hamper initiative for the local church soup kitchen. Engaging in these acts of charity gave me a sense of purpose. As my parents entered retirement, I involved them in the shoebox collection, and they found joy in assembling items for under privileged children.

This endeavor soon became a cherished family tradition that we eagerly anticipated. Through our ongoing collections, we witnessed the profound impact that even the simplest items could have on individuals' lives. A pencil or notebook could open doors for a child striving for education in a developing nation, and a food hamper could provide nourishment for those facing homelessness or poverty within our community.

Through our actions, we also felt a sense of community and connection with others who were enthusiastic about helping those in need. We met other volunteers, donors, and recipients, and I learned about their stories and experiences. Our efforts may have been small, but they influenced the lives of others. We learned that giving back helped others and filled our hearts with joy and purpose. Today, as I continue to volunteer, give back, and spread kindness, I hope to inspire others to do the same.

Christmas is, to me, a time for reflecting on our blessings and considering how we can be effective in helping others. It is not about the gifts we receive but the gifts we give, whether that is our time or kind words. Helping others fills my heart with joy, and I am thankful for the unwavering support of my family and friends, who also value these principles. Reflecting on my journey, I appreciate the significant lessons I have learned. The essence is in spreading love and kindness during the holiday season and incorporating these values into our everyday lives.

In my case, I was caught between two vastly different religions. Hinduism was a complicated and complex religion, whereas Christianity was less restrictive. However, both religions taught me that no matter what path one follows, everyone should encompass empathy, love, kindness, and a sense of service to society. I honestly believe in letting people choose their faith and religion. The act of coercing or mandating someone's adherence to a particular religion does not garner any additional merit or favor. True blessings come when someone willingly and wholeheartedly serves one chosen faith without imposition or constraints.

However, in our upbringing, our parents compelled both Rani and me to attend church and the temple, leaving me with a sense that the compulsion to comply detracted from the true purpose of these religious sanctuaries. Instead of focusing on these essential aspects of these spiritual visits, I found myself consumed by fatigue, boredom, or drifting into daydreams as a means of escape. My firm conviction is that traditions and culture can exist independently of religion. One does not need to relinquish their culture or traditions to adhere to a particular religion. Some people, like my parents, believe that traditions and culture are integral to religion, but it is important to understand that culture and religion are distinct.

When I reflect on those Christmas celebrations of the past, a wave of nostalgia and warmth washes over me. I am deeply grateful for the traditions my father passed down to me, and I intend to continue them with my children. To me, Christmas will forever embody sentiments of love, family, and the joy of giving generously with a thankful spirit. Our Christmas festivities were simple yet cherished customs, such as baking Christmas cake with my mother and adorning the tree as a family. Over the years, we introduced new traditions, like watching beloved holiday classics such as 'A Christmas Carol' and my personal favorite, 'A Charlie Brown Christmas.'

I also remember attending school in the evenings for drama and singing practice. My parents would come to watch the Christmas plays put on by our class, and sometimes, they would even bring friends or relatives. Our family celebrated Christmas together as we wrapped gifts for those less fortunate and visited Santa Claus, a Canadian tradition our family embraced. Our house would become alive with festive decorations, the aroma of my mother's cooking and baking filling the air, and everyone overflowing with joy.

Rani would spend hours making her Christmas list. Mine was much simpler; I was grateful for whatever Santa would bring me. The whole family would come together, whether stringing the lights, decorating the tree, or the kids placing the ornaments and candy canes. My father would invite his friends and neighbors over to enjoy treats and give gifts. We were too excited for Christmas and could not wait for Santa. We left milk and cookies for him; Father always complained to Mother about the milk as he was not a fan of drinking milk. He tried to tell us that Santa did not like milk, but our mother put a stop to that and said to Father there would be no changes in the new traditions.

On Christmas day, the entire family would eagerly rise - early, brimming with excitement to discover the surprises Santa - had left beneath the glittering tree. The mornings were filled with the comforting aroma of our mother's freshly brewed chai, complemented by her delectable baked goods and renowned fruit cake, creating the perfect setting for us to huddle around the tree and unveil our gifts.

Each of us took turns receiving a special present from her, relishing the anticipation of slowly unwrapping them. Following the gift exchange, we experimented with our new toys and indulged in timeless Christmas movies together. Amidst the laughter and merry chaos, the core values of Christmas. These values of love, kindness, and generosity encompassed our hearts even as we celebrated, reminding us of the importance of sharing joy and spreading goodwill during the festive season.

We would take the time to call our relatives and friends, wishing them a happy holiday season. We would often visit the local charity of our father's choice and spread joy to those less fortunate. In the afternoon, we would sit down to enjoy a delicious Christmas feast around the table. Our father would then take us out to play in the snow while our mother cleaned up and took some time to relax.

In the evening, we would gather around the fireplace, engaging in conversations and genuinely enjoying each other's company. The warmth and love of our family were truly palpable. As the day came to an end, we continued to bond by playing games and sharing stories. We felt grateful for the love and kindness we had received. It was a truly magical time filled with laughter, joy, and abundant love.

As I grew older, I became curious about why we celebrated Christmas even though we were not Christians. When I asked my father about it, he explained that it was not solely about religion. He believed that Christmas was about helping others and being generous. He emphasized that the spirit of Christmas transcended religious beliefs, culture, and social status. He wanted us to understand that spreading love and joy was something that everyone could relate to, regardless of their faith or background.

My father's response impressed me and provided me with a fresh perspective on the meaning of Christmas. It was not just about the religious significance or the commercialized aspects but rather about doing good for others and connecting to everyone around us. This sentiment stayed with me throughout my life, reminding me of the power of small acts of kindness and their impact on others. When I look back on those memories, I feel incredibly lucky to have had such a wonderful family.

Our gifts may not have been the biggest or the most expensive, but the love and warmth we shared made Christmas truly special. It is easy to get caught up in the materialistic side of the holidays, but we should remember that the most valuable things in life cannot be bought or wrapped in shiny paper. The moments we spent with loved ones, the memories we created, and the love we shared were what truly made the holiday season magical and meaningful.

The Future holiday seasons will be different due to all the deaths and trauma. I am grateful for the memories of my childhood and the opportunity to create new ones in the future with my own family. I appreciate the trivial things even more now the smell of fresh pine trees, the twinkling of lights, the joy of wrapping gifts, and the warmth of being surrounded by family and friends. Regardless of how our traditions may change over time, the one constant is the feeling of love, warmth, and joy that comes with the holiday season.

Months would go by, the snow would melt, and everything around us would turn into slush. I did not particularly enjoy that part, as it was messy and inconvenient, making it difficult to play outside without getting my shoes wet. However, I knew the snow would return again next year, and I eagerly looked forward to it all year round. That fluffy, white stuff was so magical that it made me feel incredibly happy and free. Even though the scenery may have changed, and the snow has melted away, the love we had for each other and the memories we shared will always remain the same.

Our family spent so much time together, creating joyful and heartwarming moments. I recall my father driving my mother, Rani, and me to see the beautiful Christmas lights in Vancouver. When we returned home, my mother would make chai tea for everyone, along with her fancy homemade samosas. She was always busy cooking or baking, and seeing her the happiest in the kitchen was truly special. She loved making Indian treats like jalebi or ladoo to share with the family and our neighbors. These moments became some of the happiest memories of my childhood. Even though we did not have much money, we always had each other, which was more than enough.

As I reflect on those cherished memories, I am reminded of the true spirit of Christmas. It is not about the presents or the grand gestures but about the love, warmth, and joy that we share as a family. It is about the little moments and the simple traditions that brought us together. I have come to realize that the most precious gifts we can give are the love, joy, and kindness we share with others.

It is essential to acknowledge and respect the distinction between cultural characteristics and religious views, particularly in situations where contrasting beliefs can lead to conflict. A person's beliefs that differ from other religions, affiliations or people can breed animosity. I have witnessed this firsthand as my parents decided to reduce their interaction with my family due to our differing religious beliefs. This period posed challenges for my family, especially for my children, who felt the absence of their grandparents. It is a vital aspect for children to have a connection to their grandparents, particularly in Indian families. Grandparents play a significant role in shaping a child's behavior, cultural identity and passing down traditions. Witnessing the destruction of a potentially meaningful relationship that could have brought diverse personalities together in a nurturing environment was devastating.

Chapter 7

Tragedy, Moving, and Gender Biases.

O ur mother received a call from our father's work alerting her that he had been injured and taken to the hospital. We were shocked and scared. Our mother, accompanied by a family friend, rushed to the hospital. The doctors immediately took him into surgery. The family was informed that he had lost his right eyesight, and they could not save it. In the following months, there were endless hospital visits, consultations with doctors, and physical therapy sessions. The news was devastating, as we never expected such dire consequences from his fall. Seeing him lying in a hospital bed, connected to machines, was heartbreaking. Despite the challenges, we held on to hope for his recovery.

We knew that our father was a fighter, and he had a strong will to live. As time passed, we saw slight improvements in his condition. The doctors slowly started weaning him off the machines, and he began to show signs of consciousness. It was during this time that our mother's strength and resilience shone through. She spent every day with him, advocating for his needs and ensuring that he received the best care possible. Rani and I visited our father, bringing him his favorite foods and keeping him company.

After several months, our father was finally well enough to leave the hospital and come back home. Although he still had a long road to recovery to be with us, we learned to adjust to a new way of life, where we had to take extra precautions to keep him safe and comfortable. The experience taught us to be grateful for our health and the time we have with our loved ones. We learned that life could change in an instant and that we need to be prepared for the unexpected.

We also realized the significance of having a dedicated support system and the value of resilience and perseverance. Despite the hardships, our mother adamantly refused to give up. She acknowledged that it would be a tough road ahead but stood firm in the commitment she had made to our father. Her determination to navigate through this challenging period and her readiness to do whatever was necessary to aid his recovery were unwavering. Confronted with obstacles, our parents came together to collaborate and support each other through the highs and lows.

Our mother was a constant source of strength and encouragement for our father as he struggled to come to terms with his injury. Over time, things began to get better. He learned to adapt to his new condition, and we started to rebuild our lives. Our mother's constant support and dedication made all the difference. In the end, her decision to stand by our family paid off. We were stronger and closer than ever before, and we continued to support each other through life's many challenges.

Following our father's injury and subsequent recovery, our family decided to buy a new home that symbolized stability and security. Gone were the days of cramped living in a basement or constantly shifting from one place to another. The new house offered us a sense of space and comfort, and we were grateful for the yard that allowed us to enjoy the outdoors and host family gatherings. Living in a safe and tranquil environment enabled Rani and me to embrace our childhood and fully appreciate our new surroundings. Without the interruptions of our previous living situations, we flourished and were able to pursue our interests and excel.

The community that came along with our new homes was undeniably one of the greatest advantages. In our neighborhood, which was mostly comprised of Europeans, we warmly embraced everyone. This open-mindedness allowed us to forge new friendships and establish connections with our neighbors. There was something about them that made Canada feel like our true home. It must have been their genuine kindness, which now is a rarity.

Our new home in Vancouver was a symbol of the new life that we had created in Canada. It stood for hope, opportunity, and a fresh start. We were grateful for the chance to build a new future in our new home. I interacted with the people in our new neighborhood and felt a sense of community. By offering my help in mowing lawns or clearing snow for the elderly, I aimed to make a positive impact on their lives. Without any expectations, I genuinely connected with them through love and compassion.

Among them, there was a kind-hearted elderly Italian - couple whom I referred to as Uncle Joe and Aunt Cecilia. In their sixties, they exemplified love and generosity in their relationship. Tragically, they experienced the loss of their only son, Nick, who was a friend of mine. After Nick received a brand-new sports car as a gift from his parents upon graduating high school, a tragic accident occurred.

Nick collided head-on with a garbage truck and, sadly, lost his life. This devastating accident had a profound impact on our family. To provide support during this tough time, I prioritized visiting Uncle Joe and Aunt Cecilia. I aimed to help them by taking care of tasks like mowing the lawn or shoveling snow. Witnessing Uncle Joe's heartbreak and grief made me realize the significance of being there for others in their darkest moments.

I will never forget the piercing agony that was etched into my soul when my father shared the heartbreaking news with me. The heaviness in his voice spoke of a pain so deep that words could hardly encompass it. At that moment, I could not help but feel the raw ache in my own heart, as if the weight of their tragedy rested - on my shoulders. How could such a cruel twist of fate steal away their only child, leaving them shattered and helpless and their - world crumbling in despair? The sheer injustice of it all was overwhelming, a relentless reminder of life's unyielding cycle. Months later, Uncle Joe passed away, followed by Aunt Cecilia. The loss of these remarkable individuals deeply saddened me, but I will always cherish the beautiful memories I shared with them.

In 1976, my mother welcomed a baby boy named Michael into the world. The joy on my father's face was undeniable as he finally had a son and namesake. Since my little brother was born, our family dynamics have changed. My parents became more focused on traditional gender roles stemming from our Indian heritage. They started to enforce old-fashioned views that a woman's primary role was to take care of the home, learn cooking and cleaning, and look after the family. This shift in expectations based on gender norms highlighted a contradiction within our family dynamics. It was evident that there were contradictions in the expectations and roles assigned by my parents based on traditional gender norms.

While these roles and expectations were rooted in cultural beliefs and norms, it was important for me to question and challenge them. I was questioning why certain tasks are assigned based on gender rather than ability or interest, engaging in open conversations with parents about these roles and expectations, and expressing my feelings and beliefs about gender equality and individual capabilities. By sharing my thoughts and challenging traditional gender roles, I tried to foster a more inclusive and balanced family dynamic. My thoughts did not matter to my parents as their beliefs never changed.

Though I did not understand this concept, as I was always helping my father with any jobs he needed help with, whether it was yard work, painting, or renovating homes, I thought these were male jobs. Yet here I was doing them. So, when considering gender roles according to my parents' rules and traditions, why were they letting me perform these tasks but not allowing me to do other things? This was a shock to me, as I had always believed that my parents valued and empowered all their children equally, regardless of gender.

However, there was a sudden shift in expectations. I believe that when my father thought he could not have a son, he treated his daughters with more freedom and liberties. Later in life, I noticed that my parents started to allocate more resources towards Michael's education and activities. At the same time, the girls were expected to spend time helping with household chores and cooking.

This caused tensions within the family, and it was frustrating to see Rani and I cast aside while our brother got all the attention and support. In Canada, I saw that such outdated notions failed to match up with the values I hold dear. Tension in our home increased as I began to question these preconceived notions. Striving for gender equality in our family was a continuous and challenging battle since absolutely nothing changed. Rani and I were still seen as invaluable assets in our family. Gender norms and social expectations are things that motivate me to speak out against them. I am devoted to pursuing my passions and desires in everything I do, including my career, and I refuse to let my gender restrict me to any one profession. I intend to go beyond these boundaries and the restrictions that society has imposed on women, not just for myself but also for other women.

Despite efforts to promote gender equality, gender biases still exist within some families. Therefore, it is crucial to have open and honest discussions with parents about your feelings and concerns. It may benefit from involving a trusted family member or a close friend to facilitate discussions. It is crucial to ensure that all children are provided with equal opportunities for growth and development. Every child deserves the same level of assistance and encouragement, regardless of their gender.

It was not until 1996 that my parents became Christians, as my mother was paralyzed, and my father took her to various temples for healing. The visits to the temples did not help her recover. After trying for a long time and running around to different temples, they finally gave up on Hinduism. They came across an advertisement for a Christian healer at the local church and decided to attend the service. During that day, God blessed my mother, and she was miraculously healed. This incident cemented their faith in God. While everyone does not need to experience divine healing as my mother did, I do believe that miracles happen and that having faith can bring about such miracles.

As my parents embraced a more modern perspective that values equality and respect for all genders, they began shedding their traditional views. This change was evident in how they treated Michael and Elizabeth, while Rani and I experienced different treatment. For instance, where Michael and Elizabeth were given more freedom and liberties, in contrast, societal expectations pushed Rani and me, at age sixteen, towards the traditional path of a forced arranged marriage.

The stark divergence between Elizabeth's life and our life served as a poignant reminder of the contrasting paths we had unknowingly embarked upon. Rani and I had fought our own battles and faced countless obstacles. We fought and struggled for years. Our sole purpose was to attain the freedom and equality we yearned for, but Elizabeth seemed to effortlessly inherit all that we had fought so hard to achieve. Her life radiated with opulence and ease, a stark contrast to the challenges and sacrifices we had endured. It was as if our shared upbringing had shaped us in contradictory ways, molding us into individuals who would forever tread separate paths. Elizabeth was sheltered by wealth and was not aware of the difficulties and tribulations we faced along the way.

In hindsight, it is evident that Elizabeth never inquired about our upbringing or the circumstances surrounding our arranged marriages. She consistently showed disinterest and dismissed our concerns with her trademark phrase, 'not my problem.' While we fought tirelessly for equality, justice, and better opportunities, she effortlessly reaped the rewards of our collective fight. It was disheartening, to say the least, to witness the stark differences in our circumstances, a constant reminder of the disparities that existed within the same family.

It was not a matter of resentment or envy but rather a poignant realization of the intricate complexities of life. We had been molded by the same hands and guided by the same parents, yet fate steered us into vastly different realms. It was a reminder that paths and upbringings, despite starting from the same roots, can diverge drastically, resulting in vastly contradictory outcomes. As we observed Elizabeth's life unfold before us, we could not help but reflect on the raw power of circumstance, privilege, and opportunity. It served as a poignant reminder to cherish the battles we fought and the progress we made, even if it was not reflected on the same gilded stage that she danced upon.

I can still vividly recall those tumultuous nights that resonated with heated arguments between my parents one night etched itself deep into my memory, surpassing the others in its intensity. Amid their stormy dispute, my mother, cradling Michael tightly in her arms, along with Rani, abruptly stormed out of the house. I hurriedly chased after her, tears streaming down my face, desperately pleading for her to stay.

As I caught up with my mother, she turned to me, her words leaving an indelible mark on my heart: "Stay with your father, as you are dark like him." This statement challenges the hurtful connotations that suggest that when she fell in love with my father, she failed to consider his darker features and the possibility of passing them on to her children. If she had elevated expectations when it came to physical appearance, perhaps she could have married someone with features she could proudly showcase to the world.

At that moment, a whirlwind of emotions engulfed my young mind. Confusion, fear, and a profound sense of loss set in as my mother's words cut through me, casting shadows of doubt and painting my father in a negative light. Father, consumed by anger, struggled to find the right words to console me, and a flicker of understanding began to emerge within me. We silently retreated into our home, the weight of shattered harmony leaving us with a heavy weight on our shoulders. As we settled down, my father tenderly took a seat beside me, his face reflecting a blend of remorse and empathy.

With an emotional voice, He began to speak, unraveling the complexities of adult relationships. "Beta," (child), he started, his words slowly seeping into my wounded soul, "disagreements do not signify the end of love." Even the strongest of bonds face turbulence and turmoil at times. Sometimes, out of frustration and anger, adults express themselves in ways that may seem harsh or confusing. But we must remember that it does not mean they do not care. Love can coexist alongside strife, and we must navigate through the storms while holding onto the thread that unites us.

As my father's words gradually began to heal the cracks in my heart, a glimmer of hope kindled within me. I started to comprehend that beneath the tempestuous battles, there was a love that endured. Despite the arguments that tore apart my parents, they still shared a love that refused to be extinguished. And with that realization, an inner strength blossomed within my young heart, reminding me that even in the darkest of nights, love possesses the power to prevail.

My mother finally came back home after hours of being out. My father went to work without saying a word about what had happened. I still did not fully understand, but I felt a little better after talking to him. I knew he would always be there for me, no matter what happened. It was a scary lesson to learn, but I realized that even families have ups and downs, and we just must stick together and support each other through them.

I vividly remember the mischievous moments when Rani and I would engage in fights and end up locked in the furnace room. This small space, located downstairs in our house, became our temporary prison, with its only escape being a narrow window. However, it was Rani who hatched an escape plan, slipping through that very window. Despite her successful getaway, I made a conscious decision to face my punishment honestly and with pride. Unfortunately, when I revealed Rani's escape plans, our father swiftly sealed the window shut, cutting off any future getaways. It was humbling knowing that she would be facing punishment as well. In fairness, he decided my punishment was paid in full.

Our mother's struggle to handle us led to a troubling pattern of discipline. She resorted to locking us in the furnace room as a means of punishment, as it was the only way she could manage our defiance. Sometimes, we would be punished with no dinner and trapped in the room until 11 p.m., and our mother would inform our father about her issues and struggles. He would be angry after a long day at work. The confrontations would escalate, causing him to use a belt to discipline us, leaving us in tears, exhausted, and sometimes prompting us to fight back in a desperate bid for relief. This cycle - of abuse stemmed from our mother's inability to cope with the challenges of raising two defiant children. The furnace room became a symbol of our confinement and the toxic environment created by our parents' struggles to manage our behavior.

Finally, Rani and I were given the freedom to walk to school on our own due to our mother being busy with Michael, which made us both thrilled. Our father permitted us to take a newspaper route. He believed that it would keep us busy and out of trouble, but little did he know what Rani was capable of. As we finished our deliveries, Rani suggested we make a quick stop at the corner store on Kingsway Street. Excitedly, we entered the store with money in our pockets and the intention of purchasing candy treats.

However, to my surprise, she had a different plan in mind. She grabbed a tempting ring-shaped sucker and swiftly slipped it into her newspaper bag; the store owner had caught sight of her actions. Suddenly, the air filled with the owner's enraged voice, threatening to summon the police. Caught amid the panic, I implored Rani to pay for her candy so we could escape this dreadful situation.

But before I knew it, she dashed out of the store, leaving me behind, frozen with uncertainty. Fear of being connected to her behavior, even though I had done nothing wrong, overwhelmed me. After what seemed like an eternity, Rani finally returned to rescue me from the paralyzing grip of fear. Together, we hopped on our bikes and rode back home, my heart pounding with anxiety. Seeking solace, I hid under my bed, overwhelmed with worries about how our father would react to this incident. Even though I was not the one who had stolen the candy, I was still consumed by the fear of being associated with Rani's actions. Our watchful mother soon discovered my hiding spot and opened the door to a conversation that brought clarity and a solution to this troubling experience.

The following day, our father took us back to the store to confront the situation. The same woman was working there, and he made Rani apologize for stealing the candy. When we arrived home, he was visibly upset with both of us. He sternly warned us that any disrespect, dishonesty, or theft would not be acceptable and would result in severe punishment. It was a distressing ordeal for me, and it was all because of her mistake.

Even though my father is no longer by my side, his wisdom continues to guide me in every decision I make, whether for myself or my children. I always find myself reflecting on whether my actions align with the values he instilled in me and if they are something he would be proud of. I strive to conduct myself in a way that brings honor to his legacy and always consider the impact of my choices on those around me. These fundamental principles -

serve as my compass, helping me navigate life with integrity and accountability.

I may not have taken the same path and approach as my father, but his teachings have helped me with my values and morals. I strive to be kind, empathetic, and compassionate to everyone I meet, regardless of their background or beliefs. It is amazing how a few small acts of kindness can lift a person's spirit and make their day brighter. I am grateful to my father for instilling these life lessons in me, which have become the foundation for the person I am today. When I think about the lessons he taught me, it is not just about what he said but also how he led by example. He demonstrated the importance of hard work, honesty, and perseverance. He never gave up on his goals. This should be an incentive for future generations: that you can do anything and accomplish anything; the only thing stopping you is your mind.

One thing I appreciated most about my father was his ability to see the good in people. He was not quick to judge or criticize others, and he always went out of his way to help those in need. He showed me the value of empathy and compassion and taught me that kindness can make a significant difference in someone's life. As I navigate my journey through life, I try to live by these same principles. I want to be a source of light in this world, to be an example, and to leave a positive impact on those around me. Every day is a reminder to stay true to myself and always to make choices that align with my values.

The only question that still bothers me is: why was he so indifferent toward his girls? And treated us better before his son was born? After the birth of his son, gender biases started to show. Was it a matter of societal norms or a personal choice for him? I guess we will never have the answers, but the lesson for me here is to evaluate the experience and see where changes are needed.

I was determined to incorporate gender equality and acceptance into my parenting style. From this experience, I supported my daughter in taking an active role in her future career, and she trained to be a welder, which is a male-dominated field. If more parents try to support their children, they too can help to break the cycle of gender biases and create a more equal and accepting society for future generations.

I strongly believe that providing the necessary tools for success is a good start, but building a support system to encourage everyone to fight for equality is a long journey. A famous quote comes to mind: "You can lead a horse to water, but you cannot make it drink." I think something similar applies here. Not only pointing out where things need fixing or restructuring will not help; everyone needs to be an active participant.

Whenever my father took on remodeling jobs, I always found myself sacrificing my evenings and weekends to help him. In return, I was sometimes allowed to go out with my cousins to the drive-in movies. This was very rare when my father would allow this, and I came to realize that it was only when he needed alone time or did not want me hanging around. Radhika Reggie and all of us would cram into Radhika's car. The tight space made me uncomfortable, and I found myself wishing I had stayed at home. Deep down, I just wanted to be the only cousin accompanying them. Despite being out and free from Rani's constant presence, I could not shake the feeling of homesickness, even though all I truly craved was freedom. It seemed bittersweet to enjoy the outing when I felt that Rani should have had the opportunity as well if only she had worked as diligently as I did. At times, I did not understand why I was so reliant on Rani or the comfort of our home. The strict upbringing and sheltered life affected me more than I realized.

Chapter 8

Fiji and Summer School

In 1977, it was time for a visit to our relatives in Fiji. Our relatives were quite curious about our family. The trip involved visiting relatives. I remember our father mentioning that we did not have sufficient time to visit everyone. His younger half-brother's wedding kept everyone busy. Hindu weddings lasted a week, and it became tiring to socialize with unfamiliar relatives, especially when there was a language barrier for those who did not speak English.

Fiji exuded a captivating charm with its stunning landscapes and hospitable people. The island seemed to transport you to another era. The sight of towering coconut trees swaying in the wind created a melody that resonated with the soul. Once in Fiji, the allure was undeniable, making it hard to contemplate leaving. I relished the strolls amidst the sugar cane fields, the gentle caress of the ocean breeze enveloping me, evoking a sense of déjà vu. Despite having no recollection of ever visiting before, Fiji's enchantment held me in its spell.

Transitioning to the lifestyle in Fiji posed challenges for both Rani and me. Venturing into remote areas inaccessible by car, we met relatives living in impoverished conditions without modern amenities like indoor plumbing. The cuisine was a stark contrast to what Rani and I were accustomed to back home, as we missed the familiar tastes of burgers, bread, and cereals. Finding these staples in Fiji without a readily available source of income proved difficult. To alleviate our discomfort, our father arranged for relatives to help us with shopping. Despite our efforts, the absence of fast-food outlets in Fiji left us feeling a sense of longing and disappointment.

In the small town of Wayabi, where my mother's relatives lived, we were warmly welcomed by our grandparents for the first time. They greeted us with kisses and hugs, showing their excitement about meeting our family. Our grandfather "Nana" was a skilled tailor who operated his business from home, specializing in crafting leather bags and purses. His work fascinated me, particularly the bags he created. To our delight, Nana gifted us backpacks for school, which he had made himself.

However, the visit took a dark turn when Rani, in a malicious act, intentionally stabbed Nana in the butt with a pair of scissors. Shocked and horrified by Rani's actions, our parents rushed to the scene, and the severity of Nana's injury led our father to decide that it was best for us to leave. Our mother, along with Michael, decided to stay and deal with the issue. Our mother later informed us that Nana needed medical attention, including stitches for the injury.

We visited our grandfather (Ajja) on our father's side of the family. The place was so big that it looked like a school with so many rooms. There were so many adults and lots of kids. We were introduced to everyone, and then we went to play outside. The adults were in the house talking about everything. Ajja finally forgave our father for the marriage and accepted all of us. As we were leaving, Ajja told me I looked like Grandmother (our father's mom). He gave us hugs and kisses as we left. We saw Ajja crying; our father said he never saw him cry.

It was time for us to leave Fiji - the place that holds a special place in our hearts. All the relatives were at the airport to see us off. It reminded me of a church gathering or an assembly at school. Everyone was hugging and crying. The plane arrived in Vancouver, and we realized that we could not live without burgers and fries. We were excited to be back home, sleeping in our beds and watching television.

As school started again, things changed at home. With more homework to do, we found we were spending less time playing and more time studying. To make things even more difficult, our father was unable to help us since he did not know the subjects we were learning. Our father enrolled Rani and me in summer school. We were so angry and upset about it. While our friends were enjoying their summer vacation, here we were, begrudgingly walking to school. It felt like such a punishment at the time.

Despite our initial reluctance, when summer school began, we were pleasantly surprised to find that many of our friends had enrolled as well. We had expected the worst, that we would not have any fun or enjoy school at all. But, as it turned out, we were wrong. Summer school turned out to be much better than we had anticipated. Being with our friends made the experience more enjoyable, and we were able to support and encourage each other as we learned. It felt good to know we were not alone in our studies and that everyone was working hard together.

What made the experience even better was that our favorite teacher was teaching the summer classes. Having a teacher we knew and trusted made us feel more confident and comfortable in the classroom. Plus, he made learning fun and engaging, and we looked forward to each lesson with excitement. It was like we were all discovering something new and exciting together, and we felt proud of our progress as the weeks went on.

By the end of the summer program, we realized that it was not just about getting better grades or catching up on missed work.

It was about the experience of learning and the confidence it instilled in us. We had all come together with a common goal and worked hard to achieve it. It was a lesson in perseverance and determination, and we were grateful for the opportunity. We learned that sometimes the things we dread or fear can turn out to be the best experience of our lives and that with hard work and the support of others, we can achieve anything we set our minds to.

I attended summer school every year because my father believed education was important for success in life. This summer, in addition to my studies, I began tutoring a second-grade student named Johnny. He was struggling with both speaking and writing in English, and his father, who was a friend of my father's, asked me to help. Over several months, I dedicated my time to tutoring Johnny, and his father witnessed significant improvement in his language skills. Impressed with the progress, his father expressed a desire for me to continue tutoring him daily.

My father intervened, explaining that I had my homework to focus on and could not commit to daily tutoring. He suggested the idea of Johnny attending summer school while I would assist him on weekends. I did not ask for any payment for my tutoring services, as I believe that helping others is an inherently good thing to do. As Johnny attended summer school, I was elected to help him register for school and walk him back and forth. The downside was that after Johnny lived far away, approximately 10 blocks from our home, on

Fraser Street. I recall Rani was upset that we had to go out of our way to do this favor.

Rani never seemed to have any interests beyond staying home or going shopping with our mother. It was clear that she tended to prioritize her own needs and would not lend a hand unless there was something in it for her. She missed out on so many valuable opportunities to learn and grow at a young age, mainly because she was overly sheltered and overprotected by our mother. Reflecting on it now, I believe that experiencing a variety of situations, both good and bad, can teach us important life lessons during childhood. If only our mother had allowed Rani to face these challenges, her life could have possibly taken a different path. It might have changed the course of my life, too.

Chapter 9

Biases and Elementary School

My mother began to display a bias toward me. Despite weighing 80 pounds, she frequently criticized my weight. She made comments about my skin color and questioned my intelligence. This treatment made me feel as though she was not my biological mother. I felt hurt and angry. How could she say harsh words like that to me? I was her child as well. Throughout my life, I have been all too aware of my mother's biased treatment of me. During this period, the stark differences in our physical appearances struck me with full force. Unlike my mother, Rani, or Elizabeth, my body shape was pear-shaped, as was my darker complexion. I had prayed every day to look like Mother. Over time, it became painfully clear that such a transformation was beyond my reach.

A feeling of crushing disappointment overwhelmed me as I grappled with my parents' inability to fully accept and appreciate me for who I was. Instead, they seemed to yearn for me to mold myself into Rani's image. The stream of negative comments about my appearance undoubtedly took its toll on my self-esteem, leaving me feeling depleted and devoid of worth. I did not want to be like Rani. I did not appreciate her qualities; she was selfish, arrogant, and vain.

Gradually, I started to interact with my mother and Rani less. This caused me to be around my father more. I struggled to find my place within my own family. Facing my reflection in the mirror became disappointing, as the sight of my features filled me with an insurmountable sense of unease. Nevertheless, I look back on that period as a turning point in my life; it was when I discovered that my worth could not be defined by other people's opinions but rather by my strength and determination. I learned that true beauty extended beyond physical appearance and encompassed confidence and self-love.

I channeled my energy toward developing my skills, pursuing my passions, and chasing my dreams. I realized that my worth was not dependent on anyone else but myself. This realization stayed with me as I grew older; my appearance and attitude became a part of my identity. I no longer felt the need to shield myself or conform to societal standards of beauty or behavior. I grew comfortable in my skin, celebrating my unique qualities and embracing my individuality.

I am grateful for the journey I have undertaken and the person I have become. I take pride in treating others with kindness and compassion and in fulfilling the promise I made to myself to be a better person than those who mistreated me. Also, by extending a helping hand and showing empathy to everyone I encountered, regardless of their race, gender, or social status, I discovered the fulfilling nature of being a good person. This gave me a positive feeling and left a lasting impression on other people's lives. It also guided me through the challenges, allowing me to remain true to myself while treating others with kindness and respect.

Reflecting on my childhood, growing up, and my experiences has significantly shaped who I am today. Despite facing challenges, I discovered strength within myself and the power of compassion. Through it all, I have learned that true beauty is found not just in physical appearance but also in a person's character depth and resilience to overcome obstacles. In essence, true beauty is in a person's self awareness and the deep sense of self worth they nurture.

In fifth grade, I sneaked up onto the stage behind the curtains at school to catch a glimpse of the sock hop dance. At that time, the event was exclusively for sixth and seventh graders. Some of my friends and I were not technically allowed to attend. However, our curiosity got the best of us. I remember the gym being dimly lit, with music blaring so loudly that it drowned out any other sound.

Peering down from my hidden spot, I could not help but chuckle at the sight of Rani showcasing her dance moves. Dressed in an elegant dress, she was aiming to impress her friends. Everyone was not dancing, to my surprise. A few kids lingered on the sidelines, observing and chatting amongst themselves. I could not grasp why they chose not to participate in the enjoyment. However, being involved in something forbidden heightened the excitement of my small escapade.

I divided my time between playing every sport I could at school and helping my father with remodeling homes, while Rani stayed home to help our mother. I often questioned why I had to perform all the hard work while Rani enjoyed the comfort of staying at home. I was told that Rani's tiny stature meant she could not handle challenging tasks. I disagreed with our mother's explanation, although I chose not to dwell on it.

My love for sports and the thrill of competition helped me maintain my focus on my interests. However, as time went on, I started to notice a pattern. Rani seemed to be treated special despite not contributing much to the family in terms of helping or going with our father to remodel homes. She was always the first to get new clothes, and I often found myself left out. Throughout my childhood, there was a constant sense of emptiness that I could not shake.

However, as I grew older, I began to rebel against these gender norms and expectations. I started asking questions and challenging the so-called "rules" imposed on us. I wanted to be able to do things that boys could do, and I felt that I deserved that same freedom and opportunity. I talked to my parents about my feelings and concerns, but they were unwilling to change. They believed it was in our best interest and that girls should not be involved in certain activities.

I must also acknowledge a stark contrast in my parents' initial intentions. At first, their purpose in migrating was to provide their daughters with education and opportunities. Regrettably, as time passed, they chose to abandon these aspirations and arranged for both Rani and me to be married off at the tender age of sixteen. Neither of us was given a chance to finish high school or any prospect of a better future through education.

If we fast forward to the 1990s, Michael and Elizabeth graduated, and our father decided to pay for their education, but both declined. The change in their perspective casts a shadow of disappointment and disillusion over our cultural beliefs and the different paths life can take. Despite their initial hopes for our education, their actions emphasize conflicts that can arise within the intricate fabric of our familial and societal expectations.

Reflecting on my parents' sacrifices highlights the complexities of immigration. It reminds us of the various aspects that influence our lives, including culture, economics, unexpected events, and changing perspectives. Exploring further into their experiences, I realized that their choice to move was complex and had many facets. The conflicts and drama within the extended family led them to seek a more stable life in Canada. Additionally, the prospect of better economic opportunities motivated our father to pursue a new life in a foreign country. Their varied cultural backgrounds were a substantial factor, as their traditions defined their approach to gender roles and expectations.

Looking back, I am grateful for the lessons I learned and the strength I gained from my experiences. Although it was challenging at times, I am proud of standing up for myself. Through my educational journey, I started as a security officer and enrolled in school to secure an education. I gained experience in the criminal justice field by volunteering at the police station. This is what ultimately led me to pursue my college aspirations. I studied Psychology, Law, policing, and sociology. I graduated from the criminal justice program in two years. I secured a job in the surveillance field, and I ended up taking the private investigator course and receiving my private investigator license. I want to inspire my children and others to break barriers. It starts with pursuing your dreams. Education is a powerful tool for empowerment and positive change. Let us continue to strive for a world where women are recognized for their contributions and have equal opportunities to make a difference.

When it comes to my mother's bias towards me, I struggled to understand it when I was young. My Aunt Baby once told me, "Beauty comes and goes, but what you learn stays with you forever." Those wise words have motivated me to continue learning and expanding my knowledge. Initially, I was confused, as I believed everyone to be beautiful. Unlike my mother, her sisters did not resemble her in looks and did not hold biases or define beauty as a necessary attribute.

Unfortunately, discrimination and biases based on gender and physical appearance are all too common. It is vital to recognize that these attitudes are unjust and unacceptable. Having a support system and a safe environment is crucial, and seeking help from a mental health professional can provide more resources to process these feelings and develop effective coping strategies.

Remember that your worth and value are not determined by external factors such as physical appearance or societal stereotypes. You are valuable and worthy just as you are. Remember to be your cheerleader, as this will make you feel motivated and determined to push through any obstacles. Remind yourself of where your family came from and where you are headed in your life. By making positive changes a little at a time, you will get to your goal. Surrounding yourself with positive influences and getting a support system, whether it is a professional, family, or friend, is a good start.

From my perspective, I constantly reminded myself of the sacrifice and resilience of my ancestors, who were enslaved and fought for a brighter future for generations to come. Their struggle inspired me to carve a path of success and be proud of my career. I pursued education with determination, knowing it would be a source of pride for my children and me. It was my way of honoring the legacy of my ancestors and ensuring a better future for my family. This drive propelled me to overcome obstacles and achieve my dreams. My father told me something similar: that learning never stops. My father was physically here but was not present when I needed him to be by my side during my pre-teens.

I never understood why my parents were biased toward me. My parents would tell me I looked like my grandmother, and I thought my father would be more inclined not to comment on my appearance. As far as my mother, I understood her approach when I grew up: to assimilate into Canadian society. She thought one had to have light skin and be beautiful to be accepted. My thoughts did not matter, as I was not significant when it came to them discussing me. I overheard my parents saying it would be easy for Rani to find a husband because she was beautiful, slim, and intelligent. However, they mentioned that I might have a more difficult time because of my physical appearance. They questioned whether anyone would want to marry me. At that moment, it hit me how much emphasis my family placed on beauty, being slim, and intelligence.

However, as I progressed through high school and formed friendships, I began to develop my interests and values. I learned that beauty, for me, was different from my parents' expectations. I discovered my unique qualities and that I was beautiful in my own way, despite what others may think. My father regularly visited our elementary school to check on Rani and me. I vividly remember playing tag with the boys in my class while my father casually strolled through the halls. These moments were some what embarrassing, as I had to pretend not to know anyone, and they had to pretend not to know me.

My father felt obligated to protect his daughters' welfare. These were his deep-rooted values derived from his traditions and culture. He believed that any social interaction with boys, especially within the school environment, could jeopardize our virtue and reputation. I wanted to blend in and be treated just like any other student. I understood that my father's actions stemmed from both traditional beliefs and his fears and anxieties. Having grown up in a different era, where gender roles and societal expectations were more rigid, he felt the need to shield us from harm and negative influences.

As I matured and gained a deeper understanding of the world, I could not help but recognize the limitations of my father's beliefs. His actions were driven by love, but they were also anchored in outdated notions of gender roles and purity. The longing for independence and the freedom to forge my relationships, regardless of gender, grew stronger within me. Yet, my father remained unwavering in his stance, shutting down any attempts for further discussion. Our relationship did not falter, but I could not help but notice how deeply the restrictive ideas about gender roles and purity had split us apart. All our treasured moments were tarnished because my actual self was hidden from my father's sight. I so badly wanted him to break free from his constraints and accept me for the person I was becoming—a secure, self-sufficient youngster who was free from the shackles of conventional conventions and gender stereo types.

Today, I reflect on those embarrassing moments with a mix of nostalgia and empathy. My father ruled his household according to traditional beliefs. And these beliefs were also a testament to his dedication as a father. Although our understanding of gender roles has evolved, I will always cherish those memories as a reminder of the deep care and love that shaped my upbringing. In hindsight, I now understand why my father was always so overprotective—his traditional beliefs shaped his protective nature.

He held traditional philosophies. These deeply ingrained cultural ideologies supported severe limitations for girls and women, denying them any chance of self-identity or autonomy. I did not adopt or embrace this mindset. I did not conform to these aspects of our tradition and culture. I believed that such thinking was outdated and that change was necessary to align with the values of modern society. It is essential to recognize that adopting empowering measures for girls and women does not compromise or disrespect anyone's religion. However, I firmly believe in granting children the full range of youthful experiences and not depriving them of any. I think empowering measures are more conducive to their future growth and development.

When my parents changed their religious beliefs in 1996, they embraced a more modern concept of equality. This trans-formation was reflected in how our younger siblings were raised. A modern parenting style was developed by my parents, leading them to adopt a relaxed parenting style without resorting to abuse or discipline. In the future, my parents became more accepting of dating, children born out of wedlock, and sleepovers with boys for their youngest daughter.

Looking back, I acknowledge the significant role tradition and culture played in shaping my father's behavior. He had a deep-rooted sense of duty and responsibility toward our loved ones. In our family, cultural traditions emphasize family unity and protection.

For my father, ensuring our safety and security was also an act of love. He was upholding the values and principles passed down through generations. In our culture, parents are expected to watch over the well-being and actions of their daughters. This vigilance was perceived as a way for my father to show authority and control. It was how my father upheld his responsibility as a provider and guardian, ensuring our safety and protection from any possible dangers. Our cultural legacy is deeply embedded with a sense of duty that drives these behaviors. It was his method of respecting and safeguarding the principles and beliefs passed down to him.

My father's steadfast dedication to our culture has profoundly shaped my perception of family connections and the importance of ensuring the safety of our cherished ones. Through his consistent communication and backing, driven by love, tradition, and culture, I have cultivated a deep sense of obligation and accountability towards my dear ones. His deeds have highlighted the crucial role of maintaining customs that nurture cohesion, security, and assistance in our community, shaping my life in a lasting way.

My father's commitment to preserving our cultural heritage has greatly influenced my identity. Seeing how he is dedicated to upholding our traditions, values, and rituals has made me deeply value our cultural roots. This awareness has connected me to my past and ancestors. It has also given me a sense of belonging and identity in a diverse, globalized world. My father's commitment has taught me the importance of preserving and celebrating cultural heritage, empowering me to pass on these traditions to future generations.

When I was young, I saw how my father's strong work ethic positively influenced our family's well-being. Inspired by his determination and his indefatigability, I followed in his footsteps and strived for the best. Whether studying for exams or engaging in extracurricular activities, his example has taught me the value of wholehearted dedication and going the extra mile. In times of defeat or simply feeling like giving up, I find strength in recalling the hardships my ancestors and parents faced to secure our freedom. This reflection grants me the support and motivation needed to persevere through challenges.

From my father, I have learned invaluable lessons about family, respect, and responsibility, which have shaped my beliefs and actions. His wisdom and insight surpassed his years, leaving-me forever grateful for our shared moments. Consistently holding himself and us to high standards, he embraced life with commitment, faith, and integrity. I recall his selflessness in prioritizing our family's needs, even at the expense of his own.

His legacy lives on, not just in my memories of him but in the way I approach life with courage, compassion, and humility. Now that I have my own family, I have raised my children with core values like respect, trust, honesty, and gender bias. My father never discriminated based on a person's race or religion. He believed in fairness and justice for all, and he instilled that belief in me. That is why I am committed to raising my children and future generations with the same values, treating others with kindness and compassion and promoting gender equality.

My father showed more empathy, kindness, and understanding to strangers than to his flesh and blood, his daughters, Rani and me. If our father had shown understanding to us, our worlds could have connected. We could have avoided clashes of perspectives and ideologies. Perhaps we could have salvaged the peaceful family life we all deserved. His abusive nature led to negative consequences and rebellions in our formative years. Instead of showing us the right path with love and nurturing us to grow and learn, he asserted his authority as the head of the household. He imposed unrealistic goals for Rani and me, using fear, coercion, and abuse as leverage.

As you establish your own family, it is essential to confront and overcome any prejudices or stereotypes you might have encountered. Take deliberate steps to treat all your children fairly and impartially, regardless of their gender. Children should explore their interests and not be stopped because of gender norms. Engage in honest dialogues with your partner about your shared approach to parenting, ensuring alignment and promoting gender equality within your family. Cultivate an atmosphere where your children are valued and respected as individuals, regardless of their gender.

Remember that you can shape your family's values and principles. By actively fostering a gender-neutral environment, you can lay the foundation for a more inclusive and socially equal future for all children. It is crucial to raise your children as advocates for gender equality by exposing them to diverse perspectives and experiences. Motivate them to develop empathy, tolerance, and respect for others by engaging with different cultures. Promote them to form friendships with people from diverse backgrounds and to challenge stereotypes and assumptions. By taking these steps, you will empower them to advocate for equality and justice for everyone. It is equally important to model gender equality in your behavior. Divide household and parenting responsibilities equally, treat your partner with respect and equity, and challenge gender stereotypes in your attitudes and actions. As a role model, you can instill in your children the values of fairness and equality they will carry with them for the rest of their lives. Remember that every action, word, and value you hold will shape your children's perceptions of gender equality. Therefore, make every interaction count.

Although our father was not emotionally available to Rani and me during our youth, he tried to make up for it during my adult life. My father remained a steadfast pillar of unyielding support, standing resolute beside me in the face of daunting challenges and glorious moments of joy. His unwavering dedication has continuously shown through his empathetic support and guidance during challenging times. Only when I became a parent did the profound magnitude of my father's love become evident. He witnessed the intimate exchanges between me and my children and had a profound realization that deeply moved him.

This moment happened when I started driving my father to his dialysis appointments. It was not solely about giving physical aid; it was equally about providing profound emotional support. As I held his hand, he finally understood how much I had contributed to his well-being. Although it was a simple gesture, it had a powerful impact in demonstrating my care and love for him. This experience brought me and my father closer together and solidified our bond. As the days passed, he began reciprocating the love that I had yearned for my whole life and that love had been neglected for too long. My father, seated next to me, said, "Beta, you have done so much for me, and I am truly proud to call you my daughter." This epiphany did not happen overnight; it happened gradually over months. It was a journey filled with emotional turbulence and perseverance.

Each day presented new challenges and obstacles, but I remained steadfast in my commitment to caring for my father. Through all the highs and lows, I never gave up hope. Finally, after months of unwavering dedication, my father began to change. His heart slowly opened, and he started to show love and appreciation. It was a bittersweet victory, one filled with tears of joy and relief. The transformation that took place was not just in my father but also within myself. It taught me the power of love and forgiveness and the importance of never giving up on the ones we hold dear.

Despite the positive change in my father's perception of me, it is essential to acknowledge that it did not erase or compensate for the abuse I endured from him. He never spoke about the abusive behavior, and it remained a closed topic for him. However, he gradually started to express his love and appreciation for my dedication to caring for him as he aged. Despite the silence on past issues, his actions spoke volumes and helped heal some wounds, laying the groundwork for a more positive and supportive relationship.

Through this newfound connection, I was determined to pave a path devoid of abuse, prioritizing the well-being of my children. I aimed to create a safe and nurturing environment for them to grow and develop, listening actively to their needs and concerns and providing guidance and advice as needed. Encouraging their independence while setting clear boundaries, I aimed to nurture-their self-worth, self-esteem, and respect for their opinions and beliefs. Above all, I wanted to demonstrate unconditional love and acceptance to my children, assuring them they could always rely on me for support and guidance.

In addition to my appreciation for the values and lessons my father taught me, I also acknowledge the challenges and struggles that came with his traditional beliefs and protective nature. While I am grateful for his love and concern for our family, I must also acknowledge the negative impact that his abusive behavior had on our relationship. It is hard to reconcile his actions with the lessons he taught me. I realized that naively following beliefs, traditions, religion, and culture can sometimes enable or justify harmful behavior.

This realization opened my eyes to the importance of promoting critical thinking and individual autonomy rather than enforcing conformity. The experience taught me that forcing others, especially children, to comply with strict beliefs without question can breed resentment, erode trust, and damage future relationships. I have learned to have open and honest communication with my loved ones, to respect their beliefs and values, and to find a balance between tradition and modernity.

Disco fever had taken over the nation, captivating people of all ages. The infectious beats and groovy melodies of disco music made even the most reserved individuals engage spontaneously in dancing. Everyone wanted to join the disco revolution, from youngsters to adults. What surprised many was the growing popularity of disco among elementary school kids; they could not resist the catchy tunes and the pulsating rhythm. Sock hop became a regular event at school, where children would gather in colorful outfits, letting loose and moving to the music. The school hallways were transformed into discotheques, filled with laughter, joy, and energetic dance moves.

The disco era captured even me, and I eagerly anticipated every sock hop that came my way. Determined to enjoy my passion for disco, I devised a clever plan to fund my adventures by saving my milk money. I had a distaste for milk and a devotion to the groovy disco beats. When the day of the sock hop arrived, excitement filled the air. It was time to boogie, get down, and let loose on the dance floor. I learned all my moves from Soul Train on television and was ready to bust a move. I would wear my shiny pants adorned with glitter and sequins and tie a vibrant bandana around my head. Ready to strut my stuff, I joined my classmates, who were all equally enchanted by the disco beats.

The dance floor erupted into a vibrant playground of energy and groove. We unleashed our best moves, spinning and twirling with unbridled enthusiasm. We sought to imitate our idols' electrifying dance styles while grooving to the iconic Bee Gees, Donna Summer, and Abba tunes. Time seemed to stand still as we lost ourselves in the blissful pleasure of movement. Disco provided a unique sense of freedom and the opportunity to express ourselves fully. The afternoon transformed into a magical escape, allowing us to let go of all inhibitions and immerse ourselves in the pure joy of dancing. As the music intensified, so did our passion for dancing. The energy was infectious, spreading from one person to another. The music affected everyone in the room; teachers were dancing, uniting everyone in the universal language of dance.

When I was in elementary school, our sixth-grade teacher sent a note to all the parents informing them that our class would be participating in dancing. I vividly recall my father coming to school to talk to the teacher about his concerns regarding dancing. He was upset and thought it was inappropriate for his daughters to hold hands with boys at such an early age. However, unbeknownst to him, Rani and I had already been dancing during gym class and the occasional sock hop. Unfortunately, my father's perception of the situation was based on outdated notions. Dancing was not considered inappropriate, and specific dances required holding hands with boys. We were only having innocent and harmless fun, as children do at school.

The sock hops were innocent and enjoyable. These casual dance events allowed us to socialize and dance with other students. Everyone, irrespective of gender, would form groups and dance. The whole thing was a worry-free and joyful experience for us. My father expressed his concerns to our teacher. He wanted to ensure we were not exposed to uncomfortable situations or harmful influences. Rani and I were already well-acquainted with dancing with boys in supervised settings. We understood boundaries and knew how to handle ourselves. Despite the teacher's clarification of the benefits of dancing, including exercise and socialization, my father remained unconvinced. He decided not to send Rani and me to gym class.

He later spoke with the principal and requested that we be excused from any classes involving proximity to the opposite sex. The principal did not fully agree, but he did approve our exemption from dancing, allowing us to participate in other sports activities. While my father was not entirely satisfied, it was a step towards achieving his outcome. Consequently, Rani and I became the targets of ridicule and bullying. The students laughed and teased us, making us feel ostracized and different. Even the teachers openly discussed us, questioning our origins and why girls were treated this way in Canada. This incident deeply affected us, and my father instructed my mother to keep a closer eye on us. Despite our parents' efforts, the bullying continued for weeks, eventually reaching a point where neither Rani nor I wanted to go to school anymore.

Looking back, those sock hops were more than just innocent school dances. They were an escape, a chance to experience dance, music, and freedom. The whole day seemed magical and enticing to express myself without being confined by the rules within my home.

Little did my parents know that the milk money they entrusted me with was being used to create cherished memories that would last a lifetime. So, let us reminisce about those days when disco ruled our hearts and feet. Let us remember the joy it brought, the freedom it instilled, and the unity it fostered. Let us groove once again to the timeless beats of disco. It is time to dance like it is the disco era all over again. It is time to boogie, get down, or whatever phrase jives with you. It was time to put on your shiny pants and bandanas and hit the floor. The sock hop was so popular at our school that it became a regular event every Friday and was incorporated into gym class.

We mustered the courage to confide in our teacher, who showed immense sympathy and understanding. She heard our issue, and she assured us that she would investigate. The following day, she addressed the entire class, emphasizing the significance of kindness and respect towards everyone, regardless of a person's nationality or background. Our classmates began treating us with respect and compassion. The bullying that had plagued us for weeks finally ceased, and we were able to regain a sense of normalcy. The intervention of our teacher sparked a positive change, allowing us to feel once again safe and valued amongst our peers. This experience taught me the power of speaking up and seeking support from others. It showed me that I do not have to face challenges alone and that speaking up can be effective. I now understand the importance of exposing children to physical activities and social environments for their psychological well-being.

Exposing children to diverse experiences helps them develop a broader perspective and gain insight that assists them in making informed decisions. This exposure enables children to understand and appreciate diverse cultures, backgrounds, and perspectives, fostering empathy and respect. Thus, it provides children with the skills to manage demanding situations and teaches them how to navigate social dynamics and stand up for themselves. This experience has taught me the value of seeking support, fostering inclusivity, and providing children with a well-rounded upbringing that prepares them to be compassionate, empathetic, and resilient individuals in the face of adversity.

Parents must let their children explore and learn through various experiences. Differences in race, religion, and nationality sometimes hinder children's learning experiences. Parents can teach their kids the value of respecting others by encouraging them to ask questions and learn. By opening children's worldviews, parents can help them develop empathy, understanding, teamwork, communication, and problem-solving skills.

While our parents' restrictions sometimes felt suffocating, these clandestine activities allowed us to claim autonomy and self-expression. The littlest things that satisfied us—involved in dancing to a disco beat, scoring a goal on the soccer field, getting lost in the pages of a Western novel, or indulging in watching TV shows—became outlets for us to let go and be ourselves. Our parents denied us the right to express ourselves or even laugh at something; they saw it as suspicious activity. They felt that showing emotions was somehow associated with being devious and that you were doing something inappropriate.

Those moments of rebellion and escapism were essential steps in our journey toward independence. They taught us the value of seizing possibilities despite being faced with limitations. Though our parents may not have agreed or even approved of our choices, those clandestine nights with "Three's Company" and "Happy Days" remain special memories that remind us of the resilience and resourcefulness we had as pre-teens.

As a parent, I learned the importance of setting clear boundaries in my household. I allowed my children to choose their shows and movies as long as they adhered to my rules and were age-appropriate. I encouraged my children to socialize with friends, go on dates, and enjoy their youth. I did not want to be overly strict or controlling, as I believed that could lead to rebellion or the suppression of their thoughts and emotions. Instead, I prioritized open communication and trust with my children, which helped us develop a strong and respectful relationship.

In contrast, my parents seemed to thrive on control; as parents, we all come to realize that nothing can truly be controlled, as there will always be room for rebellion. They restricted something as simple as dancing, English music, or an activity that allowed children to express themselves. They also limited our participation in Canadian activities, and these are typical childhood experiences. We were restricted from activities like hanging out with friends and going to the movies. We were compelled to find ways to defy these rules. We were aware of the severe consequences, and we believed it was necessary to have these experiences to live our childhood.

Growing up, I constantly clashed with my parents' strict rules and high expectations. I struggled to conform to my parents' strict rules and high expectations. To assert my independence, I started to rebel in small but significant ways. In search of belonging, I began to smoke and hang out with friends, testing the limits set by my parents. It was an exciting and invigorating experience that fueled my desire for freedom. Skipping classes and Rani forging notes became a routine act of rebellion, sending a clear message of defiance.

However, the consequences eventually caught up with me. The school discovered my actions, informing my parents of my consistent absence from gym class and at the principal's office, facing disappointment and concern in their stern gaze. My parents reacted with understandable anger and disappointment. They realized that their attempts to impose order and structure were not respected. In response, they laid down their ultimatums, warning of severe repercussions. It was a defining moment, a crossroads that forced me to evaluate my actions.

Instead of succumbing to the pressure, I remained determined and resolute. The unexpected consequences that followed served as validation for my choices, further solidifying my belief that I was carving my unique path, one that few had dared to tread. Each admonishment from my parents only fueled the flames of my rebellious spirit, propelling me to resist even more fiercely.

Reflecting on the journey that lay behind me, I can now see that my defiance was not a rebellion for the sake of it but rather a quest for self-discovery and a challenge to societal norms. Each act of defiance became a catalyst for personal growth and expanded my perspective beyond the confines of my parent's expectations. However, this rebellious streak within me persisted.

Despite the gray clouds foretelling the arrival of fall in September in Vancouver, I found myself befriending a new classmate, Larry. He was unlike anyone I had met before, with a slender build, brown hair, and hazel eyes. Larry's light brown skin set him apart from my Caucasian friends, yet we discovered a shared bond of common interests that drew us closer. I found out Larry moved a few houses down from my house.

My parents were to be informed of our friendship, or worse, Rani was vindictive and would not stop at anything to seek retribution if she discovered it. The whole prospect sent chills down my back. The repercussions I would face would not be at all enjoyable; they would cast a shadow on my joy. And yet, despite my anxiety, I persisted. It was a delicate dance, accepting my friendship but being wary of the possible blowback. Happiness and fear swirled together, weaving a tapestry of feelings that directed my movements. And I hoped it would stay hidden as I made my way through the unknown.

A group of friends decided to seize the opportunity of a professional day to visit Queen Elizabeth Park in Vancouver. I had always dreamt of going there with friends, but deep down, I knew my parents would never allow me to go. Determined to make it happen, I resorted to improvisation and decided not to inform my parents about the professional day. With my friends by my side, including Larry, I embarked on this daring adventure, hoping to keep it all a secret.

During the brisk, cool days of early autumn, as raindrops started to fall on our heads, we began walking home together. Too cool for umbrellas, we embraced the rain, laughing and running through the wet streets. I was not allowed to talk or walk with any boys except John or Henry; my father knew them. Rules were strict: straight to school and straight home, with no exceptions unless approved by my father, which was rare.

On that rainy walk home, amidst the refreshing rain, I was stunned when Larry offered to carry my books. My heart raced with excitement as he took the heavy load off my hands. The scent of damp leaves filled the air as we walked down the street, enhancing the ambiance of our friendship. Larry became my best friend; here he was, walking next to me, giving me a warm, fuzzy feeling amidst the changing seasons.

During our walk to school one day, Larry expressed curiosity about my nationality, noting that I looked different from everyone else. When I told him I was Indian, his laughter surprised me, as he mentioned being called "Native" in Canada due to his mixed Native and Caucasian heritage. While his background did not bother me, it highlighted the racist behavior my father often spoke about. With every day that went by, Larry and I became closer. We became attached like two peas in a pod as we spent more time together. I found comfort in him as we walked home. Our lunch breaks blossomed into moments of connection and laughter. It was an unexplained feeling; nervous worry lingered in the recesses of my heart like a persistent, silent presence.

Larry's mother lived in constant fear of the government taking her children. My heart ached for Larry and his family and the fear they must have faced every day. In stark contrast, while Larry's family had Indigenous roots, my family hailed from Fiji, with ancestors originating from India. Despite our different backgrounds, the bond between Larry and I grew stronger as he confided in me about their impending move. I could sense the anxiety in his voice, knowing that his mother's strict belief in never staying in one place for too long governed their lives.

The day my father spotted Larry outside, a surge of unexpected panic washed over me. I could not believe my eyes as he welcomed Larry into our yard, defying all expectations. We walked toward the backyard to talk. The moment we embraced, tears filled my eyes, overwhelmed by the depth of our connection. Little did I know that this heartwarming reunion would soon turn into a devastating revelation. As Larry poured his heart out, I felt a knot tighten in my stomach. The truth about the government taking children from Native families shook me to my core, though I could not fully comprehend the gravity of the situation just yet. Just as I was trying to process Larry's move, my mother emerged yelling and demanding Larry leave.

Due to my immature age and lack of understanding, I was completely unaware of the Native children being forcefully taken away. As I struggled to process this heartbreaking revelation, I could not help but worry about my father's potential interaction with Larry's mother. The thought of any consequences or conflicts arising filled me with overwhelming fear. I informed Larry that his mother was waiting for him in the front. As Larry and his mother departed, my father pulled me aside. The weight of Larry's situation fell upon him, mirroring our journey and struggles.

Intrigued, I pressed for an explanation, only to learn that Larry's family shared a connection to the land as Indigenous people while our family maintained our Indian heritage, with our ancestors hailing from India. The realization hit me like a ton of hot bricks, understanding the reasons behind their constant moves and the deep-rooted fear that haunted them. Larry's mother's plea for us not to identify ourselves as "Indian" weighed heavily on us, knowing the historical precedent of authorities taking "Native" children in this country. The extent of their struggles was overwhelming, leaving my father feeling powerless to ease their pain. Despite our limitations, I knew deep down that my father's compassionate nature would have moved mountains if he had the means to help.

Witnessing strangers approach my father with an in explicable familiarity has always fascinated me. It was as though his kindness and goodness radiated from within him, drawing people towards him with their burdens and stories. This captivating quality illuminated his character, making me admire him even more. At that moment, I understood the significance of his heartfelt gestures and the impact they had on those around him. As I grew older, I began to follow in my father's footsteps, seeking ways to help others and paying it forward. Whether it was buying a coffee for someone who could not afford it or giving money to a homeless person, I developed the mindset that it wasn't about what you received in return but rather about doing good for the betterment of society.

In later years, during school, I recall learning about Christopher Columbus in my social studies class. My teacher explained that Columbus had mistakenly used the term "Indian" to describe the Native people he encountered in America, believing that he had reached India. How easily do people accept Columbus's words and follow his example without questioning or understanding the cultural and historical context? It made me realize the importance of critical thinking and seeking knowledge beyond just accepting what is presented to us.

Though I never crossed paths with Larry again, his impact on me lingered, for he was the friend who opened my eyes to a world I had never known. His genuine kindness and lack of judgment towards others based on appearance or culture left an indelible mark on my soul. I often questioned why the government seemed to fear children like Larry and how people allowed such injustices to be tolerated. I hoped and wished for his family's safety, and I fervently wished that he would find happiness and fulfillment in his life. Larry's memory served as a constant reminder for me to strive for empathy, understanding, and a world where no child feels marginalized or mistreated.

Larry's friendship had a profound impact on me, teaching me invaluable lessons about the significance of empathy, compassion, and embracing diversity. Through our friendship, I learned the importance of breaking down cultural barriers and treating every individual with equal respect and understanding. Despite our age, his influence was transformative, shaping my perspective on the world and the way I interacted with others. I will forever cherish our friendship and be thankful for the profound impact he had on my life. Larry taught me to appreciate the beauty of our differences and to strive for a more inclusive and understanding society.

As I grew older, I became more aware of the plight of Indigenous Peoples, now recognized as the original inhabitants of their respective territories. In Canada, they are collectively known as First Nations, Inuit, and Métis. It is essential to understand that many Indigenous Peoples prefer to be addressed by their specific nation or tribe name as a way of honoring their distinct identities and celebrating their rich cultural heritage. This recognition is a crucial step towards acknowledging and respecting the unique histories and traditions of Indigenous Peoples.

I recall my father and I going to my cousin's place after finishing a renovation job. Father decided I could go out with my cousin Reggie and his sister Radhika roller skating. The roller rink was playing "Night Fever," and everyone was dancing on their skates. I was not good at dancing on skates, but it was thrilling just skating and watching the people. At that point, I realized that life has much more to offer than just school and chores. I asked my father if he could buy me some roller skates, and a couple of weeks later, Rani and I had roller skates. My mother did not like the skates and did not want us rolling around on them. My father told her that cuts, bruises, and scars were all part of growing up and learning.

I was always falling and hurting myself, dislocating my shoulder or arm. However, that did not stop my enjoyment of my new-found activity. I remember the doctor making home visits and telling my mother, "It seems like she is always falling and breaking something." My mother told my father about the doctor's visits and talked to me about being more careful, but being a kid was about doing things that involved falling and getting hurt. Roller skating may have started to escape home, but it became a source of joy, confidence, and friendships. It taught me the value of persistence and the rewards of taking risks.

Looking back, I'm grateful for the experiences and memories that roller skating brought into my life. It taught me to push myself beyond my limits, never give up on my goals, and embrace the joy of living in the moment. Roller skating remained a passion of mine, and I would often go out to the local rink with my cousins to unwind and have fun. It was a reminder of the carefree days of my youth when anything seemed possible and the world was full of excitement.

Ah, grade 7 was a time of both excitement and trepidation as I embarked on a new chapter of my life. It was during those formative years that I encountered numerous "firsts" that filled me with a blend of anticipation and nervousness. Adolescence had just begun, and I found myself caught up in the thrill of rebellion. I vividly remember the first time I dared to take a puff from a cigarette, trying to project a sense of maturity and independence. At that moment, I felt a surge of adrenaline mixed with a hint of guilt, a combination that both thrilled and scared me.

As the days passed, my spirit of adventure led me to another first: skipping classes. It was both a daring act and an escape from the monotony of textbooks and routine. The anticipation of freedom and secret adventures added an extra layer of excitement to my everyday life. Those moments of truancy gave me a taste of independence and a glimpse of the possibilities that lay beyond the walls of my school or home. Grade seven was also the time when I experienced the exhilaration of having a crush. The butterflies in my stomach, the stolen glances, and the clandestine notes passed between desks were all part of this newfound territory. Every heartbeat felt amplified, and the fear of being caught added to the intensity of these emotions.

Reflecting on the "firsts" I experienced in seventh grade, they resembled brushstrokes on the canvas of my teenage years, creating a vibrant landscape of experiences that molded my self-perception and perception of the world. I believed in the abundance of inspiring places, diverse individuals, and experiences waiting for me to explore, eager for the journey. During this time, I was fixated on pursuing a career in the criminal justice field, not pondering beyond immediate goals as marriage and adulthood appeared distant and unimportant. In seventh grade, my mindset revolved around cherishing my childhood, savoring the simplicity of innocence, and engaging in childlike activities.

Chapter 10

Rebellion and High School

I n a modern country, we are surrounded by traditional customs and practices that make our home life challenging. Under our mother's guidance, Rani and I learned essential household skills like cooking and cleaning. One memorable experience was our first attempt at making Indian dishes like dahl. Unfortunately, we ended up burning the pot, and in a moment of panic, we threw it onto the patio. Thankfully, our father arrived just in time to extinguish the flames. Despite his initial anger and strict instructions not to cook unsupervised, we persisted and honed our cooking skills over time.

Our mother also taught us how to sew, cook, and perform various household chores. Though it was frustrating at times, we understood the importance of these skills. Her sewing skills were so incredible that she could look at a dress or any other piece of clothing, and a few days later, Rani and I would be wearing a new outfit. She belonged to an era where women were expected to stay at home and take care of the family and house. I did not believe that skills like cooking and sewing were necessary for every girl. I yearned for something beyond the traditional domestic tasks, and Rani shared those same aspirations and goals.

However, our desires did not align with the expectations our parents had for us. They had certain expectations and beliefs when it came to our roles as girls. We were raised to be polite and obedient, with a strong emphasis on domestic duties. However, Rani and I had unique ideas and desires that did not quite align with these traditional expectations. It was challenging and disheartening to witness the inequality, especially when we saw boys like our cousins or our brother being encouraged to engage in sports and pursue their interests freely. At that time, we did not have the awareness or understanding to challenge these gender norms.

As I grew older, I began to question these traditional roles and cultural expectations. I learned to pursue my interests and fight for the same opportunities as boys. This led me to rebel, which my parents did not appreciate. They did not understand that it was not out of disrespect but rather my difficulty grasping their outdated views. It seemed as if my parents had forgotten that we were no longer living in Fiji. While they saw my actions as a rebellion, it was my way of asserting my identity and individuality.

Our household was a mix of conflicting values, breakdowns in communication, and parental restrictions that challenged my sense of autonomy and individuality. It was through this struggle that I began to understand the true meaning of freedom and the importance of forging my path despite the obstacles that stood in my way. My parents exerted complete control over every aspect of Rani's and my existence, deciding where we could go and who we could interact with and even forcing us into arranged marriages against our will in the future.

The experiences led to a stark realization that the freedom and equality we were taught in Canada was an ambitious concept. As I navigated the journey from childhood to adulthood, I grappled with the disparity between these ideals and the practical constraints I faced within my own family. It was in later years that I began to question and challenge these oppressive circumstances. This newfound understanding further highlighted the significance of upholding and protecting freedom, not just as an abstract idea but as a fundamental right that should be available to all individuals without exception.

Observing my church friends with loving families made me feel like I had entered a fairy tale. The genuine connection and trust they shared was something I deeply desired. I wanted to know when my parents would show me the same level of trust and respect. Their negative attitude and hostile demeanor left me puzzled, as it seemed like they did not trust anyone, not even their child. Their response to any birthday party invitations was always a firm "no" without explanation. Only after much reluctance would they allow me to attend, but only if my brother Michael could accompany me, and even then, it was limited to daytime outings.

My parents never allowed me the slightest bit of independence, whether it was during the glaring light of day or in the mysterious depths of the evening. The rules, ever-changing as I grew older, only served to ignite a smoldering rage within me—a resentment that burned towards my parents and the suffocating grip of Indian culture they imposed on me. All I ever yearned for was a chance at a normal childhood, an opportunity to bask in the sweet liberation and joy that other children effortlessly experienced. While my friends were allowed to socialize with boys and girls and had a curfew of nine p.m., I was deprived of these privileges. While they indulged in movies and hanging out with friends, I was permanently forbidden from such activities. Rani and I were restricted from attending church as our parents deemed our questions about the church teachings were exposing their restrictive and manipulative behavior, which they did not want to discuss or confront.

These contrasting experiences only heightened my sense of frustration and isolation. I yearned for the liberty my non-Indian friends enjoyed, allowing them to make their own choices and express themselves freely. It was during this moment of clarity that

I realized true freedom encompassed not just physical liberty but also mental and emotional liberation. To truly experience genuine freedom, I understood that I needed to liberate myself from the oppressive Indian traditions that hindered me. I discovered that rebellion does not always have to be confrontational; it can serve to voice our concerns and challenge outdated norms with tact and sensitivity.

The disheartening silence from my parents before their passing regarding their motivations for migrating to Canada, as well as their unwavering enforcement of gender-based rules and forced arranged marriages, weighed heavily on me. It was perplexing that they deliberately chose to evade these crucial topics and provided no explanations whatsoever. Perhaps toward the end, as they witnessed the failed marriages, divorce, separations, cheating, betrayals, and enduring trauma inflicted upon their daughters, they could have, even if belatedly, acknowledged the wrongness of their decisions to marry off Rani and me as teenagers.

I continued my journey of introspection and exploration to address these unresolved matters. It is important for my growth and healing to find a way to reconcile and seek closure for these significant aspects of my life. This was a frustrating and disheartening experience for me, but I did not give up. Instead, I persevered by seeking answers from other sources; I talked to immigrant relatives. Gradually, I started to understand the complexities of migration and the impact of culture on gender roles.

During my conversations with Aunt Baby, she informed me that arranged marriages exist in Muslim culture as well. She enlightened me about their prevalence in numerous religions. Contrary to common belief, these unions are not haphazardly thrown together. Couples often have a say in the matter, and their interests and compatibility are taken into consideration. She also mentioned that potential couples are given a chance to get to know each other and spend time together, contributing to the final decision-making process. Individuals are even allowed to choose their partners within the boundaries set by their families.

We must remember that arranged marriages differ significantly across cultures, and the level of individual choice and input can vary greatly. While some arrangements may prioritize family compatibility or societal factors, modern arrangements often prioritize the preferences and desires of the individuals involved. From my personal experience, I tried to understand my parents' ideologies and traditions. The more it caused rifts in our relationship, the more adamant they became about making their arranged marriage a reality. Whether or not I was willing, it would still take place. My parents stood by their decision, leaving me with no choice, and the matter was closed. It would have been easier to conform to societal expectations and pressures. The decision they were making would affect my life. This was not something they cared about or wanted to dwell on.

In my journey through life, I have confronted the suffocating weight of oppressive regulations that confined me in every aspect. My dreams and aspirations were being overshadowed—by society's biased expectations for girls. Breaking free from the confines of prescribed gender roles and societal norms required me to challenge the limitations placed upon me. From my parents' strict rules and traditions to the confinement of my thoughts and ambitions, the struggle to overcome these gender biases and societal expectations has been arduous. Yet, it also propelled me towards discovering the importance of trusting my judgment and following my instincts, even when they diverged from the norm.

Traversing the intricate web of familial expectations, societal pressures, and personal evolution has been a profound voyage of self-realization. This expedition has led me to challenge deep-seated convictions, defy oppressive norms, and celebrate the richness of diversity. With each stride forward, I am forging a path toward authenticity, comprehension, and inclusivity. The quest for self-awareness and empowerment is a continuous endeavor that requires tenacity, empathy, and an unwavering belief in our inherent ability to craft the stories we portray. I want to strive for a future that encompasses freedom and liberty, compassion, and self-fulfillment while navigating the web of my heritage via reflection, investigation, and a commitment to personal growth.

However, fast forward to the future, and my journey has been marred by the stifling constraints enforced by my parents' rigid beliefs and traditional customs. Escaping the grip of these gender-biased prejudices and expectations has proved to be an ongoing battle. Their authoritarian mandates cast a shadow over my existence, restricting my autonomy and confining me within the walls of my own home for the simple act of having a boyfriend. These arbitrary regulations acted as a painful echo of the numerous hurdles I encountered as a young teenager in Indian society. Adding to the burden, I found myself coerced into a forced arranged marriage, yet another manifestation of the restrictions placed on me solely due to my gender.

Despite these challenges, I was determined to forge my path and break free from the confining grip of cultural norms and societal expectations. My rebellion has been an act of defiance against the restrictive ideologies that have held me back. Through this process, I have come to recognize the significance of individuality and the value of embracing diversity. By challenging the confinements of gender roles and expectations, I aim to motivate others to question and challenge these outdated norms. Together, we can work towards building a society where every individual is valued and respected for their true essence, regardless of their gender.

We can start by breaking free from the limitations of gender roles and striving for a world that honors and embraces the diversity and individuality of all people. Together, let us stand against gender prejudices, demolish the boundaries set by tradition, and nurture an inclusive, welcoming, and liberated society. It is essential that we expand our perspectives and wholeheartedly embrace the notion that women can compete and thrive against men. Through our combined endeavors, we can forge a path toward a future where gender equality is not just a dream but a reality, where individuals are evaluated solely based on their skills and potential.

Starting high school in eighth grade was an incredibly intimidating experience for me. In the first week of school, I found myself in a tense encounter with two boys as they approached me near my locker. Suddenly, the taller of the two forcefully pushed me into my locker and locked it shut. Panicked, I called out for help, and fortunately, the principal happened to pass by and heard my cries. Acting swiftly, he arranged for someone to cut the lock and release me. Filled with anger, I wished for the perpetrator to face the consequences, but I did not even know his name. To my surprise, the principal identified him as Pal, who had been committing such acts against other students regularly.

I began spending time with Rani and her friend Dee, engaging in activities like smoking and skipping classes. The consequences at home, should our parents discover our behavior, were of little concern to Rani or me, given the strict and controlling environment we lived in. Our parents seemed like wardens, tightening their grip as we rebelled more. The school served as our only respite from the suffocating control enforced at home.

On professional development days at school, Rani and I would sneak off without informing our parents, relishing in our fleeting taste of freedom. We would hang out with friends, explore Queen Elizabeth Park, or swim at the recreation center, daring to wear bikinis despite knowing our parents' disapproval. Our aim was simple: to blend in with the other kids at the pool. We encountered no judgment or unwanted attention, possibly influenced by the accepting and diverse environment in Canada.

After school during the first week, a fight erupted on the hill. It all started when Rani began taunting two East Indian sisters, embarrassing them in front of everyone. Though she was the main target, I found myself in the middle of the escalating tension. I felt a strong urge to stand up for her to prevent potentially dire consequences at home. The spectacle at the hill's peak almost seemed comical, with Sita and Rani circling each other, throwing punches in the air that always missed their mark—to the surprise of many, no teachers or administrators intervened to diffuse the conflict, allowing students to observe the unfolding drama eagerly.

Suddenly, as I turned around, an unexpected blow landed on my face—it was Sita's twin sister joining the mayhem. The fight between Rita and me intensified rapidly as I struck Rita with a punch, resulting in her receiving a black eye. Our physical altercation led us to roll down the treacherous hill, where Rita was screaming in painful agony. Upon examining my injuries, I noticed my lip was bleeding from a deep cut, and my nose was broken and bleeding profusely, with no signs of stopping.

As I watched in shock, Rani forcefully pushed Sita down the hill, causing her to cry out in agony. The sisters, fueled by anger, turned their attention towards me, but I retaliated with equal force. My counterattack left Sita with more injuries while I punched Rita, and she fell to the ground, struggling to rise. Everyone started to run away as the principal and teachers were observed heading towards the hill. The fight finally came to an end. We all started to inspect our injuries, and Rita started yelling that she could not move her arm.

We were escorted to the principal's office, and our parents were called. Sita and Rita blamed Rani for the fight, but she was standing at the top of the hill "like a queen on her throne," and she had no visible scratches from the fight. The principal, upon seeing the blood and injuries, became furious. We were then given a lecture on how girls were expected to behave, and this kind of behavior- was deemed unacceptable. The principal expressed disbelief, questioning, "I cannot believe this is the timid girl I rescued from the locker." I responded by explaining that after realizing the consequences of not protecting myself, I decided to look after my well-being.

The principal proceeded to record our names and declared that he never wanted to see us in his office again. To protect Rani from being caught, I deliberately kept my response vague and omitted any mention of her involvement in the incident. This decision was made with the realization that secrecy would ensure her safety and prevent any potential retaliation from her in the future. Little did the principal know he would be encountering me more frequently, as I left a lasting impression on him. Consequently, all of us were suspended for a week from school. Our parents were not thrilled about the suspension, especially since we were just starting high school. The drive home was full of harsh remarks, like 'Who taught you to fight?' and 'Are you going to school to learn Dada Giri?' Indian meaning: goondaism, gang rule, intimidating behavior. I thanked God that I had been beaten up enough and was spared a belt whipping.

Rani began discussing the fight as though it were impressive, and I felt a surge of anger because she had not offered any help. I was in agony, every part of me hurting, and her voice only seemed to irritate me further. I instructed her to stay quiet, warning that if our parents discovered what had happened, we would both face a belt whipping. Out of frustration, I urged her to leave if she valued her safety. Reflecting on the situation, I realized that my actions consistently led to trouble for others, whether it was through my honesty or my tendency to inform people. My father's words, "Sundi rani logo ki karti harani," meaning in Hindi that Sundi causes people grief, now resonate deeply with me.

Finally, I was back after my suspension. During lacrosse practice, I noticed an unfamiliar guy with wavy hair cascading to his shoulders. He stood tall and had a distinct East Indian appearance, which intrigued me. Though I did not recognize him, my friends informed me that he had been regularly attending our games and was a grade 9 student at our school. At that moment, I did not pay much attention to it.

One day after school, I decided to linger a little longer and convinced Rani to stay with me. We ended up watching the football game, where I spotted Nikhil, the charismatic captain of the team, showcasing his skills on the field. Dee joined Rani, and they headed to their favorite spot, the corner store. As my friends and I began to walk home, a voice called out, demanding our attention. "Hey, girls! Can I speak to Sundi?" Initially, I thought he must be referring to someone else, but to my surprise, he was indeed talking to me. He asked if he could accompany me on my way home. Seeing no harm in it, my friends agreed and left us alone.

As we walked side by side, he mustered the courage to reveal his feelings for me. The sudden confession took me by surprise, leaving me feeling a blend of astonishment and uncertainty. Unsure of how to react, I chose to take things slow and let our friendship unfold naturally. I could not help but question why he was drawn to me, especially with numerous girls seeking his attention. Given his status as the popular football captain, many desired to be his "girlfriend." Despite my initial doubts, our bond deepened towards the middle of eighth grade and blossomed into a relationship.

Amid the bustling hallways and fleeting class periods, our interactions turned into enchanting moments. A simple glance between us would spark an uncontrollable smile, filling us with a warmth that reached deep into our hearts. The air crackled with nervous excitement as our laughter resonated through the corridors, drawing curious looks from our peers. In those instances, our smiles spoke volumes, conveying a blend of infatuation and admiration that forged an unspoken bond filled with thrill and intensity. We blushed and giggled, our faces perpetually lit up by the joy that seemed to surround us, transforming the world into a brighter, more magical place. The laughter that bubbled between us carried the weight of pure affection, weaving a connection that felt like the start of something extraordinary.

Nikhil and I decided to walk home together one day after school, but our journey led us to the Annex school near my house.

It was a mistake to head towards home, yet we found ourselves gravitating towards the school grounds. We made our way to the tall tree on the premises, etching our names on its trunk before settling on a nearby bench to chat. Lost in conversation, we wandered towards the back of the school, oblivious to our surroundings. A quick glimpse: I observed my father and the family driving towards home. As they approached, I saw Rani with her head hanging out the back seat window of our father's brown Ford Pinto. At that moment, I was sure she saw us.

Quickly, I made my way back to the house before they arrived. Sitting on the back patio stairs, engrossed in a book, I was startled when Rani came up to me and said, "We need to talk." Instantly, I knew that she wanted to discuss what she had seen. Later, we had a conversation, and she was not going to tell our parents because she wanted favors from me; at this time, she never mentioned what the favors would be. She went on to say, "Now I understand why you are so happy all the time." She started to show her true side, saying, I wonder what our parents would think about what you are doing and what this is going to cost you.

During my tenth grade, our relationship took a turn. While Nikhil was in grade 11, he expressed a desire for a more serious, mature commitment—being open and honest about our relationship, not hiding it, going on dates, and hanging out with his friends. He stood there, confessing his love for me. I got scared and ran away, leaving him in shock about what had occurred. We never saw each other or spoke about the incident again, feeling incredibly sad about the situation and not wanting to end things. Unfortunately, the issues we faced could not be resolved due to the expectations and rules in my home, making it difficult for our relationship to move forward.

A month after our breakup, I was caught off guard when Nikhil approached me in the hallway at school. He expressed his desire to get back together, stating he could not bear the thought of our breakup and was upset. He went further to say we can start over and forget everything I said to you that day. I was shocked by his confession, but I accepted our breakup and realized that it was for the best. While I sympathized with his feelings, I knew that getting back together would not be fair to either of us. I explained that I had already moved on and wished him the best. It was a bittersweet moment, as a part of me felt a flicker of nostalgia and longing for what it once was. But deep down, I knew that I was not ready for a serious, mature relationship. I had changed during our time apart. Our paths had diverged, and it was important for us to continue forward on our journeys.

Reflecting on the situation now, I understand that disclosing the long-term relationship with my parents would have likely resulted in serious consequences for everyone involved. This was particularly unusual for Rani, as she typically used such information as leverage for personal gain. The fact that she chose to keep this secret added a level of complexity to the already confusing circumstances that left me puzzled.

Life at home was far from easy. My parents were exhibiting signs of emotional distress. No one in our family ever openly communicated their feelings. This lack of emotional expression seemed to have been inherited from our parents' upbringing, where showing vulnerability was frowned upon. I felt helpless and trapped in this toxic environment. It seemed that every day, there was some outburst or argument. I spent my free time in my room, trying to stay out of my parent's way. I did not understand why my parents were like this. They had once been happy and in love, but something had changed. They fought about everything from money to chores, even what to cook for dinner. It was exhausting and draining to be around them all the time. They were too caught up in their issues to see how it was impacting their children.

Living at home was toxic, and with every breath I took, I wondered what was next. Straying from the rules meant facing harsh consequences. Seeking a bit of rebellion, Rani and I found solace in smoking whenever we could. We talked about how we could fight for our rights and force our parents to understand. I told her it seemed like a losing battle, but we tried to be positive and continued the fight for our freedom no matter how long it took. Eventually, Rani wanted me to repay the favor for keeping my secret. She told me to buy her cigarettes and do her share of household chores. In those days, buying cigarettes did not require showing ID, and our go-to excuse was that it was for our non-English-speaking grandfather.

One day during gym class, we were instructed to run around the perimeter of the school for the entire hour. Despite my best efforts, I found myself at the back of the pack, often needing to stop to catch my breath. On that fateful day, something truly terrifying occurred. As I continued running, a dark-colored Trans Am suddenly pulled up ahead of me, facing the wrong side of the street. My heart raced as I watched the driver, an old East Indian man who was balding and chubby, step out of the car. Before I could react, he tried to pull me into his vehicle forcefully. Panic gripped me, and instinctively, I fought back, shouting for help desperately. In that moment of sheer terror, a classmate who had noticed the commotion sprinted towards me. Reacting swiftly, she called out for the gym teacher. The sound of her voice appeared to startle the man, prompting him to quickly retreat to his car and speed away into the distance.

Understandably concerned, my father was informed about the incident. However, he made the decision not to share this information with my mother, wanting to shield her from reliving a past traumatic experience. I understood his fear and shared his desire to protect my mother from enduring another terrifying moment. It did not feel like we were keeping a secret; rather, we were determined to keep her safe. My father's support helped me heal and provided me with a sense of security.

In response to this alarming incident, the school implemented additional safety measures for all students. Enhanced staff presence was implemented during pick-up and drop-off times, with a focus on ensuring students were not walking alone. During gym class, students were to run in pairs for added security. Parents began to walk or drive their children to school. Children were asked to have open communication with their parents and report any unusual incidents promptly. The incident served as a stark reminder of the importance of being vigilant and prioritizing safety in our everyday lives.

Despite the fear and danger I faced, I could not help but feel grateful. I had managed to escape unharmed, and that was a miracle. This harrowing experience served as a stark reminder for me always to stay vigilant and aware of my surroundings. Even during seemingly safe activities like running in broad daylight during school, I realized the importance of being cautious. During the period from the 1970s to the 1980s, attempted abductions were underreported or addressed on a broader scale due to limitations in sharing information. The lack of advanced computer and data collection techniques during this period meant that information about the incidents was restricted to individual schools or local authorities.

However, despite the bond that formed between Rani, Dee, and me, I never shared the dark encounter that haunted me, not even the near-miss abduction I experienced. My father warned me not to tell anyone, not even Rani. There was a silent understanding that all our different issues, even untold, bonded us three together. These incidents were too heavy to bear, and perhaps we each feared judgment from our peers. As a result, the incident remained buried, hidden beneath the façade of the three of us and in our everyday struggles. It makes me wonder how many others out of there have similar untold stories concealed by the weight of their fears and shame.

Rani and Dee devised a plan to go shoplifting from the corner store, but I opted out of participating. Rani grew agitated, cautioning me that I would miss out. Disappointed by their need to steal once again, I walked away. Upon returning home, our mother questioned me about Rani's whereabouts, and I reassured her that she would be back soon, though I was unsure when. As I waited for her to return, our mother scolded her for taking so long. Rani deceived her, stating she had to retrieve a forgotten book from school.

Living in this family was scary. If the slightest thing was out of place or if you said something inappropriate, the belt would be there faster than saying sorry. Our parents found out about Rani's drinking, smoking, and her boyfriend. Rani fought with our parents, and in the morning, I found out that she had run away from home. It took the police and our parents a week to track her down, and she was forced to come home. My parents started yelling and swearing at me as though it was my fault and I was not the one who ran away. It took me decades to realize that I could not blame Rani for her actions as it was not her fault. It was the negative environment that we lived in that showed in our behaviors.

The oppressive atmosphere within our family home mirrored that of a military boot camp rather than a nurturing home. Our parents imposed rigid regulations and a controlled disciplinary approach that left no room for tenderness or compassion. The repercussions of Rani's transgressions were unjustly extended to me, leading to both of us enduring the brutal consequences of the belt for the slightest hint of defiance. In moments of pain and suffering, tears streamed down my face as I pleaded with my father, "Why are you subjecting me to this torment? I have not done anything wrong!" Regrettably, my plea was in vain, as it appeared that they had already decided on what they believed we deserved.

This retaliation by our father had negative consequences on my emotional and mental health; it created a severe dislike for Rani. It also caused me to have negative behaviors like skipping classes, hanging out with the wrong crowd, participating in drag racing, smoking, and arguing with my parents. These self-destructive behaviors stemmed from the environment I grew up in. I wish my parents had sought out support from the community or professional resources to assist them in overcoming the challenges of raising us.

I began to question their motives, pondering why they subjected us to such endless regulations. It appeared that we had parents who could exhibit love only to their son and not to Rani or me. In moments of silence, I would lie on my bed and contemplate, "Is this how childhood is supposed to be? Is it possible to find joy when everything we do is scrutinized?" Despite my deep contemplation, the questions lingered without answers. However, as time passed and days turned into weeks and weeks into months, I gradually started to comprehend the importance of self-discipline and respecting authority.

Eventually, as I matured, I took time to contemplate all that transpired. Though challenging, I recognized that the adversities my parents subjected us to had a negative impact. It changed my character and heightened my sense of protectiveness over my children. I firmly reject any form of violence or mistreatment toward others. Through these experiences, I discovered that following guidelines and respecting different viewpoints, even when in disagreement, helps us to see other people's perspectives.

Reflecting on my strict and conservative upbringing, I appreciated the emphasis on hard work, discipline, and respect for authority, which have shaped my work ethic and personal values. I also recognized the importance of maintaining a nurturing and loving environment while imparting these virtues. Which in my upbringing was not shown or provided by my parents. The emphasis on diligence and perseverance has particularly influenced my drive and determination, propelling me towards the relentless pursuit of my aspirations.

This value has also given me a sense of structure and order, enabling me to work within rules and guidelines without feeling the need to rebel against authority unnecessarily. These values have been instrumental in my personal and professional development. While I may not agree with every aspect of conservatism, these values have proven to be invaluable in various aspects of my life. As I reflect on my journey, I realize that strict parenting is not a conducive parenting style, but it should always be balanced with love, support, and understanding. It is important to set boundaries and teach responsibility, but it should never come at the expense of a child's emotional well-being.

Strict parenting was difficult and painful for me, but it did teach me a valuable lesson about perseverance and the importance of balance in parenting, not wanting my children ever to feel neglected or go through abuse. I created a nurturing environment for my children where discipline was tempered with love and understanding. The government should recognize the challenges parents face by making non-voluntary parental classes before any children are born. This will help parents learn about parenting and provide ongoing resources to help them in their parenting journey, especially within interfaith families and those struggling with societal pressures. This can make a child's life better and even save their life.

I have come to understand the negative impacts of strict parenting and realize that each child possesses distinct strengths and challenges. Exposing a child to turmoil as a means of dealing with personal issues is unjustifiable. Parents play a key role in providing a safe and supportive atmosphere where children can flourish. It is important to balance discipline with love to create a positive and encouraging space for children to thrive; in today's rapidly changing society, parents should encourage their children to explore their unique interests and values while also teaching them responsibility and respect.

By setting ground rules and boundaries, parents can help children make good choices and decisions while promoting a culture of acceptance, inclusivity, and diversity. Additionally, focusing on children's emotional and mental health, supporting their interests, and providing positive reinforcement can help build their self-esteem and confidence. Through an open and honest relationship based on trust and respect, parents can guide their children with positive behavior and sound decision-making without the need for harsh punishment, strengthening the parent-child bond in the process.

As a parent myself, I have learned the importance of fostering an environment that encourages children to express themselves and learn from their mistakes. Instead of resorting to strict discipline, I have chosen to engage in open communication with my children, encouraging them to share their thoughts and collaborating on finding solutions together. By promoting a supportive and understanding atmosphere, my children feel comfortable coming to me with their concerns, even if it means discussing something that might lead to consequences.

Through this approach, we work as a team to address issues constructively and strive for positive outcomes. This approach helps build a strong bond between parents and their children, which is important for their overall development. When children feel that their parents are on their side, they are more likely to trust them - and seek their guidance when faced with difficult decisions or challenges. By providing a supportive and sympathetic environment, I created a foundation for my children to become confident and independent adults who can make their own choices and solve their problems.

My parents, coming from two distinct religious backgrounds and striving to meet the expectations of extended families and society, may have internalized a new set of perceptions or ideologies regarding what is considered acceptable parenting. As a result, they established impractical objectives and physical punishments that ultimately led to their failure as parents. Their parenting style exhibited physical and emotional abuse and gender biases rather than nurturing or understanding. The use of belts as a form of discipline could potentially be a remnant of the abusive mentality prevalent during the colonial era. This parenting style was learned from their parents and handed down through generations. Rani and I deserved a childhood free from pain and fear. Where we could grow and learn as normal teenagers.

It is crucial to recognize the damaging effects these behaviors can have and the need for parents to foster a safe and encouraging environment that promotes healthy growth and unbiased opportunities for all children. I may have biases regarding this issue, but others may see this as a good sign that the person has succeeded in life and has a career, family, and stability. However, it is the journey that is the downside, not the outcome. I believe that a more nurturing and supportive approach could have been taken instead.

Towards the middle of the year, summer arrived. My original plan was to spend time with my friends on the sly, but our father insisted that Rani and I attend summer school. It felt like we would never catch a break! Despite our reluctance, we signed up for classes. The tough part was waking up early and walking the long distance from Kingsway and Knight Street to East 41st Avenue in Vancouver. During summer school at John Oliver High School, I noticed a significant presence of children from various countries. In contrast to my high school, which lacked diversity among its students, Rani and I were among the few representing diverse cultural backgrounds.

The other children frequently inquired about our proficient English and lack of accents. Communication proved difficult as their English skills were lacking. Rani proposed that we keep our distance from them, but I could not shake the thought of why our school had so few children from different countries. Rani wanted to go back to our school as she enjoyed her usual hangout spot, where she knew more students. On the contrary, I was curious and eager to interact with a wider range of people.

After conversing with the students, I developed an interest in attending John Oliver. When Rani and I returned home, we discussed the individuals we met with our father. I expressed my desire to attend that school, but he refused, insisting that I remain at my current school and focus solely on my academics. He believed that I did not require any friends and should prioritize my school work.

This year was rough. Rani was sent to live with extended family in hopes that it would resolve the problems our parents were having with her. Our uncle's family was a very strict Muslim family due to Rani's disregard for our parents' rules and frequent running away from home. Instead of finding a resolution themselves, our parents decided to pass the problems on to our mother's brother.

As a parent, I must take ownership of addressing and resolving family problems instead of passing them on to someone else, even if they are family. I strongly believe in actively seeking resolutions and fostering open and honest discussions with our children. In my own experience, my parents never engaged in such conversations with anyone. I cannot help but think that having those discussions could have positively impacted our lives, shaping our futures in profound ways. Taking a proactive approach like this is crucial for the well-being and growth of all children.

With the absence of Rani, my home life became quiet. I focused on my homework while also assisting my mother with chores and taking care of my younger sibling. However, I could not help but constantly wonder why my parents kept us apart. Was it truly to protect me from becoming like Rani? I found it hard to believe that any situation could be so severe that they could not share the reasons.

Furthermore, I was utterly bewildered by the unfathomable violence and abuse inflicted upon us. It was as if our fundamental rights to self-expression and freedom were callously stripped away. I found myself constantly wondering where they had learned such twisted parenting methods, as our family dynamic bore no resemblance to anything I deemed normal. These continual thoughts forced me to confront a startling question: Was this appalling mistreatment of Indian girls a tragically common occurrence in families like ours?

As the year went on, I began to feel the absence of Rani more and more. Despite her habit of causing trouble, she brought a certain liveliness to our family that I had taken for granted. The house now felt empty without her. It was when she moved away that I realized just how much I truly needed her in my life. Although her behavior could be confusing and sometimes aggressive towards others, she was still family. Our family gatherings lacked the same energy and excitement without her.

It felt as if a vital piece was missing from our dynamic. Rani always kept us on our toes, bringing laughter and chaos wherever she went. Her mischievous ways were a mix of amusement and frustration for those around her. There was always a mischievous glint in her eyes as if she relished the thrill of pushing boundaries and defying convention. While her actions often led to disagreements or even physical altercations, her boldness had a certain charm. She exuded an unwavering fearlessness, approaching life with vigor and never shying away from a challenge. Deciphering her behavior was like solving a puzzle, as her tantrums, outbursts, and confrontations added complexity to her seemingly fearless persona.

At times, dealing with the aftermath of Rani's troublesome behavior was both exhausting and draining. However, upon reflection, I recognize that her actions were a form of communication—her way of expressing herself and seeking attention. Ultimately, her behavior was a manifestation of the abuse we endured in our upbringing. There were moments where I felt sympathy for both of us, as siblings trapped in the same cycle of abuse, unable to protect ourselves.

Our parents were informed that Rani had run away. It was a distressing situation, as she was going to be sent back due to her negative influence on the other children. Our parents were furious and upset with her behavior. However, the aftermath of her actions took a toll on my own life. Their anger and emotions were unleashed on me, with accusations of me being just like Rani despite them never fully explaining the events that had unfolded regarding Rani. I was confused and hurt by their reactions. I wondered why our parents were so cynical and temperamental.

On Valentine's, I received a large card along with a flower taped to my locker. As I looked around, I did not see or hear anyone.

I opened the card; it was a nice gesture. However, I did not know who it was from, so I intended to leave it in my locker. My friends put it in my backpack without my knowing. As I arrived home, my mother opened my school bag and found the card. What a big mistake! She made such a commotion about it.

My father ripped the card and flower from her hands. I tried to explain that I did not know the person at all. I pleaded with my father to call my friends, who were present when the card was put in my bag. My parents would not listen; they asked, "Why did you keep it instead of throwing it away?" I explained that I intended to discard it, but my friends slipped it into my bag without my knowledge. In response, my father resorted to punishment and administered a belt whipping.

Despite my hopes that the punishment would end with Rani's absence, the household responsibilities of cooking, cleaning, laundry, and babysitting persisted. I worked diligently to adhere to all the rules and obligations assigned to me, but the outcome remained unchanged. Although I was relieved that Rani was no longer subjected to the abuse, I continued to endure the harsh treatment inflicted on me.

Later, I learned that the card and flower had been given to me by a new Grade 8 student from India who was learning English as a Second Language. Despite this revelation, I could not shake the feeling of not owing him anything, especially considering the punishment I faced from my father because of his gesture. It weighed heavily on me, but I was resigned to the fact that my life was governed by my parents, particularly my father. Keeping the events to myself, I refrained from discussing them with my friends, fearful of being subjected to judgment.

I always felt like I could not live up to my parents' expectations. No matter how hard I tried, it never was sufficient. I often pondered my existence and purpose in this world, especially as the treatment of Rani and me by our parents reinforced my sense of inadequacy and hopelessness within our household. Our family life was shrouded in secrecy and inner turmoil, known only to us. Despite the outward appearance of a perfect family unit with caring parents and two daughters, the truth behind closed doors was starkly different from the idealized image.

Back in high school where I wanted to be seen as a cool person among my peers, so I did not participate in sports in grade 10. This desire led me down a risky path of skipping school. During the lunch break, I was by my locker when this unknown guy, a couple of lockers down, was staring at me. I looked at him and arrogantly asked what his problem was. He walked over and said that he did have a problem! I was puzzled and a little agitated. He then went on to say his problem was he did not know how to ask me out. The revelation changed my outlook, and I thought this guy

"Jay" was so forward. After that, we started to see each other all the time and spent every school day together.

Months later, I decided to skip school, and to my surprise, Jay, who did not like skipping school, showed up unexpectedly. Not wanting to face the day alone, my best friend Sita, "Yes," it is the girl with whom I fought in grade eight, joined me in this rebellious escapade. We were drawn to the river on Marine Drive, finding comfort in its soothing presence. As Sita's anxiety mounted, we reluctantly decided to depart from the park.

However, just as we began our retreat, the menacing presence of the police descended upon us, whisking us back to school as we left without permission. The ride back to school was filled with a mix of anxiety and curiosity as the officers interrogated us, trying to uncover the reasons behind our truancy. Our shared desire to break free from the suffocating grasp of our overbearing parents, we confessed our longing for a taste of freedom.

In an unexpected turn of events, the officers, in a negative display of authority, had advised us to run away from our troubles. It was a suggestion so absurd it sent a surge of disbelief through my veins. Escape was never our goal; all we wanted was a taste of liberation and respite from our parents. Returning to school, our hearts sank as news of our unexcused absence reached both of our parents' ears.

Both of our parents' wrath descended upon us like an unforgiving storm, leaving us trembling in fear of the consequences. I am grateful yet fearful that the authorities kept our accomplice's identity a secret. I knew, deep down, that divulging this information would only lead to a labyrinth of turmoil and difficult explanations, as though my life was not complicated enough.

As the night wore on, my father's anger reached its peak, his voice resonating through the walls as he recounted the incident in Hindi to my mother. I silently thanked my lucky stars for the secrecy surrounding our partners in crime. However, my relief was short-lived as my father's clenched fist reached for the belt ominously hanging on the wall. Its harsh sting served as a stark reminder of the repercussions of my rebellious actions, leaving me to grapple with the intense drama unfolding because I pursued freedom.

Although my rebellious attitude brought me temporary satisfaction, it was short-lived due to my frequent skipping out of school. My parents grew exhausted from the constant suspensions. I learned that no matter how rebellious I was, it did not justify abuse. My parents did not want us to engage in normal teenage activities that they deemed unacceptable, like having friends or even a boyfriend, which warranted punishment. As a teenager, it is natural to rebel and push boundaries, but in our family, there were to be no exceptions to the rules. Even though I found satisfaction in my rebellions, the fleeting moment of freedom was cut short as I faced my father's anger, and it was not a pleasant feeling.

Rani was back home from Edmonton; she excluded palpable anger, hinting at a significant shift in our relationship. It became clear that a gap had emerged during her year-long absence while I struggled to pinpoint the root cause of this strain in our connection. A fundamental lack of trust tainted our interactions. The trust had always been a vague concept between us, overshadowed by caution and skepticism. Our parents' enforced communication restrictions on us further solidified the belief that trust was a scarce commodity in our relationship.

Now, Rani seemed like a distant figure compared to the familiar presence I once knew. Subtle changes in her behavior had been noticeable even before her departure. Despite sharing physical proximity, an emotional distance existed between us, creating a contradictory sense of closeness and isolation. The circumstances leading to our separation remained shrouded in mystery, our parents' imposition of silence acting as a barrier between Rani and me, potentially driven by motives of concealment. This imposed silence weighed heavily on our relationship, serving as a constant reminder of the widening void between us.

Rani and my confinement started within the same room and year. Rani found herself restricted in all forms within the walls of our home. I felt the walls closing in on me after my return from school. The event that unfolded after coming home was truly a nightmare. Our parents restricted every movement, controlling everything, but one thing they could not control was our thoughts.

At this point, we were truly broken. Rani and I fought for our right to be treated as normal children, but unfortunately, our parents did not see this as an acceptable demand. Despite sharing the same physical environment and meals, a palpable lack of communication tainted our daily interactions, enveloping our existence in solitude and loneliness. The suffocating silence within our shared room appeared to cement an unspoken pact to keep our distance, leaving me burdened with a heavy sense of isolation.

We were bound together by our common circumstance of home confinement. Day by day, the barriers surrounding us grew taller, entangling us in fear and uncertainty. Tip-toeing around each other and the looming threat of parental repercussions, we were unable to breach the walls that constrained us. Through stolen glances, fleeting smiles, and rare moments of warmth exchanged in passing, those fleeting gestures bore testament to the silent bond that tied us together. Trapped within the confines of our shared space, burdened with unvoiced questions and unexpressed longings, we endured. While our lives stood still and the future remained uncertain, I vowed to shield myself from Rani's apparent fate, holding onto a thread of hope that the barriers separating us would one day crumble, freeing us from our shared silence. During school hours, I embarked on a secret relationship with a guy named Jay. Unfortunately, my parents discovered the secret through Rani's meddling, and their anger erupted with explosive force. Swearing and yelling filled the air, their insults cutting deep as they hurled hurtful words like *"bitch"* at me. Overwhelmed and seeking refuge, I hurried to my room, hoping to find solace within those familiar walls. Yet, to my dismay, my father followed, clutching a belt in his hand, a chilling emblem of our father's chosen disciplinary tool. The irony of their approach struck me, as violence seemed to be their only way to confront this situation.

Despite the knots of fear tightening inside me, a small, bitter laugh escaped my lips. My father's strikes intensified until exhaustion finally forced him to relinquish his futile efforts. That night, the laughter faded, and my body paid the price. The pain and welts served as a reminder of the violence that had been inflicted on me. Amid my anguish, Rani entered the room, expressing her apologies. However, my anger consumed me, making it impossible to meet her gaze or utter a single word. My parents made the decision that we should go to Jay's house and speak to his parents. Cruel and painful, my father grabbed hold of my long hair, pulling it and kicking me repeatedly in the butt as he dragged me to the car. The physical abuse only added to the turmoil I was already experiencing.

Our search for his house took us on a long and winding journey throughout Vancouver. Desperate to find the right address, my father approached random East Indian people, hoping they could provide some assistance. After what felt like an eternity, he finally encountered an old lady who knew the family my father was looking for. She shared the new address with him, offering a glimmer of hope in an otherwise tumultuous situation. We arrived at the address, and his parents were home. The entire ride leading up to the moment was filled with swearing and degrading comments directed towards me. I was insulted and belittled, with remarks like, "You must have liked his ass!" What did he see in you? You are fat, dark, and ugly, not even smart.

When Jay finally came back home, my parents displayed an overwhelming fury towards him and adamantly insisted that he immediately marry me. This situation induced fear within me as I pondered the potential consequences we would face, and it left me unsure about how to handle it. His parents made it clear that they understood my parents' desires, but they believed that rushing into marriage simply to appease them would not be in our best interest. They acknowledged that we were both very young teenagers, recognizing that we were still growing and maturing before making such a significant decision. By emphasizing the importance of waiting until we were older, his parents wanted to ensure that we had the necessary life experiences and emotional maturity to handle the responsibilities that come with marriage.

His parents wanted us to explore our paths, chase our dreams, and discover our own identities before committing to a lifelong partnership. His parents emphasized that marriage is a serious commitment and should never be entered into lightly. They wanted everyone to understand the gravity of the decision and ensure that we were ready for the challenges and sacrifices it entails. At that point, I realized his parents were more willing to listen, and their advice was making sense. However, unfortunately, my parents were not receptive to the idea and demanded that we get married. My parents were unwilling to deviate from their goal of immediate marriage and nothing less.

At that moment, I recognized the openness of his parents and the validity of their advice. Regrettably, my parents seemed resistant to the notion, insisting on no alternatives. Their unwavering stance left no room for compromise or discussion. Both our parents told us to go into the room and talk over everything that was discussed. I feel trapped between my parents' anger and my desire to make the right decision for my future. I knew we had to come to an agreement and give our parents an answer. We sat down, holding hands tightly, as we discussed the situation.

After deep introspection and heartfelt discussions, we came to a profound realization of the strength of our love for each other. However, we also acknowledged the importance of considering practical factors, such as our ages, limited financial resources, and the inevitable pressures from my parents. With an abundance of caution and a focus on personal growth, we made the deliberate choice to prioritize our paths for the time being. By seizing this opportunity to pursue our education and gain the necessary skills and knowledge, we believe that we can build a strong foundation for our future. This compromise allows us to prioritize our individual growth while also maintaining a strong foundation for our relationship.

Also, acknowledging that rushing into marriage without being fully prepared may lead to additional stress and challenges. By giving ourselves the time and space to mature and achieve financial stability, we can enter marriage with a clearer understanding of ourselves and our goals. By focusing on our education and personal development, we can acquire the skills and knowledge necessary to navigate the complexities of life. This will empower us to make informed decisions, handle challenges effectively, and contribute to a healthy and fulfilling partnership.

I am grateful for having learned the wisdom of carefully considering the importance of marriage. Impulsively tying the knot often leads to regret and disappointment. Sadly, this lesson rings all too true in my own experience. It seemed as if the people I called family only cared about forcing me into an arranged marriage and did not have much concern about anything else. It was confusing to witness two people, my parents, who had married against their family's wishes, begin making unreasonable demands. I struggled to understand how two individuals who had fallen in love could be so negative and cause both Rani and me physical and emotional pain. Their behavior was something that I never imagined that two-people who claimed to love me would inflict. It was beyond comprehension, both cruel and unyielding.

Ultimately, their intolerance and prejudice were evident in every aspect of their actions. My parents were comparing me unfavorably to Rani; they went on further, saying if you are going to get married, marry my older daughter. She is everything men want in a wife, and she is light-skinned, beautiful, slim, and very smart. This shocked Jay's parents, and they even asked if I was adopted. They reminded my parents that love should not be based on caste, religion, or skin color. I was utterly shocked by my parent's behavior and did not want to be around them at all.

My parents were unwilling to bend because they were determined to have an immediate marriage. Jay's parents said that there would be no marriage until the children were older, and my parents became angry. After hours, we eventually left Jay's house. On the way home, my parents continued to shout at me, calling me a disgrace and a shame to the family. My father said, "He used you" and "asked whether you felt good about it." I said we did nothing wrong. My father said, 'Wait until we get home; I will show you.' I thought, here we go again with the belt syndrome.

We arrived home, and I went straight to my room. Rani was curious about what happened. Our father yelled at our mother, shouting. "Your daughters are both garbage; they deserve nothing, and no one will ever marry them." The ranting kept going on like a broken record. Our home became a place that felt like boot camp. My father wielded the belt as a means of discipline, consistently hitting me. In those moments, I attempted to distract myself by thinking about other things, anything, to escape the physical pain. Thoughts of fleeing and never returning consumed my mind, providing a glimmer of hope amidst the chaos.

My lack of reaction only fueled my father's anger, intensifying his assault. It was as if I had shut off my emotions, feeling nothing as each blow landed. Eventually, he grew tired and gave up, but the toll on my body had already been paid. The dark bruises and swollen welts served as visible proof of the brutality of what I had endured as I silently wept as tears came down my face and dried up, keeping the true extent of my pain hidden from those around me. I eventually fell asleep from all the emotional and physical torment.

After the incident, Jay and I never spoke again. My friends had all vanished, leaving me to grapple with everything alone. Rani tried to check on me, but I rejected her attempts at communication. I was consumed with hurt and anger towards her for exposing my secret and causing such turmoil. Days turned into weeks, and our lives reverted to being confined in our shared room. The ordeal left a profound rift in my relationship with my parents. I grew more distant, avoiding their outbursts and harsh punishments. I also distanced myself from Rani, realizing I could no longer trust her with my secrets, even though I had no secrets left. My father refused to let me go to school, and the situation got worse at home. My father told everyone to ignore me, and no one was allowed to talk to me.

Rani and I made a bold decision to run away from home. Excited at the prospect of escaping the abuse we endured, we headed to Vancouver to enlist in the army. However, our hopes were quickly dashed when the recruiting officer informed us that we were too young to enlist and required parental consent. Knowing our parents would never agree, we felt defeated. Rani suggested obtaining a signed note from our mother, but the officer firmly rejected the-idea. Heartbroken, we returned home, anxious about facing the repercussions. Our parents had not yet returned from their outing and provided us with a momentary reprieve.

Rani decided that marriage was the way forward as she cited it to gain more freedom from our oppressive home environment.

Concerned about the prospect of exchanging our father's rules for those of a husband, I voiced my hesitation. Despite my reservations, she informed our parents that she would follow their rules and get married. Our parents began searching for a husband for her, though Rani did have some say in choosing a man. Her newfound sense of freedom, however ironic, was a decision I did not fully comprehend but respected as her choice. I felt her momentary sense of freedom was not worth saying yes or giving up.

Through many experiences that took my freedom away in my late twenties, I learned a valuable lesson about the true essence of freedom and independence. I came to understand that true freedom does not rely on external validation but on yourself. I tirelessly fought for my freedom. Additionally, I learned that with freedom comes accountability. I must take responsibility for my decisions and their consequences without blaming others. Furthermore, I recognized the importance of respecting my choices and fighting to be free from my parent's unrealistic rules.

In my youth, I often equated independence with rebellion, breaking rules, and doing whatever I wanted. However, later in life, I realized that true freedom is not about breaking rules and doing whatever I want. I also learned that interdependence is just as important as independence. I also learned to collaborate with and work with others to achieve common goals. No one can achieve anything great alone. Overall, I am grateful for the lessons I learned about freedom and independence. I will continue to treasure and protect my independence while respecting the freedom of others.

Two months before the end of tenth grade, the situation at home had gotten worse. I was taken out of school, and the principal was told I would be going to Fiji. The principal did not do anything about the situation, and I wished he had taken a more proactive approach to the issue at hand. I was not allowed to talk to anyone by myself as my parents went with me, so there was no way to tell anyone the truth about my home life or any other problems. I was already under house confinement by my parents. My parents told me that I would be getting married soon. I was upset and angry, and I thought the older we got, the beatings would stop. This was not the case; the beatings kept going on.

I felt like I was only there to serve a purpose without feeling loved or accepted by my family. I helped the family with everything they needed: laundry, cleaning, and cooking. My time was not my own; it was whatever my mother needed. I was locked in the house with no way out. I never imagined things could deteriorate to such an extent; it was unbelievable. This situation was difficult because I had never fully grasped life before. I had no one to talk to or share my feelings. I was not allowed to communicate, not even with my extended family. Feeling lost and desperate, I did not know where to find comfort or someone to listen to me. Each morning, I woke up feeling sad and frustrated, knowing another day of being insignificant.

I felt trapped in a repetitive time loop; the rest of the family seemed preoccupied with their own lives, completely unaware of my existence. I longed for someone to notice me, listen to me, and understand. Each time I tried to engage in conversation, it felt like my words were being ignored. They would nod carelessly, never truly listening or showing any genuine interest in what I had to say. Despite my attempts to console myself, the feeling of emptiness persisted. I craved genuine connections, meaningful conversations, and a sense of being acknowledged and understood. It felt like a part of me was dying, consumed by the feeling of being unwanted and unloved.

Although the scars of feeling invisible would always stay with me, I learned to assert my voice, stand up for myself, and demand the recognition I deserved. I realized that I was never meant to be invisible; my thoughts and emotions were valid and worthy of being understood and recognized. I was tired of going through this situation; it was not getting better, and things were getting worse with no end in sight.

I decided to commit suicide. I ate the silicone gel that comes with new shoes. I held the small packet in my palms and opened it, not knowing what would happen. I put it in my mouth and swallowed it. I did not taste anything, maybe because I was so emotional. The whole day and event felt weird, and I did not want to feel like this. I was taking a risk; things could get drastically worse. But I just wanted to be free from this life; it was making me miserable, and at this point, any way out was a solution.

I thought death would come quickly, but nothing happened. At that moment, a realization struck me like lightning: What was I doing? How selfish was I being? Oh, my god, grandmother died from suicide! Was this the only way to cope with my situation? My mother had been watching me incessantly, closely monitoring my every move. As soon as she saw me, she rushed to my room and urgently called for my father. In response, he angrily shouted, "Let her die like her grandma if that is what she wants." My mother recalled my adverse reaction to eating ripe bananas, which caused me to get nauseated, and she urgently fed me a banana to induce vomiting and alleviate the potential consequences. Throughout the night, I experienced waves of sickness and repeatedly vomited. It was a long and uncomfortable night, but eventually, exhaustion took over, and I drifted into a restless sleep. When morning arrived, I found myself in the same confined space, within the walls of my room, with no significant changes to my situation.

Despite my struggles while under house confinement by my parents, I received no emotional support from them or Rani. I want to encourage anyone going through a similar situation to seek help, as there are people who are willing to listen and offer support. It is important not to face these challenges alone, even though you may feel like it is the only option. When emotions cloud our judgment, it can be difficult to see other possibilities. This is why it is crucial to have a new set of perspectives to guide us on where and how we can fix the issues. Give yourself a chance, and you will see other ways to navigate your problems. It is also worth noting that everyone's situation is different, and finding someone who has gone through something similar can provide different viewpoints and support. Back in the 1980s, there was no hotline for suicide; today, there are more options to seek help and support.

I longed for a solution, a miraculous revelation that would mend the shattered relationship between us. Each day felt like a battlefield, with tension lingering in the air, threatening to ignite at any moment. I yearned for compassion and for my parents to understand the turmoil within me, but it felt as if they were trapped in their world of expectations and disappointments. We were like ships passing through the night, our paths diverging further with each passing day.

The divide between us seemed insurmountable, a gaping chasm that no bridge could adequately span. I wondered if we were destined to live forever amid this suffocating cycle of misunderstandings and unspoken words. But deep down, a flicker of hope remained. I clung to the belief that love had the power to transcend these barriers, to bridge the gap, and to bring us together.

I yearned for a breakthrough, a moment of vulnerability that would shatter the walls we had constructed around ourselves. For now, though, we remain trapped prisoners of our egos and pain. The silence between us grew louder, drowning out the possibility of reconciliation. It felt like an endless loop of heartbreak, each day depicting a new chapter in this tragic narrative. Sometimes, in moments of quiet reflection, I would imagine what life could be like if we could find a way to break free. I envisioned a home filled with laughter where understanding and acceptance prevailed.

A world where love triumphed over stupidity and compassion mended the wounds that time had inflicted. What happened to those days when we were a close family? Where did we go wrong? These questions haunted my thoughts, relentless in their pursuit of answers. But until that day arrived, I refused to let this suffocating cycle define me, for I knew that there was strength within me—a determination to find a way to mend what was broken. In these moments, I could not help but wonder how different things could be.

Breaking free from the suffocating cycle became an unattainable dream, slipping further from our grasp each day. In these moments, I pondered a different reality, where we could escape the never-ending cycle's suffocating grasp. I yearned for a way to bridge the widening gap between my parents and me, to find the compassion and understanding we desperately needed. But, for now, we remained tangled in heartbreak. Each of us carried burdens of unresolved emotions, burying the love that once bound us beneath layers of hurt and disappointment.

One thing was certain: the snarling web could not hold forever. Although it felt unbreakable, I refused to accept our destiny of bitterness and sorrow. This journey was far from easy. Breaking the chains demanded strength, courage, and a willingness to let go. We had to confront our pain head-on, acknowledge the scars it left, and actively work toward healing and forgiveness. So, I clung to that glimmer of hope, nurturing it with patience and determination. I vowed to keep searching for a way to bridge the divide, even when it seemed impossible.

Rani talked to me about how our parents' wishes were a top priority; this left me feeling trapped and helpless. She mentioned the pressure to conform to these wishes by getting married or living in confinement indefinitely, which only added to my feelings of despair. If Rani and I had only talked sooner, maybe we could have formulated a plan to diffuse the notion of our parents' forced arranged marriage. To this day, I still do not understand what could motivate parents to abuse their children and force them into arranged marriages.

Why would you willingly give society control over your family? It raises an important question about the legal protections in place to protect individuals who oppose or resist arranged marriages. Additionally, it prompts us to consider how communities and support networks can better assist those facing pressure to enter arranged marriages against their will. Education and awareness are crucial in challenging and potentially changing the practice of arranged marriages, ensuring individuals' rights and well-being are respected.

My journey with an arranged forced marriage occurred in a surprising context: a modern country like Canada, where freedom and individual rights are highly valued. While it is true that Canada champions the principles of personal freedom and choice, my experience highlights the harsh reality that these values are not always extended to everyone. The question then arises: what about my freedom? I as an individual living in a progressive society, have the right to make decisions about my own life, particularly when it comes to such intimate and personal matters as marriage.

By sharing my story, I aim to challenge the notion that forced arranged marriages only happen in traditional or less developed settings, emphasizing that all societies must strive to ensure the preservation of individual freedoms and protect individuals from such unjust practices. As a teenager, I found myself unexpectedly facing the intricacies of a forced arranged marriage. The sheer magnitude of this decision was overwhelming, surpassing my ability to grasp it, let alone cope with it fully.

At the age of 16, even simple choices like deciding what to eat presented a challenge. Yet, I was suddenly thrust into a situation where I was expected to make a lifelong commitment. Additionally, I was burdened with the responsibility of supporting my husband due to immigration restrictions on work visas, as my parents no longer wanted to bear the financial responsibility for us. It was an overwhelming and deeply unfair burden that I carried. In my darkest moments, I found myself yearning for an escape, and the thought of death seemed like a preferable alternative.

Reflecting on this, I cannot fathom how modern society continues to accept and perpetuate such practices. I firmly believe that it should be illegal for anyone under the age of 20 to enter marriage. The notion that individuals at such a tender age possess the maturity, life experience, and emotional development necessary for such a profound commitment is unrealistic. It is only through experiencing and living life that one can truly develop a sense of their identity, understand their desires, and make informed decisions about their future.

By enacting laws to protect young individuals from forced marriages, we can uphold their rights, ensure their well-being, and grant them the opportunity to grow and discover their path in life.

My parents signed a consent form to allow the arranged marriage. If the government had the power to intervene in arranged marriages involving minors, my parents would not be able to sign a consent form for my marriage without my input. We should enact laws that make it mandatory for governments to investigate any marriages involving minors.

As my thoughts raced, a persistent question consumed my mind: Why go through the trouble of bringing us to Canada? If they had intended for us to be married anyway, we could have simply remained in Fiji, cherishing and upholding our profound traditions. It would have spared us the disruption, the uncertainty, and the abuse to conform. Why present us with a glimpse of this new life only to snatch it away? Each inquiry lingered unanswered, fueling my restlessness and confusion. Neither of my parents felt compelled to address my concerns. After all, my father held the reins of power within our household while I struggled to find my rightful place.

Chapter 11

Rani's Arranged Wedding Societal Pressures

I t was 1984, and as Rani's façade of excitement filled the air, our parents went to great lengths to make their wedding dreams a reality. It felt like every ounce of their energy was dedicated to this elaborate spectacle while Rani's and my desires were dismissed and overlooked. The cruel irony was not lost on me, as I knew she shared my reluctance towards this arranged marriage. They believed that arranging a marriage for me following Ranis' wedding, would fulfill their societal obligations and secure our family's honor. In their eyes, my dreams and desires were irrelevant.

In this distorted reality, Rani and I found ourselves ensnared in a situation we never asked for. Both of us were victims of circumstances that ignored our desires and trampled over dreams. Our aspirations lay broken and ignored as we were coerced into conforming to societal expectations and familial pressures. The dysfunctional household had become a battlefield, with unspoken resentment poisoning the air and fractured relationships left in its wake. We became prisoners in our own homes. Our rights are blatantly stripped away as if we were nobodies.

Our voices and choices were silenced, our hearts yearning for freedom and autonomy in a world that seemed determined to shape our lives for us. Amid this turmoil, we longed for understanding, compassion, and the chance to pursue our paths, unburdened by the expectations of others. My thoughts were simple: nothing good would come out of this wedding, as they were doing it for themselves and not for us. If they had thought about us, they would not have gone through with this charade.

It was summer; Rani was getting married, and it was a huge event. People came over to our house every day. Our mom and I had to do the cooking and cleaning. I was making and serving tea to everyone. Rani was not allowed to do anything, and our parents said her job was to look pretty. On the day of the wedding, the temple, a two-story building in Vancouver, was filled with unfamiliar faces, creating a scene reminiscent of a Bollywood movie. It seemed improbable that my parents knew so many people in Canada, except for those back in Fiji.

Among the vibrant colors and rhythmic beats, my heart ached for Rani. I yearned for her to break free from the constraints of societal expectations and find happiness on her terms. I wanted her to share in the sense of pride and duty towards our heritage that I had developed over time. It was important to me that she had the opportunity to embrace our roots while still maintaining the freedom to make her own choices.

This strong connection to our culture was cultivated through the bond and cherished moments I shared with my father. I was always around him, whether it was listening to his music interests or hearing his stories, assisting him in the yard, or remodeling homes. These shared moments were never explicitly expressed, but rather, it was the unspoken things that made me realize my father was unique. I often wished for a gentler father figure—someone who was not so closed off and did not resort to physical violence as a means of control over Rani and me.

Suddenly, I found myself back in reality, facing Rani's marriage rituals. This is not where I wanted to be, nor was it what she wanted. We were not close and did not talk about anything anymore; it was as if we had stopped being sisters. We were not even friends; we were strangers living in the same space, and that was it. I knew her marriage would be short-lived, as the writing was already on the wall. Unfortunately, I was the only one who could see the outcome, as nothing good comes from forcing someone against their will. However, our parents adhered to traditional customs and would never allow Rani or me to deviate from the path they had set for both of us.

Amidst a whirlwind of emotions that swept through my soul, I made a conscious choice to cherish the fleeting moments that emerged amid the relentless storm. Seeking solace within the hallowed halls of the bustling temple, I found respite in its tranquil ambiance—a sanctuary that offered refuge from the chaos that raged. Nevertheless, beneath the surface serenity, an unsettling fear gnawed at my core, casting shadows of doubt over my path. Yet I clung to a glimmer of hope.

Rani was dressed in expensive attire, adorned with gold bracelets, and surrounded by the splendor of a haldi ceremony and engagement party. The enchanting ambiance created by the expensive flowers and beautiful decorations and the looming reality of my upcoming forced marriage overshadowed everything. Amid the grandeur, I could not ignore the feeling that my desires and dreams were being disregarded. My simple attire served as a stark contrast to the opulence around me, a constant reminder of the sacrifices I was expected to make.

The loud music and commotion made it almost maddening. As the guests settled into their seats, the prayers began, followed by rituals. Though the ceremony was fascinating to observe, I found myself becoming tired. Throughout the entire wedding ceremony, I was assigned the role of an errand runner, responsible for attending to various needs like getting selected items for the prayer like flowers and incense. As I tirelessly fulfilled everyone's requests, my energy gradually diminished.

The hours seemed to stretch on as I patiently waited for the priest's announcement, signaling the conclusion of the wedding and the departure of the newlyweds to prepare for the reception. Finally, my relief arrived. However, it was short-lived, as the reception brought a new wave of chaos and a fresh set of tasks for me to-tackle. Amidst the lively atmosphere, it appeared that everyone was fully engrossed in the festivities. I was overwhelmed by my responsibilities, and it only added to my sense of unease when my parents proudly boasted to acquaintances about the staggering sum of over $40,000 they had spent on the wedding.

Later that year, we were moving to a brand-new house in Port Coquitlam. It was a spacious two-story home with three bedrooms upstairs and two bedrooms downstairs. Rani and her husband settled into the downstairs area while I moved into the spare room downstairs. Reflecting on our previous living arrangements, where we never had our rooms, I could not help but notice that my brother Michael and Elizabeth now had their separate rooms. It made me realize how easy their lives were to ours.

At this point, my parents underwent a significant transformation—they became more compassionate towards their younger children. They became more relaxed with their rules and overall demeanor. I cannot pinpoint exactly what prompted this change, but it was a stark contrast to the upbringing that Rani and I had experienced. It felt as though this was a completely different family altogether. I was feeling unhappy and constantly sulking around the house.

It was bewildering to see how our parents were now treating Rani and me as though we were insignificant. I never heard the words "I love you" addressed to me or anyone in the family. It felt as if there was no way out of my situation. Instead of considering alternatives, my parents resorted to marrying me off against my will, leaving me, a teenager, to fend for myself and figure everything out later! How could this happen to me? The only mistake I made was falling in love, or so I believed at the time. All I wanted was a normal teenage life—going to school and hanging out with friends; however, that was never an option.

I felt trapped in the thought of my arranged marriage, with no answers on how to escape. The yearning for freedom to make my own choices and chase my dreams consumed me. Questions swirled in my mind—how could I fix this and restore balance? There was no one to turn to, only my jailers, with no end in sight. "Where is society now?" I wondered, feeling alone in my struggle with no one aware of the turmoil within. What has become of liberty and freedom?

How can the government allow parents to marry off a child? Especially in Canada, where everything is taken seriously, why is this overlooked? Not only was I deprived of a carefree adolescence, but I also had to navigate the intricacies of society, traditions, and culture. Throughout my upbringing, my parents stressed the significance of fulfilling societal duties and upholding cultural norms, leaving scant space for pursuing my dreams and aspirations.

Their main concern revolved around maintaining a certain image in front of our extended family and friends, always disregarding my desires and goals. As a result, I grappled with the conflicting pressures of conforming to societal expectations while striving to find my path in life. They wanted us to be perfect and well-behaved Indian girls, never allowing us to express our opinions or thoughts. It did not make sense to put on this perfect princess exterior when the opposite was happening in real life.

Our parents seemed like such hypocrites. Not only were we not allowed to express ourselves, but we were also restricted from having conversations with boys or unknown people. Everything was monitored and controlled, and it felt suffocating. I saw other Indian families, and none were like ours, so strict and embedded in the old traditions and culture. Why are we the guinea pigs demanding that we give up our rights for the sake of our family's dignity? What right does anyone have to force this behavior and attitude? What did society or the Indian culture do for me or my family? That I was being told I had to comply with forced arranged marriage.

To escape from this suffocating reality, I turned to books and music for solace. They provided a temporary refuge, offering a brief respite from the confines of my existence. Amidst the restrictions and control, reading books and listening to music allowed me to discover new worlds, explore different perspectives, and experience emotions beyond the constraints imposed on me. However, as I closed a book or turned off the music, the harsh reality would come crashing back, reminding me of the limited freedom within the walls of my home.

The boundaries were not limited to my choices of entertainment but extended to the very essence of my being—my thoughts, opinions, and aspirations. It felt like my imagination was caged, restricted to a narrow spectrum of stories and narratives deemed acceptable. The struggle was not just physical but internal, a battle between societal expectations and personal desires. It was a clash between tradition and modernity, between duty and freedom. The weight of these conflicting forces pressed down on me, threatening to crush my spirit. Yet, amid this turmoil, a spark of defiance ignited within me.

I realized that true freedom could only be found by asserting my agency, standing up for my beliefs, and challenging the limitations that bound me. This realization was both terrifying and liberating, as I understood that breaking free would not be easy, but it was necessary for my sanity and well-being. And so, with a sense of determination and courage, I set out on a journey towards self-discovery and liberation, ready to confront the obstacles that stood in my way and reclaim my right to live a life of my choosing.

I never lived the life of a carefree teenager, but I am older now with my children, and I am content with where I am. I am grateful for my children and for the progress we have made as a family. I know that I am not alone and that my voice matters. I learned that one needs to express their views and opinions, even if no one is willing to listen. I have learned the importance of self-care and taking time to recharge. It is easy to get caught up in the hustle and bustle of life, but it is crucial to take a step back and prioritize our well-being.

One of the most valuable lessons I have learned is that life is full of difficulties. There will be good times and bad, but how we respond to these challenges defines us. Overall, I am grateful for the life I have lived and the experiences that have shaped me into the person I am today. I believe that every experience, good or bad, has taught me something and made me stronger. And for that, I am thankful.

As the year ended and it was snowing heavily and freezing outside, Kris arrived in Canada. I felt confused and thought maybe Kris could protect me from the abuse. When we went to pick him up at the airport, my parents told me to be friendly. However, Kris never came out of the customs area, and we later found out that he was being sent back to Fiji. At that time, I thought it was a good thing, and maybe God heard me. My father rushed to the immigration area to try and get Kris released while I sat there, feeling overwhelmed.

My mother got upset with me and warned me that I would have to deal with my father if things did not work out. We waited for what felt like hours, but finally, we saw my father and Kris emerging from the airport together. In hindsight, I felt like they were blaming me for the events unfolding. I never had any connections to make this possible or a direct line to God. Even in some profound way, I was wishing he would be sent back. I thought that would not solve my problems; evading an arranged marriage was not possible.

My heart pounded in my chest. Meeting this guy for the first time, knowing that our union was not by choice but rather forced through an arranged marriage, filled me with a mixture of fear and trepidation. The moment I laid eyes on him, I could not help but notice his striking afro, complementing his dark complexion. It was the unexpected details that somehow intrigued me amidst my overwhelming emotions. He stood there, towering over me, with a slim physique and broad shoulders. I could not deny that his physical appearance held a certain charm, but it was far too early for any feelings of love or attraction to arise.

In hindsight, I started to realize the kind of man I liked was tall, dark, and handsome with an educated mindset. This propelled me to get to know Kris and to give him a chance. No matter how much I tried to push aside my reservations, the weight of this forced arrangement lingered, overshadowing any potential connection. It was a tumultuous mix of curiosity, fear, and an innate need to protect my own heart. Only time would reveal whether our relationship could transcend the boundaries of obligation, allowing for genuine love and affection to blossom.

As we started our journey, I could not help but feel a mix of emotions. Unlike the typical love stories portrayed in movies or the dreams of every girl, no butterflies were fluttering in my stomach or singing or dancing moments like in Bollywood movies. It was not the fairy-tale romance I had envisioned for myself. In a way, it felt like my life had taken an unexpected turn. I had desired to experience that unmistakable feeling of falling in love and meeting the person I would marry, just like every girl's dream. But it seemed that fate, and my parents had something different in store for me.

Despite these initial uncertainties, I could not deny the curiosity building within me. What would our journey together unveil? I wished that he would change his mind about marrying me and go running back home to Fiji. But this did not happen; it seemed like he was enjoying his adventure. At this point, my parents warned me that they would be watching how I treated him and what I said to him. Little did I know that our acquaintance would evolve into a bond of friendship and understanding.

Regardless of whether it was my choice or not, the key was to show courtesy and respect. It felt repetitive, with everyone constantly reminding me that I was going to marry him. He was always present, speaking a language I could not comprehend. My father seemed to have a good relationship with him; I was not interested in getting to know someone I did not choose for myself.

After a day of ups and downs and an emotional roller coaster, we finally went home. Despite everything, I still felt apprehensive about marrying this guy. I could not help but wonder why he could not find someone in his own country and had to come here. I found it hard to believe what was happening, and it still felt like a never-ending nightmare that I could wake up from at any moment. Furthermore, societal expectations weighed heavily on my shoulders as I struggled to maintain composure and be polite to him despite my doubts. The pressure to appear happy and excited about the upcoming marriage was suffocating.

It was winter, and since Kris did not have any warm clothes, I gave him my jacket and boots. Despite the cold weather, all the kids were outside playing in the snow, having snowball fights, and making angels. Kris was curious about why we were "sleeping" in the snow, but we all insisted it was fun. However, Kris started to shiver and ran back inside to warm up. We remained outside for hours, taking quick breaks to warm up. Later, when I was leaving, my mother noticed that I was not wearing a jacket and scolded me, saying, "You guys will never learn."

However, I eagerly took on the role of teaching Kris hockey, and unfortunately, he ended up using my brand-new hockey stick without my permission and breaking it. I could not help but feel a profound sense of disappointment, even though he offered to replace it. I had a sentimental attachment to the hockey stick my father gave me. My family told me that you do not need the hockey stick anymore as you would be married, and women do not play hockey. This left me puzzled and angry that I was being told what to do again; it seemed like I lived in a dictatorship.

As time went by, we all learned to adapt to our new living situation and worked together to make it work. We learned to communicate better and appreciate each other's contributions to the household. Although life at home was more complicated, we were grateful for our family. Kris shared my brother's room upstairs for a month. Eventually, we decided to share my room since we were going to be married anyway. My parents were angry, but I left them no choice; after all, I was doing a little "Sundi brand justice." Maybe it was a form of payback, but they deserved it. The feeling of gaining some form of control was good, even if it was temporary. The best part was looking at their faces and the anger, knowing they could not physically abuse me in front of Kris.

My parents were opposed to the idea of Kris staying in my room. They were concerned about traditions and societal norms. However, I stood my ground, and I decided to oppose them. Choosing to go against their wishes was my way of making a statement, asserting my independence, and demonstrating that this was my choice. Sharing my room with Kris felt like a form of "Sundi brand justice," a subtle way of reclaiming control and asserting my autonomy. It may have been a small act of payback for the times they controlled me and abused me.

My parents were furious about Kris and me being intimate and feeling dishonored in their home. They threatened to send Kris back to Fiji, which left him scared and caused him to stay away from me. I grew angry, questioning the pretense, as we were soon to be married, and I could not understand why they were making such a big deal out of it. What a tumultuous year it has been, and it is not even close to being over.

My relationship with Rani was never strong; although her husband seemed friendly, we never had a close relationship. They had left a few months before, but now they were back; I was living in such close quarters with them that I felt trapped. In addition to conforming to societal expectations, I now had to navigate the complexities of this living arrangement. I failed to connect with Rani because of our interactions and her habitual lying. The fear of inadvertently saying something wrong loomed over my head, causing me to withdraw from interacting with her and her husband.

However, the strained dynamics within our household prompted my parents to call a family meeting, specifically to address the mounting extra costs associated with our living situation. This brought to light the financial strain we were all under, forcing us to confront our shared responsibilities and work towards finding solutions together. After the wedding, our mother expected the responsibility of caring for her teenage daughters to be gone.

Rani and I were instructed to work to support our husbands, as they could not work due to immigration regulations. This was unfair to me, especially since Kris and I were not officially married yet. Despite the circumstances, I diligently sought employment every day, often walking long distances due to a lack of money for transportation. One day, Kris and I walked from North Road in Burnaby to Port Coquitlam; I applied for jobs without success. The experience was disheartening, and I could not help but feel discriminated against due to my age and marital status. Kris and I spent the beginning of 1985 living with my uncle and aunt, even though we came from different religions. I was relieved that they accepted us with open arms, never judging us. It was a comforting stay, and we felt secure in their home. I was especially grateful to have my uncle and his family, people who I knew would treat us with love and respect. Eventually, the time came for us to return home, but it was still a summer that I remember fondly.

During our stay, my uncle and aunt talked to Kris and me about how young we were to be getting married. I informed them it was not my choice and a decision my parents would not change. They expressed that it was not something they would allow in their own family, saying they would not get their daughter married as a teenager. I will always cherish the memories of my time with my kind and accepting relatives. At that time, I did not fully comprehend the concept of marriage, nor did I have any desire to be a part of it. However, one aspect that weighed heavily on me was the sense of obligation toward Kris—to provide him with a home and ensure his well-being.

It was as if I was bound to this person with no means of escape, especially since we were living with my parents. In this situation, I felt torn between the expectations of being the perfect daughter and soon the perfect wife, with age being a factor that seemed to fade into the background for everyone. I began to feel a protective shield forming around Kris as if I had suddenly become his guardian, shielding him from anyone who sought to harm him. It was not a role I had willingly taken on; I never signed up for this responsibility. However, circumstances led me to assume it.

I simmered with anger as I realized my parents were orchestrating my marriage. Now, they would have to face the consequences of their actions and learn to tolerate Kris. It felt like it was an opportunity for them to confront the fallout of their decision, which they never admitted was wrong. The frustration and disappointment I felt towards my parents grew as they failed to see the turmoil they had introduced into my life. I had expected them to protect me, especially since I was still a teenager.

Yet, their unrealistic demands and manipulation of my life left me feeling betrayed and vulnerable. It was as though they were playing a reckless game of poker with my future, blind to the pain and confusion they were causing. A sense of self-justice may have driven me, but that does not mean I was a vengeful person. It was my way of asserting my brand of justice. Normally, my father would have dealt with my disobedience by using the belt as a form of punishment, but in this situation, Kris was present, and he could not take the risk of anyone knowing what went on in his home.

The summer of 1985 began with troubling news when Rani informed our parents that she was deporting her husband and divorcing him. It came as a shock to all of us, as we had always believed her marriage was strong and enduring. Witnessing the breakdown of her relationship made me question the institution of marriage and the complexities that come with it. I had hoped that my parents, after witnessing Rani's divorce, would reconsider their stance on my marriage.

I believed that our parents would realize that forced marriages are not a guarantee of a lasting and fulfilling relationship. However, despite the connection between Rani's experience and my situation, my parents remained adamant about the arranged marriage. Throughout the year, I witnessed the profound emotional impact the divorce had on her; she was closed off to everyone. However, sadly, our relationship deteriorated. Despite my best efforts, I found it increasingly difficult to connect with her. She isolated her feelings and built a wall around herself. This gradual estrangement hurt me deeply, and so our bond as sisters crumbled.

Divorce can introduce complexities and challenges that strain even the strongest of relationships. However, by nurturing love, understanding, and patience, there is always a possibility for healing. As I reflected on my own experiences, I realized that feelings of regret and frustration often intensified my concerns about arranged marriages and their potential to breed resentment and dissatisfaction. While arranged marriages have long been a part of

Hindu and Muslim cultures and may work for some couples, they are not without their fair share of challenges.

In arranged marriages, a significant concern revolves around the potential for bitterness and discontent to flourish within these unions. Natural emotions like regret and frustration, which are common in various aspects of life, can be intensified due to the lack of choice or autonomy in selecting a life partner. Individuals feel stifled by the expectations and traditions imposed by their families, leading to a sense of being trapped or controlled. Consequently, these circumstances may give rise to heightened feelings of hostility and disappointment.

In an arranged marriage, there may be a lack of compatibility and shared values between the couple, which can further contribute to these negative emotions. Without the foundation of love and mutual understanding, a couple may feel stuck in a relationship that does not fulfill their emotional or personal needs. Furthermore, the pressure to conform to societal and family expectations can add to the potential for resentment. The individuals involved may feel obliged to prioritize the wishes of the families over their happiness and desires. This can lead to a sense of being trapped and unable to live their lives on their terms.

It is important to note that arranged marriages are not necessarily doomed to breed grudges or anxiety. Many couples have managed to build successful and fulfilling lives together, even in the face of challenges. Communication, compromise, and a shared commitment to making the relationship work can be key factors in overcoming the issues. If there is no compromise or willingness for compassion and understanding, this relationship will fail. However, it is crucial to recognize the potential for negative emotions to arise in arranged marriages and to address and validate these concerns.

Indian Society should work towards creating a more supportive environment where individuals have the freedom to make choices that align with their values and desires rather than being solely driven by traditional or cultural expectations. Overall, it is essential to consider the potential impact of arranged marriages on the emotional well-being of the individuals involved and work towards creating an environment that fosters healthier and more fulfilling relationships.

Weeks later, it was disheartening to realize that my parents remained firm about my arranged marriage. Witnessing the pain and turmoil endured by Rani served as a poignant reminder of the potential downside of such unions. It fueled my determination to assert my rights and pursue my happiness. I challenged societal norms and strived for a future where traditional or external pressures did not dictate love and compatibility.

As I embraced the new year, I carried with me a determination to take control of my future. I understood the importance of communication and following my heart rather than succumbing to societal norms. I felt disappointed by my parents' reluctance to learn from Rani's experience. This day taught me valuable lessons about emotions, parental oppression, and the importance of allowing children to make their own choices. It was not about being right or wrong but about life, commitment, and autonomy.

Chapter 12

My Arranged Wedding

O n my wedding day in March, Kris and I could not hide our lack of enthusiasm. The fact that our wedding was with just the minister and my parents amplified our true feelings of sadness. We did not have an engagement party or a haldi function, as my parents always told me I was deemed too dark, ugly, and chubby to have any form of celebration. They went on to say, "Who would want to see a dark, chubby girl get married?" At this point in my life, I was 120 pounds and standing at 5'2. My parents wanted to avoid the expenses of a grand Hindu ceremony, so there were no flowers, no wedding attire, and no extravagance to mark the occasion. It left me feeling like I was not truly getting married; instead, it felt as if it was a contract.

My mother and I started to argue about my clothes as I wore a tracksuit. She went on to say you should wear a saree, and I said, "No." Why do I have to wear a saree? You said no one would see me so why even bother? She went on to say oh, Kris expects you to wear nice clothes. Kris came by asking what was going on. After our conversation, he said you can wear what you want, but it would be nice if you wore a saree for my family back home as they are expecting you to look beautiful. Reluctantly, as I was getting dressed in my plain red and silver saree, my mother came back to my room to tell me to wear make-up and put powder on my face. Which I refused to do as I wanted them to see me as I was, a dark girl that they brought into this world.

My parents called me to their room upstairs, where they told me to borrow Rani's wedding ring and return it after the ceremony. Their reasoning for this decision was humiliating; they believed that we did not need a ring, as they did not want to waste their money on us. This hurtful comment brought tears to my eyes, making me not want to leave the house. I demanded my parents purchase a proper ring if they expected me to go through with this marriage. Initially, they were angry but eventually agreed to buy the cheapest ring in the store.

Reluctantly, we all got into the car, and the tension in the air was palpable. My father assumed the role of the driver. As we headed towards Burnaby, he started arguing about various things like the weather *(it was snowing heavily)*, finding the address, and finding parking. Finally, we arrived at the residence of the minister.

The apartment was dark and dingy; I felt that no one should have to get married in such an environment. It just made the day gloomier.

The minister said a few words, and before we knew it, we were married. However, I had to pay the fees myself as my parents refused to contribute. I refused, explaining that I would not pay for a marriage I did not want, but Kris stepped in and covered the expenses. There were no pictures of the event; Kris had no pictures to share with his family. We did not have a reception; there was no honeymoon, as my parents refused to pay. The absence of traditional wedding celebrations and the ordinariness of the day only intensified my feelings of disappointment.

As life moved forward, my marriage felt like a transaction rather than a union founded on love. It soon became clear that the reality of my wedding day did not align with the dreams I had harbored for so long. The joy and fulfillment I had anticipated were absent, leaving a void of unmet expectations. The vibrant tapestry of an Indian wedding—filled with flowers, music, a stunning gown, and shared love—was but a distant dream.

Reflecting on the starkness of that day when I reluctantly ventured into marriage, I now view it as a pivotal moment. It prompted me to realize the significance of living true to oneself and seeking happiness on one's terms. This did not represent a day for lavish parties or romantic getaways; rather, it represented the starting point of a journey toward a future defined by profound displeasure and personal growth.

All I did was clean, babysit my sibling, and work night shifts to provide for Kris and myself. It was a difficult situation, made even more challenging by the fact that I did not want to tell anyone I was married. Unlike my mother, who freely advertised it to everyone, including the places where I applied for jobs, I had to rely on her to drive me to interviews, which added another layer of dependence.

Obtaining a job was difficult, as I did not have any skills to rely on, nor had I finished high school. But the biggest setback was my age and the societal disapproval of teenage marriages in Canadian society. I had tried to secure a job at a popular fast-food restaurant, but unfortunately, the manager refused to give me a chance. He believed that hiring a married teenager would not set a good example for other students who worked there. It was deeply frustrating, as I felt judged without being heard, and I carried that disappointment back home, where I later cried about the incident.

Despite facing overwhelming rejection, humiliation, and setbacks, I persevered. Every opportunity seemed out of reach, and not being able to secure a job intensified these feelings. Despite these challenges, I took on odd jobs to provide for Kris and myself. Through my mother's help, I got an interview with her boss at a restaurant and landed a job. Working evening shifts ending at one a.m., I preferred to keep my personal life private, but my mother shared all the details about my marriage with coworkers.

While we were working together at the restaurant, my mother would keep a close eye on me. She would specifically demand the boys I worked with stay away from me, as she had noticed their flirtatious behavior towards me, which made her concerned about my well-being. One day, my mother confronted me about the situation. Baffled, I told her that I did not understand her concern, as it was just work, and we all had to communicate effectively to get the job done. Consequently, I found myself faced with personal inquiries from colleagues regarding my age, marital status, and educational background. Given that I presently resided with my parents and shared the workplace with my mother, I decided not to respond to such questions.

Upon discovering that I was pregnant, uncertainty loomed over the future of my relationship with Kris. The news brought conflicting emotions of excitement and fear. We started to have cracks in our marriage; it was not as perfect or easy as a marriage should be. We were dealing with my parents' input and decisions without our consultation. Managing the pregnancy proved to be challenging, especially since I was diagnosed with gestational diabetes and my weight posed additional complications. I continued to work full-time at a restaurant while also assisting my parents with their janitorial jobs.

Adding to the challenges, Kris was unable to work due to immigration issues. This fact ignited a feeling of anger within me, making me moody and unpredictable. My faith in the immigration process began to dwindle, as it seemed like no decisions were being made. The relentless cycle of immigration appointments had transformed into a source of continual torment. Oh, the searing frustration that coursed through my veins! And then, I was blindsided by the infuriating inquiries about the paternity of my child, which plunged like barbed arrows, inflicting unimaginable pain.

How could they dare to cast doubt on the sacred bond of my marriage? I was like a puppet on a string; I was compelled to journey to Downtown Vancouver week after week, burdened by my pregnancy; I needed rest and comfort. Immigration seemed oblivious to my hardship; their sole focus on the outward appearance of care. But what about my well-being and my emotional survival? Escape was not an option; divorce was a forbidden course of action in my tight, traditional family. I wondered what would happen to Rani and how are my parents dealing with Rani's marriage issues. I longed for a moment, just a fleeting respite, to release the suffocating weight that crushed my spirit. Overwhelmed, I was pain-ridden and drowning in distress.

During a time of financial struggle, we faced the tough choice of selling our wedding rings to cover essential expenses such as food. This decision was a hard blow as we had to fend for ourselves. Surprisingly, as the years went by, I felt an urge to keep buying new rings, as if they could reignite the passion and emotions that seemed lacking in our relationship. The words "I love you" had lost their meaning and had become hollow phrases, akin to saying "bye" or "see you later" without any genuine sentiment attached.

As time went on and I grew older, I began to recognize that no matter how many rings I acquired, they could never bring back what was non-existent. The passage of time was inevitable, and rather than attempting to cling to the past and try to resurrect some type of emotion, it was crucial to shift my focus towards rebuilding and moving forward. I came to understand that true healing and contentment did not lie within material possessions but in the process of embracing change, personal growth, and cultivating new experiences.

After realizing the limitations of relying on material possessions for emotional fulfillment, I set out on a path of self-discovery grounded in resilience and inner strength. Redirecting my focus towards meaningful experiences and relationships, I gradually released the belief that physical objects could reignite the essence of our marriage. Instead, I embraced living in the present moment, finding solace in crafting new memories, and actively pursuing personal development. This shift in perspective led me to a profound sense of joy and contentment, dispelling the idea that possessions alone could offer the emotional closeness I sought.

The prolonged absence of Rani went unnoticed and unacknowledged by those at home for several months. Her whereabouts and activities during this period seemed to be of little concern to anyone. She showed up at the front door unexpectedly. However, that fateful day, a surging wave of fury prompted her to hurl my mother's dinner plates at me in a fit of rage. In a frantic attempt to shield myself from the barrage of flying crockery, I desperately dodged each projectile to safeguard my face and head. Overwhelmed as fear and anxiety consumed me, I cried out for her to cease, and it was at that pivotal moment that Kris finally heard my desperate pleas.

In the face of my attempts to reason with her, Rani redirected her anger towards Kris and me, unfairly holding us responsible for her leaving our parents' house. Despite my efforts to explain that her actions had brought about those consequences, she remained unwilling to listen. Enveloped in anger, she hurled plates at us, showing no regard for rationale or compassion. The scene escalated into chaos and danger, prompting us to seek shelter from the flying objects. Kris, displaying bravery, stepped into the kitchen to try and diffuse the situation and soothe her emotional turmoil.

The tension in the situation continued to mount, with the argument quickly escalating into a physical altercation. Both parties seemed entrenched in a cycle of anger and hostility, refusing to yield or seek a peaceful resolution. Fear gripped me as I dreaded the possibility of the conflict escalating to a point where law enforcement would need to be involved.

The situation had spiraled out of control, and it appeared that external intervention might be necessary to ensure the safety of all those present. The sudden arrival of our parents only served to intensify the chaos within the household further. Father's face shifted from surprise to fury as he took in the tumultuous scene unfolding before him. He started directing his fury towards Rani and Kris. He was furious at both for their part in the altercation, expressing his disappointment in their behavior.

On the other hand, our mother refused to acknowledge me, blaming me for not waiting downstairs and insisting that whatever I needed could have waited. My mother's silence made me feel even more frustrated and helpless as I longed for her support and understanding in this tumultuous situation. To make matters worse, my parents forbade Kris from entering upstairs, abruptly cutting off any means of support or resolution. I felt trapped, as if there were no options available to rectify the mess that had unfolded.

The whole situation felt overwhelming, and I found myself at a loss for what to do next. Being caught in the middle of Rani and Kris's ongoing drama was a constant source of stress and tension. It felt like I was walking on eggshells, always fearful of saying or doing something that would further ignite their conflicts. Resolving their issues seemed impossible, and I found myself in a difficult and emotionally draining situation.

Rani's decision to move out had left my parents dissatisfied, prompting a return to the usual routine. I assisted with my parents' cleaning jobs and worked at the restaurant some nights. They did not pay me for the cleaning tasks, considering our living arrangement, and I chose not to raise any issues. However, Kris was unhappy with both the living situation and the assistance with the cleaning jobs. Kris believed that my parents were manipulating us and expressed a strong desire for it to end. Despite understanding Kris's perspective, I lacked the emotional strength to confront our parents about the situation.

After five months of being pregnant while napping on the couch, I suddenly felt a sharp pain in my stomach. My mother assured me that it was normal during pregnancy. But the pain persisted and worsened, making it difficult for me to breathe. That is when I asked Kris to take me to the hospital. Concerned, Kris immediately called the doctor, who advised us to go to the hospital without delay. The car ride was silent, filled with tension and worry.

On June 18, at the hospital, I went for emergency surgery following the heartbreaking loss of our baby. The following week was overwhelming sorrow and despair. The once familiar atmosphere at home now felt eerily quiet and unsettling, as if a piece of my heart had been torn away, leaving me feeling adrift and as though nothing in life would ever be the same again.

Kris's erratic behavior began to take a toll on my emotional well-being. Out late into the night, attending parties and meeting other women, he returned home intoxicated or sometimes did not return at all. I found myself emotionally drained, struggling to cope with the harsh reality unfolding before me rather than confronting the obvious signs of infidelity and addressing the issue.

I denied the truth, turning a blind eye to his actions out of fear and misplaced hope that things would improve. Making excuses for him became a daily habit as I buried my growing apprehension deep within, avoiding the inevitable confrontation that lay ahead. Deep down, I knew that I deserved better. Instead of setting boundaries and standing up for myself, I chose to remain passive. I let my emotions get the best of me, and I became emotional from the constant worry and uncertainty.

I allowed Kris to walk all over me, putting his desires and needs above my own. If I had been a stronger person, I would have put my foot down and demanded respect. If I had made it known that this behavior would not be accepted by me only, I would have dared to confront him and have an honest conversation about my feelings and concerns. I was like many women who find themselves in a similar situation—in denial. I did not want to face the reality of the situation or admit that my relationship was in trouble. I believed that if I ignored the problems, they would eventually go away.

Looking back, I realize that this was a mistake. Ignoring the truth only prolongs the pain and allows the toxic behavior to continue. I should have been stronger and demanded the respect and commitment that I deserved. At the time, I was only a teenager and already married, which added another layer of complexity to the situation. I contemplated moving out to escape the toxic environment. However, it proved to be challenging, considering my age and marital status. I felt trapped and overwhelmed, unsure of how to navigate this difficult situation.

I realized that being in such a toxic environment was not healthy for me. Individuals must have a safe and supportive environment, especially during their formative years. In my case, my parents were extremely controlling even after my marriage, which left me with limited options to cope with the abuse and dominating atmosphere. As a result, I was feeling isolated, and Kris began taking advantage of the situation as he started to show his true self with his newfound freedom in Canada.

Unfortunately, in this case, moving out may not have been a feasible option, but seeking support from trusted family members, friends, or professionals could have been beneficial. Seeking guidance and finding healthy coping mechanisms can make a significant difference in managing and eventually resolving conflicts.

As time went on, I realized that I could not keep trying to mediate and hold everything together. It was affecting my well-being and my marriage. All the constant bickering between Kris and my parents resulted in physical fights. Despite my attempts to intervene, my efforts were futile, leaving me feeling overwhelmed and helpless. In difficult situations like these, it is crucial to prioritize personal well-being and mental health.

Instead of blaming oneself or not being "strong enough," it is important to acknowledge that confronting a partner's destructive behavior is challenging. It is understandable to feel emotionally drained and unsure of how to deal with the situation effectively. However, it is essential to remember that you are not responsible for someone else's choices and actions.

Despite our desperate efforts, Kris and I were drowning in frustration and despair. We believed that breaking free from the toxicity was crucial for our well-being, like ripping off a bandage from a festering wound. But the cruel hand of fate seemed determined to keep us trapped in this agonizing situation. Each day, the pain grew more unbearable, the distress clinging to us like a suffocating cloak.

Our dreams of a fresh start, a life filled with peace, were snatched away before they had a chance to bloom. The universe seemed to revel in our anguish, taunting us with false hope and dashed expectations. The weight of our shattered aspirations crushed our spirits, leaving us beaten down and defeated. It was a painful reminder that life does not always follow our wishes, no matter how fervently we yearn for a change.

After looking back on this, I wish I had spoken up earlier about how their drama was affecting me. But, as a young bride and sibling to Rani, I felt powerless and alone. This can happen when you are in a situation where you feel helpless and powerless, especially when you have limited experience or support. It is important to acknowledge these feelings and know that you are not alone in going through a challenging time. It is important to seek support from friends, family, or a therapist who can offer guidance and help you navigate through your feelings and decisions.

They can provide you with the necessary tools and coping mechanisms to manage the situation and prioritize your well-being. They can also help you develop strategies for setting boundaries, communicating your concerns, and making decisions that align with your values and personal growth. Remember that it is okay to reach out for support and take steps towards your well-being. You deserve to live a peaceful and fulfilling life, free from toxic relationships and destructive behavior.

The situation escalated, causing tension between Kris and my parents. Kris began skipping family dinners and isolating himself from everyone. He placed the blame on me for the way my parents treated him, further adding to the strain in our relationship. I could feel his growing resentment towards me, and it deeply saddened me. It was painful to witness our connection deteriorate as he became more distant and disinterested in our family and me. I made attempts to communicate and address the issue, but he refused to listen or acknowledge his role in the problem. It left me feeling helpless and unsure of how to salvage what was left of our relationship.

As days passed, the tension in my household kept building, and it became increasingly difficult to ignore the cracks in our dysfunctional family. Arguments between my parents grew more frequent, and I could feel their resentment towards Kris growing stronger. Seeing my parents' pain weighed heavily on me, but I could not deny the bond I shared with Kris. We had been through so much together, and I believed in the good in them despite their flaws.

The bond that once grew between my parents and Kris dissipated. My mother started to restrict Kris from using the bathroom and having meals. In frustration, Kris decided to break the bathroom door. My mother ran to her room and called my father and me. My father was furious and told Kris and me to move immediately, as he did not want to deal with either of us. Here, I was held responsible for their behavior and the outcome. Kris replaced the damaged door. We ended up living with my uncle and his family.

The constant conflict between my loyalty to my family and Kris gnawed in my heart. I desperately wanted to find a way to mend the broken relationships and bring peace and healing to both sides. But I felt utterly trapped as if I had become the rope in a never-ending tug-of-war. I yearned for a solution, a magic remedy that would make everything right again. But the reality was that I had no control over the actions and decisions of others. All I could control were my own choices and how I responded to the chaos around me.

In moments of solitude, I would reflect on what truly mattered to me. I knew that love, forgiveness, and understanding were essential ingredients in restoring any broken bond. However, achieving that would require immense effort and compassion from everyone involved. Instead, I decided to take a step back and adopt a more empathetic approach. I started having an honest conversation with both my parents and Kris. I started by expressing my deep-rooted love for both sides without taking a stance against either.

As fragile as our family situation was, I remained hopeful. With time, patience, and communication, we could find a way to grow and heal together. I could not single-handedly fix everything, but I could try to bring about a positive change by fostering understanding and love between all parties involved. During the chaos, I learned that life was not about choosing sides. It was about acknowledging the flaws and mistakes of those we loved while also recognizing their potential for growth and redemption. Love and loyalty could coexist, and it was in embracing both that true healing could occur. It was truly a difficult situation, as neither side wanted to solve the issue. They were busy blaming each other for everything that went wrong in the home.

Dealing with conflicting advice from family members can be a tough situation, especially when it involves major life decisions like marriage. In my case, my parents suggested that I end my marriage and get married to another man of their choice again. I did not believe that getting married to someone else was the solution to my problems, particularly after experiencing a difficult relationship. I communicated my perspective to my parents, but they were not pleased and did not want to engage in any further discussion about it. Despite their disapproval, it is essential to remember that we must make choices that align with our own beliefs and values.

Reflecting on my past experiences has played a crucial role in shaping my understanding of relationships and what I truly desire in a partner. During my formative years, observing my parents' dynamics offered me valuable insights, both positive and negative. Witnessing their conflicts and disagreements instilled in me a determination to steer clear of such destructive patterns in my relationships. Moreover, the presence of physical and emotional abuse within my family underscored the importance of recognizing and rejecting toxic behavior. These experiences have significantly impacted my perspective, guiding me toward seeking healthier and more nurturing connections in my life.

Recognizing the importance of loyalty was a significant aspect of my journey. It evolved into a fundamental value that I held in high regard in my past relationships. Trust and loyalty were virtues that were non-negotiable in a partner for me. In shaping my aspirations for the future, I yearn for a companion who not only provides for our family but also values me as an individual. I seek a person who epitomizes faithfulness and commitment, acknowledges the importance of diligence, and strives to construct a secure and affectionate life together. This has not been true in my life; this is where I failed and compromised my values.

Through this contemplation, I have gained deeper insights into my wants and expectations in a partnership, spurring me to pursue a relationship founded on trust, loyalty, respect, and a unified vision for our shared future.

Seeking professional help, such as couples therapy or individual counseling, can provide further guidance in navigating through this challenging situation. Ultimately, it is important to trust myself and have confidence in my ability to make decisions that will bring happiness and fulfillment into my life. In times like these, we must trust our instincts and make the best decision for ourselves, even if it means going against the advice of our loved ones. Our mental and emotional wellness should always be our priority. If staying in a relationship is negatively impacting our well-being, it may be time to move on. Although it can be a hard decision to make, it can also demonstrate our strength and resilience.

Ending a relationship can be an incredibly challenging and painful process. But by doing so, we take an active role in shaping our own lives and claiming our happiness. It is an act of self-love and self-respect, acknowledging that we deserve to be in a relationship that uplifts and supports us rather than draining us emotionally. Through making difficult decisions, we reveal our strength and resilience. It takes courage to break away from familiar patterns and step into the unknown. Moving on from a relationship that no longer serves us can be an opportunity for personal growth, self-discovery, and a step towards finding fulfillment and contentment in the future.

Kris talked to me a week later, telling me he was moving by himself to Whistler for work. I asked where he was going to be staying, and he smiled and said with friends. A few days later, Kris left, and I was alone to handle the mess that was left behind. My parents came to talk to me and said to let him go and not worry about him. I still felt some type of responsibility, as he did not have any family here. This was a breaking point for me; as weeks and months passed, I received no calls from Kris. I began to worry about his well-being and could not shake off the feeling of responsibility.

I was feeling isolated, and Kris began to take advantage of the situation. Despite my parents' advice to let him go, I could not just abandon the friendship and feelings I had. As time went on, my concern grew stronger. I found it hard to focus on anything else, constantly checking for any message from him, hoping for a sign. I tried reaching out to a mutual friend to see if they heard anything from Kris, but no one heard anything. My mind started to create various scenarios, each more worrisome than the last one. Was he in trouble? Did he regret his decision to move? I felt guilty for not being able to help him or diffuse the situation that happened to make him leave.

As time passed, I realized that letting go was the best decision for both of us. I would not be dragged down; I wanted Kris to change and take responsibility for our lives. Kris needed the space to work on himself and his issues. Sometimes, for the sake of our well-being and that of others, we must make tough decisions. These choices may not be easy, but they are necessary for growth and moving forward. Although I missed Kris and our friendship, I have come to understand that letting go was the right decision to make at this moment.

Weeks turned into months, and the silence of Kris became unbearable. I could not shake off the feeling that I had failed him in some way. It was as if a part of me was missing. I was left feeling broken and alone while dealing with the shambles of my marriage, Rani's visit, and the discord between Kris and my parents. I did not know what to say to anyone anymore, but I had friends who were Jehovah's Witnesses who listened without pushing me to change my religion or beliefs. They were willing to help me deal with everything, little by little, making me feel lighter and more at peace with my challenges.

As I spent time with my new friends, I loved the way they lived their lives with a commitment to their family and husband. I found myself drawn to their principles toward family and marriage. They demonstrated kindness, compassion, and a deep sense of happiness that I was missing. These were traits I believed should be embedded in every person. Although I never became a Jehovah's Witness, I felt like I had found a new family in my friends. They helped me through some of the darkest days of my life and gave me the strength to keep moving forward. I was able to rebuild my life from the inside out. I found a new purpose, and I began to repair my relationships with my family.

One night, I heard a knock on my window; it was Kris, and I was in shock. I could not believe it; he looked tired and distant, but relief flooded through me, knowing he was okay. He went on to say he had nowhere to live and did not have any food either. I instantly let him in and got him some food. The next day, my parents found out and wanted Kris gone; they did not feel anything for him and blamed him for Rani's departure. Although it was a difficult journey, this experience taught me the value of friendship, empathy, kindness, and the importance of supporting each other through thick and thin.

Growing up, my parents restricted us from socializing with friends, even extended family, so learning how to adapt to difficult situations, whether in love or friendship, was never something that Rani or I learned. Our family never spoke about love, sex, marriage, or even the physical changes in a woman's body, like periods, menopause, or childbirth. Everything was learned later in life, either by us or through reading. My parents were so embedded in their traditions that they never talked about anything they deemed uncomfortable. This was a learned aspect handed down through generations.

However, this raises the question of how a teenager can successfully navigate a marriage when everything is unknown. The pressure to conform to cultural or familial expectations in arranged marriages can result in a lack of personal agency and isolation for teenagers. How can we, as teenagers, express ourselves when the right is stripped? How can a teenager give themselves to someone unknown, as intimacy is an emotional connection not to be handed away lightly? It is an emotion that requires trust, respect, and communication. I remember feeling trapped in my own home, with no freedom to make my own choices. My parents confined me to the house, and they forbade me from sharing any information with strangers about my home life. My parents tried to stop me from associating with my new friends. They restricted them from visiting, and they used our Hindu religion to try to control my friends and dictate what I could or could not do. It was a suffocating experience, and that left me feeling helpless and alone. I longed for the freedom to share my thoughts and aspirations with other people.

The burden of hiding the fact that I was married as a teenager was overwhelming, as I did not want to face judgment or explain that the marriage was not of my choosing. This isolation deprived me of the chance to develop meaningful relationships and left me without the support and understanding of others. Additionally, my lack of education and skills further limited my options, as I was expected to work and support my husband despite my unwillingness to comply. The absence of choice and the expectations placed on me compromised my sense of personal fulfillment and left me questioning my worth and potential.

The year started with another letter in the mail from immigration. It was getting annoying, and I was grieving the loss of the baby. The case went on for months without a positive outcome. At this point, I did not care anymore. I had other, more important things to deal with in life. Somehow, life stops when you are dealing with immigration. It consumes you emotionally and physically. You go on a solo mission, trying to appease everyone except yourself.

When Kris and I were dealing with immigration, my father would always come with us. He accompanied me to the interviews and had already prepared my responses, leaving no room for deviation. On one occasion, however, I strayed from my prepared answers, and when we returned home, my father was furious with me. It was at that moment that memories of my father's abusive behavior came flooding back, overwhelming me.

Being a teenager in this situation was incredibly difficult, as nobody, not even immigration, took me seriously. The problem we faced was that immigration doubted the legitimacy of our marriage, seeing it as a ploy to obtain a Canadian visa. I could not help but hope that if immigration continued to investigate, they would uncover the truth—that this marriage was forced and arranged.

One night, the first week of November, my mother received a call from Rani in the middle of the night. She frantically told my mother to get the baby, and she would hide him under the back stairs because the police were on their way. However, she lived in Vancouver, which was roughly 45 minutes away from our home in Port Coquitlam. Kris had just started driving and was unfamiliar with the roads in Canada; I was only 17 at the time and did not have my driver's license yet.

We drove out to Rani's place in Vancouver to pick up the baby, but there was no one home, and neighbors were peering outside. At this point, I realized that the commotion at two a.m. had stirred people out of their beds. The baby was found under the back stairs by the garbage bins, with a thin blanket wrapped around him and a pacifier in his mouth. I was so angry at Rani and did not want to see her at all. She had left no milk, clothes, or diapers for him; she just left the baby. What mother does that to a child? I was still in shock and disbelief as we drove home.

We arrived home and were so tired. We talked to my parents about everything. My father was so angry that Rani did that to the baby. My mother felt like she had no choice, and it was a good thing she called. In the morning, Kris and I went shopping with our money for baby milk, clothes, and diapers. We received a letter from welfare stating what had happened and that the child in question could not be returned to her. My mother was scared to hold the baby as Brian was only 2 pounds and 2 ounces. She said she did not have the patience or desire to raise another child and that they were too old for such situations. My mother said that she had Elizabeth in her forties and needed time for herself.

My parents manipulated and coerced Kris and me into taking on the responsibility of Brian, although we never really wanted the responsibility. I felt depressed and overwhelmed by the situation. Within a few weeks, an official welfare letter arrived, summoning us to a court hearing regarding custody. Eventually, my parents obtained temporary custody of the baby. However, since they were elderly, welfare wanted Kris and me to take care of the baby. We handled all the responsibilities and expenses without any financial help from Rani or my parents. Exploiting our grief over losing a baby, my parents shifted the responsibility to us, declaring that we were now accountable as parents.

In 1989, Mother decided to give Brian back to Rani while no one knew that she was pregnant again. Months later, we received another call from Welfare, and it made me feel like they had our number on speed dial. Kris and my mother could not understand why she kept having kids. Welfare informed us that the two-year-old and two-month-old babies had been left alone for three days. The neighbor had heard the children crying for days and eventually called the police.

Eventually, our parents dragged Kris and me along to court for custody of the kids. Despite their assurance that it would be temporary and they would eventually take the kids back, things took a different turn. After the family was awarded custody and returned home, my parents took Brian but disclosed that they could not care for Cole due to his age. It felt like another chapter of being manipulated and coerced. Living at my parents' house, we felt obligated to care for Cole in this difficult, emotionally manipulative situation where we had no real say in the matter.

After months of not knowing where Rani had gone, she finally arrived at the family home. Our father was outside tending to the garden when he called for our mother. I could hear the commotion as our father shouted for her to leave and not come back to the house. At this point, I realized that I felt the same way—angry and disappointed with her. Despite Father's warning, she began screaming and demanded her children back. Father was furious and gave her an ultimatum to leave, or he would call the police. As I approached our father to try to calm him down, Rani directed her anger towards me, accusing me of stealing her kids. Kris came out, and her boyfriend intervened, persuading her to leave.

As Rani walked away, she shouted threats about taking the matter to court. However, we knew that if we returned the children to her and she left with them, we would end up back in court with child welfare involved. This would not have been in the best interest of the children, particularly for their emotional well-being. The thought of them facing constant abandonment was heartbreaking, and we could not risk putting them through that again. Our family would not have forgiven us for allowing such a situation to occur once more.

The process of transitioning the children, especially Brian, who was older, was challenging. Despite the difficulties, we all came together to ensure a smooth transition. There were days when we felt overwhelmed and drained, but we never lost sight of the fact that our main goal was to provide a stable and loving home for the kids. As for Rani, we eventually heard from the grapevine that she has gotten herself into more trouble. It was a sad reminder of the life she had chosen to live. We knew that she would not be a part of the kids' lives, but we also knew it was for the best.

Our family received a call from Welfare regarding Rani leaving a baby girl under their care. While it was difficult for Kris and me to turn down the opportunity to take her in, considering our existing commitments, we believed it was the right decision. Our resources were already spread thin, and we could not afford to jeopardize the care of our current children by taking on more responsibility. Ultimately, we were relieved that the baby girl was matched with a family capable of providing her with the care and stability she needed.

In hindsight, it was disheartening to witness Rani having 11 children and abandoning some of them. The situation puzzled us, as we could not comprehend why someone would keep having children without taking responsibility for them. As we continued with our lives, we still felt the desire to have our own children. We did not know when or if that would happen, but we held onto the hope that one day, we would have a family of our own. Little did I know how extremely complicated having and raising children would become.

Grandfather (my mother's father) visited Canada in 1988, and the whole family was excited and waiting. Grandfather was quite a storyteller; like me, he loved keeping up to date on the latest gossip or trends. He had a tailoring business; he was making handbags for women. I asked him one time why he chose to be a tailor, and he said it has been a family business for generations. After Grandmother passed away, Grandfather became lonely and needed a new lease on life. So, my parents talked him into visiting and staying for a year to see if he could adjust to life here.

Grandfather went on to say his passion was cooking, and for decades, he cooked for weddings, birthdays, and special events. He said religion does not make a difference; I cook for everyone, and they request that I cater their events. I said to Grandfather, "That is so true. There are a lot of things that should be separated from religion. Grandfather agreed that if this had happened sooner in life, our families would have been together and not separated by religion.

As a family, we took Grandfather sightseeing all around British Columbia, showing him the beautiful landscapes and city. We also introduced him to some of our favorite local shops and restaurants. We introduced him to our friends in the community and showed him Canadian culture and traditions. We introduced him to maple syrup and pancakes. Grandfather was not a big fan; he was like my father and enjoyed his roti and curries. He refused to try burgers. I was surprised that he refused to try the famous American food, a staple for every family. I recall his breakfast of chai and puri—him dipping puri (deep-fried flatbread) into his chai- tea and eating. I found this so unusual, but I guess it was normal for life in Fiji.

Grandfather's visit showed us how we could have gotten along if only everyone had tried harder. It gave us a chance to connect with our Muslim side of the family and their traditions. He reminded us of the importance of family and how it feels when they are gone. Grandmother's passing left a void, and he did not have anyone to care for him. We learned about my mother's childhood and her growing up in a Muslim family. Their gender biases were the same as Hindus': no equality and subservient. Grandfather told us that there were a lot of similarities between both religions, and he pointed out that there were many times both religions came together peacefully.

After my grandfather's visit, my mother appeared to have a renewed appreciation for Canada, recognizing the opportunities it offered her family. She began embracing the customs and traditions of Canadian culture with pride. Grandfather expressed an interest in living in Canada but cited the cold climate and his girlfriend in Fiji as reasons against it. I vividly remember Kris and Grandfather cooking beef in the basement, a practice frowned upon in our family due to religious reasons. Recognizing the potential conflict, I preemptively assured them that it was permissible for Grandfather due to his different religious beliefs. Surprisingly, when my father eventually found out, he chose not to react, leaving me puzzled by his unexpected response.

During his visit, Grandfather shared many of his cooking techniques and recipes with us. He taught us how to make traditional dishes from his homeland using herbs and spices that he brought. We spent hours watching him cook, and I could see the joy it brought him to share his knowledge with us. One day, Grandfather took Kris aside and said he wanted to teach him a special recipe that had been handed down to him. He told us that the secret to a great dish was to cook it with love and never compromise on quality. He then proceeded to show us the procedure step by step. I loved to listen to Grandfather's stories and experiences throughout his life. Most importantly, I enjoyed spending quality time with him.

Grandfather's visit had a profound impact on me, teaching me the importance of family, tradition, and the joy of cooking. I will forever be grateful for the time we spent together and the memories we shared. As the year ended, Grandfather decided to return to Fiji to be with his girlfriend, promising to visit again. His stay had instilled in us a newfound appreciation for our family and cultural roots. Later, my grandfather called to announce his marriage to his girlfriend, which upset my mother due to the age difference. Despite this, I wished only for his happiness and realized that age was insignificant; what truly mattered was finding joy and living life to the fullest.

It was the summer of 1991, and I felt the baby was coming. We drove to Grace Hospital in Vancouver. I was admitted, and the on-duty doctor said it was not time. He said I could go home and drive back when the contractions were closer. I told him I was not going home, only to drive back, and I was no closer to giving birth. The doctor came in to tell me he was going to induce labor.

After being in labor for 24 hours, we were informed that a C-section would be performed. When I awoke, I was informed I had given birth to a baby boy weighing 9 and a half pounds. The nurse brought the baby to my room. He was so cute and had a full head of hair. He was sucking his finger, and he was so quiet. Kris was there in the room, and I did not even want to ask where he went. Kris started his speech. I have to work and cannot visit every day. I thought that all soon-to-be fathers took a day off to be there for the birth of their first child, but I guess I was wrong. Kris had somewhere more important to be at that time.

I could not help but feel disappointed and hurt by Kris's absence during such an important moment in our lives. I knew he was a hard-working man, but I had hoped he would prioritize being there for our child's birth. As the days passed by in the hospital, Kris would visit sporadically and for a short amount of time. It was clear he did not want to be here, and I could sense a growing distance between us. I tried to ignore my feelings and focus on taking care of our baby, but I could not help but feel resentful towards Kris.

Being a new mom was overwhelming and stressful, and I needed his support and presence. Slowly but surely, Kris started to keep his promise and be more available for the kids. He started to help with the baby and became more present in our lives. It was not easy, but we kept trying to work on our relationship. Later, my parents visited and told me Kris was not home at all. He left Cole with them, and he was out partying with friends. I was so upset; I did not want to deal with it. I closed my eyes when I woke up; they were gone. I got released early and went home.

The promise from Kris to be present in our lives was short-lived. I found myself left alone to care for two small children with no help from Kris. True to his habit, he spent his nights out at clubs, meeting women, and neglecting to return home. The repetitiveness of this routine was wearing me down, and I wondered when it would finally cease. Night after night, I sat by the window, tears streaming down my face, waiting for Kris to come back, but I was not a priority to him. He did not even have the decency to call and inform me that he was safe and would not be coming home. My only solace was in praying that he would at least show up for our son.

We received another call from welfare. It felt like déjà vu. They informed the family that a baby boy had been born and abandoned in the hospital on the same day. Here I was, holding my newborn baby and wondering what Rani was thinking. Why abandon these children? I was sure that no answers would be provided. My parents insisted that I take the baby, but I flat-out said "no." They could not understand why I responded that way. I tried to explain that I already had my hands full with Cole (Rani's second son) and my newborn baby. I also got stuck looking after Brian (Rani's first son). It was all just too much for me.

Kris's lack of involvement with Rani's children left me questioning his feelings towards them. My parents placed the responsibility of Rani's children on Kris as well, and I wondered why he accepted the unjust burden. There were moments when I thought he resented the situation, feeling like they were not his children and that he had been forced into this role. At times, I found myself experiencing similar feelings of resentment and understood his perspective to some extent. Cole required constant attention and supervision as he often found himself in challenging situations that needed proactive and immediate resolution.

In July, Kris and I had a major disagreement. Kris had bought a cake and stored it in the fridge. When I saw the cake, I noticed it was inscribed with 'Happy Birthday, Rachael.' I questioned Kris about it, and he brushed it off, saying it was for a male coworker. I was not convinced, as Rachael is typically a female name. In my frustration, I picked up the cake and threw it on the floor. This triggered Kris's anger. He began to physically assault me, pushing me into the wall and pulling my hair. I was so consumed with anger that I did not deal with the incident with a rational mindset.

The police arrived and instructed Kris to leave. After speaking with me, one of the officers advised me to let Kris go and focus on the children. That night, I threw out all of Kris's clothes. I was done with everything and did not want to deal with him anymore. I found myself wishing he had never come into my life. And just like that, months passed by with no contact from Kris. He never called or visited the kids. My parents came by one day and told me I was better off without him. Their words did little to soothe me. Instead, I found myself seething with anger—at Kris for everything he had put me through and at my parents for their role in my marriage to him.

While Kris was out living his life, I was left to deal with the aftermath of our fight. The police contacted me to inform me that charges were pending against Kris and that I would need to appear in court. A few days later, Kris called me to say he had been taken into custody and had spent a day in jail. Despite everything, I felt a pang of sympathy for him. However, I also knew that hitting a woman is never acceptable. Every woman should feel safe in her own home. This was a lesson Kris needed to learn.

Months had passed since Kris and I had separated. I found myself busy with the children, trying to adjust to my new life as a single mother. The situation with Kris had deteriorated, leading to our separation. The stress of managing my life and caring for the kids on my own was overwhelming. Eventually, I took Kris to court and was granted sole custody of our baby. Our relationship was fraught with conflict, and we were constantly at odds with each other. It became clear that we needed time apart. Kris needed to mature and learn to accept his responsibilities, and I had my own growing up to do as well. We were too young at the time of our marriage; this did not afford us the usual time to learn and grow as married couples do.

Kris's family called from Fiji to inform him that his mother was very sick and in the hospital. They were not very optimistic about her recovery. My father insisted that the kids and I go to Fiji with Kris. However, I felt uncomfortable going with Kris, as we were not on speaking terms. Despite his inconsistency in visiting the kids, I decided to express my concerns to my father about taking a trip to Fiji. He mentioned that if I did not go, it would cause problems among our extended family. It was a tough decision to make since my baby was barely a month old. I wondered about the potential outcomes of the trip, given the strained relationship between Kris and me.

Despite my reservations, I decided to put aside my differences with Kris and accompany him to Fiji. The reason was that I wanted my children to know their extended family members in Fiji. We packed our bags and left for the airport. On the flight, Kris and I barely spoke to each other, and it was awkward. We arrived in Fiji and were met by Kris's brothers and his family. Cole ran out of the customs area, and I had to go running behind him with the baby in my arms. Cole went under some chairs and started to play. Kris got our bags, and we headed to his mother's house. We arrived at the house; it was old and small.

We washed up and went straight to the hospital to visit Kris's mother. She was lying in bed, frail, which was heartbreaking to see. Kris was visibly upset, and I could tell that he was struggling with the thought of losing his mother. After a week, the doctors finally gave her the clearance to leave the hospital, and we were overjoyed. We helped her pack her things and went home. We were relieved to be leaving the hospital behind, and as soon as we exited the building, the fresh air felt like a breath of new life. Kris was right—it was much better outside.

As we reflected on the experience, we realized how important it is to cherish our loved ones and spend time with them while we can. Life is unpredictable, and we never know when we will need their support or when they will need ours. We were grateful for the opportunity to support Kris's mother during a challenging time, and we came out on the other side with a renewed appreciation for each other and our time together. During our visit to Fiji, Kris's mother and his sisters always went with us wherever we went, leaving us with hardly any alone time to reconnect and address our issues. Despite this, there was a moment where it felt like we could work things out. We rekindled our relationship and were intimate during our time in Fiji.

Looking back, I realize we should have discussed and resolved our relationship conflicts before jumping back into intimacy, as it only delayed addressing the underlying issues. After that intimate moment, Kris and I started to talk more openly about our relationship. We acknowledged that we both made mistakes and that we needed to work on communication and trust. We talked about our fears and insecurities and how they contributed to our problems. It was not easy, but we tried to make the most of the time we had left in Fiji. We went on adventures as a family and shared meals and laughter. It was like old times but with a new sense of maturity and understanding.

Chapter 13

Family and Discord

We ended up visiting Kris's grandfather, "Tata," and he was extremely accommodating and respectful. I guess when one gives respect, it is returned in kind. We spent the entire day and evening with Tata and his family. Tata also lived a polygamous lifestyle. When I spoke to him, he agreed that this lifestyle is not for everyone, but he managed to support all his wives and children through his farming endeavors. Tata and my grandpa (Ajja) knew each other and were part of the same social circles.

Tata said the key was to give everyone the same things, not place favoritism on anyone or anything. He mentioned everyone has a favorite item, person, or place. The goal was not to tell or show anyone your preferences. I thought, how ridiculous, and how can one hide their emotions or feelings? He further told me that having many wives made it easier to support the family and helped save money, as everyone during the colonial era worked. He further said that during this time, he was not alone in his way of thinking to accumulate wealth and expand his family. He said a lot of Indo-Fijians thought that having more children could change the outcome of their situation.

When speaking to his wives, I learned that two of his wives were biological sisters. This revelation shocked me, as I did not believe in this type of lifestyle or even one male marrying siblings. I thought that the situation probably worked because the sisters were very close and worked together as a team, whether it was cooking, cleaning, or raising the children. After talking to Tata, I learned that his first wife passed away decades ago. She left behind children that were being raised as part of the extended family. This seemed to be working, as Tata had a vested interest in all his children, whether it was educating them or teaching them farming.

Spending time and talking to Tata was a charismatic and engaging experience, and I wish more people were willing to share their stories like him, the good and the bad. Under the tree's comforting shade, embraced by the lively surroundings and enthusiastically devouring the delicious feast in front of us, Tata started weaving the tapestry of his past, revealing hidden facts about his early life and the daunting obstacles he endured during the colonial era.

With every word, his tales radiated a captivating power, effortlessly drawing us into the depths of Fiji's history, specifically the poignant chapter marked by slavery and colonization. Also known as the Girmit period by Indo-Fijians. Tata's narrative served as an illuminating window, exposing the harsh realities of the bygone stories entrusted solely to his extended family as a testament to the unity required to overthrow the shackles of British dominance. With unwavering conviction, Tata believed it crucial to honor those brave souls who made the ultimate sacrifice, placing their lives on the line in defense of their rights and the eternal pursuit of truth.

The day itself was a joyous respite, a time when Tata's love and generosity overflowed. He went to great lengths to ensure our enjoyment, treating us to an old-fashioned picnic outdoors. Tables overflowing with delectable food and coolers filled with refreshing beer surrounded us, creating a feast fit for the occasion. The farm provided an idyllic backdrop with its vast open space and endless possibilities for adventure.

The boys, especially Cole, reveled in the freedom to run wild, their laughter echoing through the air. Dev, my son, was passed around like a cherished treasure, embraced by loving arms, and showered with affectionate kisses. It was a day that reaffirmed the bond between family—a day we will cherish for years to come. For Tata, having his great-grandson "Dev" as the center of attention made the time spent together unforgettable.

I felt incredibly fortunate that Tata trusted me with his painful and personal stories. It filled me with a sense of pride to know that both my grandfather and Tata had endured and sacrificed so much to create a better life, not only for their children but for future generations as well. As the evening drew near, Tata surprised us by making kava and serving it—a traditional Fijian drink made from the root of the kava plant. I was a bit hesitant to try it, but it tasted surprisingly pleasant—almost like herbal tea. We passed the bowl around, and each person took a sip. It was a bonding experience, and we felt grateful to be included in this experience.

Tata was an amazing and very optimistic person. As the night ended, Tata thanked us for visiting and hoped we would come back again. We hugged him and his family, feeling a sense of warmth and gratitude for the hospitality they showed us. As we drove away from the farm, I reflected on the day and realized that it had been one of the most memorable experiences of my life. We learned so much about our culture, family history, and Fijian culture.

We had developed a deep appreciation for the significance of a family community and sharing with family. I also realized that being open to new experiences and challenging ourselves to try new things can lead to great memories and personal growth. Tata had lived through challenging times, but his positive attitude and resilience had left a lasting impact on his family and those around him. I felt inspired to try to live my life with the same sense of positivity and gratitude.

As we drove back to Kris's mother's place, I looked out at the beautiful landscapes of Fiji and felt a sense of connection to this place. I knew that we would never forget the warmth and generosity of Tata and his family and that we had truly experienced the heart of Fiji. Eventually, our trip came to an end, and we had to go back home. But instead of feeling resentful or anxious, Kris and I felt hopeful. We had a newfound appreciation for one another, and we were willing to put the effort into making things work.

We went for lunch or dinner at extended family homes. I found that in Fiji, the food was mostly fish, coconut, cassava, taro, and other local fruits and vegetables. Kris said that we had to adapt to the local food culture and try new things. We reluctantly agreed and started to try different dishes. Surprisingly, we found that some of the local dishes were quite delicious. We loved the lovo, which was a feast cooked in an underground oven, and found it to be interesting and tasty.

After a few weeks, we began to appreciate the Fijian cuisine more and more. We realized that it was healthy and fresh. We also enjoyed the social aspect of sharing meals with our Fijian relatives. They would often invite us to their homes for dinner, and we would learn more about their culture and way of life. It has been a long time since our trip to Fiji, and things have been better between us. We still have our moments of frustration and disagreement, but we try to be more open and honest with each other. We have learned to believe and trust in ourselves, and we are grateful for the time we spent in Fiji, which helped us to rekindle our relationship.

During our time in Fiji, we were constantly inspired by the warmth and kindness of the Fijian people. They were always willing to share their culture and their stories with us, and we felt incredibly grateful to have had the opportunity to experience it. I spent my time getting to know Kris's family, and I thought they liked me, but I guess I was wrong.

One night after dinner, an argument broke out. Kris's mother and his older sister accused me of having an affair with a teenager while in Fiji. I started to laugh and told them how disgusting they were. Kris's mother then grabbed the baby out of my arms, and his oldest sister started to hit me. Kris's mother and his oldest sister pushed me around while hitting me. I was crying and told them to give my kids back.

Kris's mother said to leave, and she was not giving my kids back to me. She went on to say I was not a good wife or a good mother. Kris said to go back to your parents, as no one could do anything to them. The whole family began saying I was crazy and the kids' safety was at risk. The police were of no use as they sided with Kris's family. Kris's younger brother Masla was returning from work when he heard yelling coming from inside the house.

Shocked by his family's cruelty, he bravely stood up for me. He protected me from harm from his family members. He also helped me gather my children, including the baby and suggested that we go to my uncle's house before leaving for Canada. Kris's youngest brother called my uncle to explain what had happened, and my uncle sent someone to pick us up. Despite Kris's mother's tactics to stop the kids from getting into the car, we managed to leave and safely arrived at my uncle's home. However, my uncle advised me to return to Canada with my children.

As we waited for our flight to be booked, the baby suddenly fainted and started turning blue. We immediately rushed him to the hospital, where the doctor informed us that he was severely dehydrated. To nurse him back to health, the doctor decided to place him on a coconut treatment instead of an IV. It was then that I was reminded that we were in Fiji, where traditional remedies were still commonly used. We waited patiently for the baby to recover enough to travel, and once he was well enough, we quickly booked our flight. However, I decided that I would rather take the baby to a hospital in Hawaii if we needed to later.

We prepared to leave Fiji; we knew that we would miss the beautiful beaches, the delicious food, and, most of all, the wonderful people. We left with a sense of gratitude and a newfound appreciation for the importance of family, community, and tradition. We knew that we had experienced something exceptional, and we were eager to share our experiences with others and to continue learning about the world around us.

We boarded the plane for our flight to Vancouver, relieved that our baby was feeling much better and drinking water. As soon as we landed, we took him straight to the hospital. The doctor performed a blood test just to be safe. Thankfully, everything came back normal, and the doctor gave our baby a clean bill of health. I felt incredibly relieved that my precious child was okay. It was a true blessing to be back home. My parents were also anxious about the baby, but they were thrilled that we made it back safely.

Our relationship has been a whirlwind of emotions, with the highs being exceptionally wonderful and the lows causing immense pain. How many nights I sat by the window, desperately waiting for Kris to come home, but sometimes he never did. I was left alone with our precious baby and Cole, my tears becoming a steady stream that could have filled an entire river. The weight of the loneliness and heartache consumed me.

Reality has a way of sneaking in, exposing the infidelities that I sometimes choose to ignore. How many times have I discovered the truth hidden in plain sight—the beeps on the pager, the lipstick on the collar of his shirt—feeling the sharp sting of betrayal pierce my heart? It was in those moments that my trust shattered, like a fragile glass breaking into a thousand pieces. I tried to mend the fractures and give our relationship another chance, yet there were nights when I wondered if it was all in vain. The pain was so deep that it made it impossible to overcome.

It felt like my heart turned into a hard rock to protect me from further pain and suffering. With every disappointment, I questioned my worth. The walls around my heart grew higher and thicker. I built a fortress to shield myself from the pain, unknowingly creating a divide between us. I became trapped behind these emotional barriers, unable to give myself to the relationship fully. Maybe it was a defense mechanism, a way to guard what little remained of my fragile heart safely. Yet, amidst all the turmoil, there were moments when I fought tooth and nail to save my marriage. At one point, I felt like I was the only one putting in the effort. I tirelessly held on to the hope that our love could withstand any storm.

As the nights grew longer and the tears stained my cheeks, I started questioning if my love alone was enough. I could not help but wonder what changed and why I stopped trying to please everyone else. It was a gradual awakening, a realization that a relationship cannot thrive with only one person's devotion. I never imagined that I would find myself in a relationship where I poured out everything and received so little in return. It was a painful lesson to learn.

I am not saying that we were necessarily bad for each other, but we both needed to grow and mature as individuals before we could truly come together on equal footing with a shared purpose. I had doubts about his readiness for commitment, particularly considering the responsibilities of parenthood. The strain of an arranged marriage, coupled with the pressure to make it work at all costs, weighed heavily on me. The combination of these factors significantly damaged our relationship.

However, something shifted. I felt it in the air, in our interactions. We finally found an understanding and a love that encompassed our children, binding us together in an unbreakable bond. It felt like we were rediscovering each other, finding a connection that went beyond the superficial. It was a fragile yet beautiful thing—this newfound unity born out of growth and maturity. And for the first time in a long while, I dare to hope that we can make it work—that this time will be different.

During a time when I desperately needed unconditional love and support, it was my son, Dev, as a toddler who provided me with solace and reassurance. His genuine love and support touched my heart and soul. Dev was the best thing in my life. He ignited a fire within me, instilling in me a deep determination to fight for the well-being of my family. Being a new mother and raising children on my own was an immense challenge, but I was resolute about not facing it alone. I recognized the importance of my son's relationship with his father and was willing to adjust and compromise to ensure he had the opportunity.

As time passed and my children grew up, I found myself in the present, with my son and daughter transformed into responsible adults. Our relationship has evolved into one characterized by respect and love. As we got older, we started to mature, not only in our thoughts but also in our actions. We decided to try to put our differences aside and work on the things that needed to be fixed. Though it was a long journey, it needed to be worked on continuously.

I was filled with hope and anticipation as I welcomed my daughter into the world, believing that her arrival would bring about a positive change in our relationship. Sadly, my expectations were shattered as the difficulties and pain persisted. Having another child does not guarantee that a marriage will survive or be automatically revived. It reminded me of my mother's advice that having a child makes everything ok between couples. I did not know where she got her advice because this was not true. It dawned on me that my mother's advice about having a child to mend a relationship was far from the truth, as the struggles and heartache persisted despite the arrival of our daughter.

Infidelity became a dark cloud, looming over my life with no apparent escape route. Each betrayal felt like a knife to the heart, leaving me questioning whether Kris cared about my feelings or our marriage. Why was I the only one who seemed to care? The hurt and sadness consumed me, like a constant reminder of the unfairness of it all. It brought me back to the beginning of our union. It felt inherently unjust as I pondered whether two married people would willingly inflict such pain on their spouses. The waves of doubt and confusion crashed over me, leaving me feeling lost and alone. I desperately sought answers, seeking solace in the belief that surely there must be a reason behind such unbelievable actions. Yet, no expectations could justify the heartache I endured.

Amid this turmoil, I could not help but question my worth and wonder if I deserved any better. The constant battle with insecurities weighed heavily on my soul as I grappled with the emotional toll of betrayal after betrayal. I kept questioning why I was putting myself through this turmoil. But during the darkness, a glimmer of strength emerged—a reminder that I am not defined by the actions of my spouse.

It was a gradual realization that my well-being cannot be dependent on someone who consistently disrespects and hurts me. I needed to take the first step toward healing and seek support from my loved ones, friends, and professionals. With their unwavering love and guidance, I began to recognize my self-worth, understanding that I deserved better in life. In this journey, the support of friends like Christine and Cindy proved invaluable, providing not only emotional solace but also stepping up to care for my children, allowing me the time and space to rest, recharge, and regain my strength.

In addition to being married to Kris for 39 years, I devoted myself to raising our children. As a committed homebody, I poured my energy into nurturing our sons and daughter, ensuring they grew up to be responsible and respectable individuals. While I may not have ventured out often, my priority was always creating a loving and supportive environment within the walls of our home. This commitment to my family instilled strong values in our children and served as a solid foundation for my parental obligations.

Throughout my marriage, I took on the responsibility of holding my relationship together singlehandedly. It was my determination and commitment that kept me going through the difficulties I faced. I devoted my time and effort to understanding and supporting Kris through the challenges and providing stability in the relationship. Despite any obstacles that came my way, I was the constant force ensuring the strength and longevity of my marriage. It should not be one person's responsibility to carry the full weight of the relationship.

I have come to the painful realization that flirting can indeed lead to an affair, and I deeply regret the indiscretion on my part within my marriage. I found myself unable to pinpoint the exact moment it all began, but a significant catalyst was a heated argument with Elizabeth. She accused me of settling and claimed that I was not deserving of love or finding my own man. According to her, no one would willingly marry me, and that was why our parents had to get an arranged marriage for me. Her hurtful words and the desire to settle a score with Kris, with a tit-for-tat attitude, may have contributed to my actions.

I wanted him to feel what it is like when trust is broken. But in doing so, I lost sight of myself. Revenge and succumbing to other people's opinions were never traits I possessed. Perhaps I was in a dark place at that time, and things quickly spiraled out of control. My heart turned to stone, incapable of feeling anything. I resorted to drinking rum straight, seeking numbness as a temporary escape. I honestly cannot recall how much I consumed, but it was never the solution to my problems. Eventually, I found myself unconscious and then woke up to a throbbing migraine.

In my disoriented state, I reached for a bottle of Tylenol, unsure of the number of pills I took, but it was enough to cause violent sickness. I collapsed while heading to the bathroom and remained unconscious. Kris discovered me in that vulnerable state when he returned from work and immediately called for an ambulance. I was quickly rushed to the hospital, unsure if my actions were a deliberate suicide attempt or a tragic accident. Upon regaining consciousness, the doctor spoke to me with concern, assuring me that things would be okay.

However, he emphasized the importance of refraining from mixing alcohol and medication. He recommended speaking with a psychologist before considering my release from the hospital. This series of events filled me with deep remorse and regret over the choices I made. After my release from the hospital, I had to have a serious conversation with Kris to tell him about the whole incident.

Whether good or bad, he needed the truth, and I could not hide the truth; it was burning a hole in my heart. The outcome was not good, as I moved out and ended up living with my parents. I was shocked that people were so full of criticism, but my parents turned out to be understanding but still angry about the situation. My parents said, "Kris had done a lot of things, and he could not expect a perfect wife after everything he has put you through." It took a long time for Kris and me to work on our relationship.

In my journey, I have come to appreciate the significance of loyalty deeply. Initially, it was a core value that I prioritized and sought in all my relationships. However, I have learned that there was a moment when I failed to uphold these values that I held dear, causing hurt and betrayal. Reflecting on those experiences made me realize that, at that time, loyalty did not hold as much importance to me as it should have.

I believe in growth and personal transformation. While also recognizing the repercussions of my actions, I worked hard to learn from my mistakes, apologized to those affected, and committed to rebuilding trust. I understood that rebuilding takes time and consistent effort. Going forward, I am fully dedicated to embodying loyalty and trustworthiness and actively striving to create an environment where these values flourish. I am determined to demonstrate, through my words and actions, that loyalty truly matters to me.

As I reflect on my relationship, I have come to acknowledge its unconventional nature, far from what one might consider a textbook marriage. To work through the challenges and strengthen the bond, I decided to seek couple's therapy. Despite attending sessions for a few months, Kris eventually expressed a reluctance to continue further.

Revisiting the present, Kris and I decided to unwind at our favorite local bar, seeking solace in the embrace of drinks and a heartfelt conversation. Summoning my courage, I broached the delicate subject and asked Kris about the exact moment he realized he was in love with me. His response caught me off guard; he meekly proposed that the surge of emotion occurred during the exchange of our vows on our wedding day four decades ago.

However, a sense of suspicion gradually cast a shadow over my thoughts, questioning the authenticity of his claim. I grappled with the notion that such a deep sensation could abruptly bloom from the mere utterance of those two seemingly ordinary words, especially in an arranged marriage. For me, love is a beautiful journey of unfolding emotions, growing and strengthening as the days go by. These past few months, my heart has been full of affection for Kris's constant presence, care, and support.

Yet, there was a part of me that longed to be sure—to know if his love for me was as profound and true as mine for him. It was important for me to give him the chance to walk away if his love did not match my own. Despite our honest conversation, I am still grappling with the perplexing question of why it is so difficult to give a straightforward answer when it comes to something as profound as falling in love.

Now, as I approach the later stages of my life, I am facing health challenges, particularly the loss of vision in my right eye and the gradual decline in vision in my left eye. Adapting to this new chapter will undoubtedly be tough, but I find immense comfort and strength in Kris's unwavering presence by my side. His support and love give me the confidence that, together, we can overcome any obstacle life throws our way. Kris prioritizes my needs above all else and helps me with tasks ranging from medical appointments to simple outings for meals.

1993 was a challenging year. One day, while I was at the bank, I received a call from Fiji. I was informed that Kris's brother, Masla, had been murdered. The news was so shocking and devastating that I fainted. To make matters worse, I was five months pregnant at the time. We later discovered that his brother had been killed for his paycheck, which he had buried in his backyard. The police informed us that the murderers had been apprehended, and shockingly, they were his friends. The two men pleaded insanity and were subsequently placed in a psychiatric hospital.

The news was devastating for all of us, especially since he was more than a friend to me; he was my hero. He stood by my side in Fiji when everyone else turned against me. Dev was teething, so Masla taught Dev how to chew on an eggplant. In the mornings, he would be outside on the grass, teaching Dev how to walk. I will never forget his pearly white teeth and his smile when Dev took his first steps. He was a kind and loving person.

His absence will be deeply felt, especially since it will be difficult to come to terms with the fact that my daughter, Cea, will never have the chance to meet him. I know he would have been an exceptional father. He was not one to shy away from getting his hands dirty, whether it was changing diapers or taking care of a baby. He would have been an excellent role model for children. I will always be grateful for the impact he had on our lives.

Looking back, I am grateful for the support I received from my family during that difficult time. It was a challenging journey, but we made it through and emerged even stronger. I am proud of how far we have come and will always be thankful for our second chance as a family. Things got more complicated. I was seven months pregnant, and still, nothing was working out with Kris.

Even though he was living at home, he was still living his life as a single man. This was my stupidity, and now I had to figure out what to do. My parents were not too happy about the situation. At this point, I was disillusioned with marriage, and it meant nothing but a piece of paper. I just wanted a man I could count on to be there for our children and me, too. He was there for our children but not for me,

I decided to have the baby, even if I had to do it on my own. He would take me to my appointments and look after the kids occasionally, but he still held on to his old ways of partying and clubbing. In the depths of my anguished heart, I found myself grappling with the enigmatic nature of our union. His avoidance of being a husband shattered our bond. This left me in a state of perpetual perplexity. The burden of being wed at such a young age, a pawn in the game of a forced arranged marriage, weighed heavily on my fragile shoulders.

I could have never imagined the immense pain and struggles that lay ahead on this difficult journey. My youthful innocence was quickly taken from me as I grieved the loss of a life untouched by such challenging trials. We walked down this path with eyes wide open, him at twenty-one and me just a sixteen-year-old, blissfully unaware of the turmoil that lay ahead. Oh, how I longed to be free to choose, to break free from the shackles that bound me to this miserable fate.

Tears plagued my nights, a regular companion in the agony I experienced. Had the gods provided me with an alternate path, I could have shielded myself from the storm of suffering and escaped the terrible cries that resonated through my empty life. Trapped within the depths of my emotions, bearing the weight of carrying our second child, I clung to a semblance of hope. The marriage union was crumbling, overshadowed by incessant strife. The cruelty of an arranged marriage, coupled with the tumultuous turmoil within, threatened to destroy all that I tried to build.

It was not my choice to get married so young, and I hated myself for not standing up against my parents or Kris. This had a bad effect on my health, as I was eating lots of sweets and drinking pop all the time. I started to not care about the way I looked or my weight. It did not help with Mother always asking me to lose weight so things would get better. I thought my weight had nothing to do with my problems and it was all their fault for getting me married to him.

I was scheduled for a C-section at the hospital in March. The pregnancy was very difficult; I was vomiting throughout the delivery. I had the flu along with gestational diabetes. I felt like I deserved it since I was not even looking after my health. I promised myself that I would cut out junk food and eat healthy, as I have kids to take care of by myself.

I held my newborn baby girl for the first time, marveling at her 7-pound, 6-ounce tiny body. Her beauty left me speechless, her tiny head adorned with an abundance of hair. As she cried out for me, calling me "Mama," my heart overflowed with joy. In that moment, all of life's worries seemed to fade away. With three children now in my care, I knew my days would be filled with the enchanting chaos of parenthood.

The years seemed to go by so fast; it was 1996 now. I did not know what I wanted in life. Being just a mother was not hard; it took heart and dedication. I wanted more in life, not just to be a mother, and I wanted my kids to be proud of me. I decided to finish my twelfth grade and ended up going to the same high school as my brother Michael. He was not very happy about it, so I ended up going to night school. After passing the 12th grade and feeling proud of myself, I decided I wanted to go to college and study criminology. It was going to be difficult because I was working and taking care of the kids.

My father felt proud of me for finishing school and looking ahead. No one in our family went to college or anything. He told me to keep going; learning never stops. He was just happy that I finally found something I liked to do, and it showed in my demeanor. I kept telling my kids that education was important and wondered how they would feel if they knew I did not finish high school. This motivated me to keep going when I felt exhausted. My days were spent going to college, and my evenings were for homework. Kris and I took care of the children.

My little princess (Cea) started preschool, and she was scared. Dev stepped up and decided he wanted to go to preschool with her. I talked with Dev about how he would still need to go to kindergarten by himself. He started kindergarten, and I felt excited for him. It was what he looked forward to every year. He was making friends, and it was nice seeing him be so positive. He was my little man, and he was growing up so fast. His schedule was pretty full: preschool in the mornings, then kindergarten in the afternoons.

My time was spent in between preschool and school. My days were so busy while I was starting college, and it was stressful. I did not know how to deal with everything. My major obstacle was juggling the kids, school, and life. Kris started to help look after the kids while I was in college. The arrangement worked out so that someone was always around to care for our children, but the downside was that Kris and I hardly spent time together. There were no arguments; it did not seem like a real marriage, like normal married couples sharing, caring, and spending time together.

Things would be normal for a few months, and then it was back to his old ways. I wanted to give the kids an everyday family life, but the fighting had to stop. I started to think that each time we got back together, it was when his life was not working out, and he needed a familiar place to hang out. My parents approached Kris and me, burdening us with Rani's fourth child, a boy. They wanted us to consider taking the child, as we had already selflessly taken in two of her kids. It was an emotional and overwhelming situation as Welfare kept calling, trying to get in touch with our family.

At first, my parents agreed to take the child on a short-term basis. However, after a few weeks, they approached Kris and me with a distressing offer: They would buy us a house if we agreed to raise the child. Filled with frustration and sadness, I firmly expressed to my parents that no amount of material possessions, not even a house or a fancy car, could make me change my mind.

Their proposition left me feeling used and utterly insignificant as if my worth and voice did not matter. It appears my sole purpose on earth was only to bear the responsibility of raising all of Rani's children. Yet, despite my repeated and heartfelt refusal, my parents persisted in pressuring me to take custody of the child, even if Kris did not agree. My parents said, "It is not like Kris is around all the time, and the kids will keep you busy."

Eventually, my parents made a decision that shattered my heart. They chose to send the child with my brother back east to live with Rani. The heaviness of the situation was unbearable. But to my dismay, it did not last long; just one week later, she called back, her words filled with indifference and abandonment. She declared that she no longer wanted the child and had coldly returned him to welfare.

When I heard the outcome, it painfully confirmed the warnings I had expressed to my mother earlier on. I had voiced my doubts about the viability of this arrangement, highlighting the fact that Rani had already abandoned the child in the hospital when the baby was born. Regrettably, my concerns were disregarded, and now, an innocent child had to suffer the consequences of the turmoil between my parents and Rani. My parents were visibly upset and angry with me for his situation, saying, 'If you had taken the child, this situation would never have happened.'

My response was one of concern for the child and for the events unfolding, but I also knew deep down that I was not responsible for Rani or her children. I had expressed my reservations and concerns from the start, but the decision was out of my control. It was a frustrating and guilt-ridden situation. I had to endure my parents' anger, even though I had tried to voice my opinion and take the well-being of everyone involved into consideration.

Welfare contacted the family to inform them that the child was adopted by a family. The family has loved the child since birth. I was so relieved that the child would have a loving home away from our dysfunctional family. I know in hindsight that all families have issues, and some problems or concerns are always overlooked, but in many cases, families need to learn to solve problems instead of pawning them off on someone else. Especially when it comes to something as serious as a young child or a member of the family, parents are coercing or forcing them to do something they do not want to do.

As time went on, I found myself growing increasingly frustrated with the way others would take advantage of me. They expected me to always bend to their will and go along with whatever they wanted without question. It became overwhelming, feeling like my own needs and desires were constantly being pushed aside. But something inside me started to change. I finally mustered up the nerve to stand up for myself. I learned to assert my own decisions and not let my family take advantage of me any longer. It was a turning point in my life—a moment of empowerment and growth. However, despite this new-found courage, I still had to navigate the complexities of living in an extended family setting with my father as the head of the household, even after getting married.

The traditional dynamics and cultural values emphasized the importance of respecting and obeying our elders, including my parents. This meant that while I had taken a step towards reclaiming my voice, the influence of my parents and the expectations of the family structure continued to shape my choices and decisions. Although I recognized the importance of respecting my parents and the traditions of our extended family, I constantly grappled with finding a balance between asserting my independence and honoring the family dynamics.

It was an ongoing internal struggle, but I was determined to carve out my path while maintaining harmony within the family. This required careful communication, compromise, and constant negotiation between my desire for autonomy and the traditional values that guided our household. In this complex web of duty, love, and tradition, I learned the importance of finding my voice without disregarding the significance of familial bonds. It was a delicate dance of asserting my needs while considering the greater whole. Ultimately, though it was challenging, this experience taught me valuable lessons about the complexities of relationships and the strength required to chart my path amidst the expectations of others.

In 1999, we found out that Kris needed kidney surgery. I paid for Kris's mother to come to Canada to visit so she could support him emotionally during his surgery. Although I wanted to remain positive, I was also concerned about his mother's visit. Nevertheless, the kids were excited about their grandmother's visit. During the day, Kris's mother and I took care of him. On the other hand, I financially supported the family by working and continuing to attend school.

At night, I took over and cared for Kris while he recovered. However, I felt frustrated because Kris continued with his old bachelor ways and did not change his attitude or habits even after the surgery. It felt like he was using all of us for his recovery. While Kris's mother watched over my children, she took it upon herself to discipline them, a decision that I did not welcome. Unfortunately, her chosen method involved physically hitting my oldest, Cole, with a spoon, resulting in it breaking.

I firmly believe that discipline is important, but we should never resort to physical violence. Through my personal experience with physical abuse, I did not want my children to suffer this trauma in their lives. As soon as I received a tearful call from Cole, I immediately headed home to address the issue. I informed Kris and his mother that I was the one who would discipline my children. Finally, I told Kris that I am always there for the kids, and they can talk to me about anything that bothers them.

In addition to Cole's distressing experience, the incident also had a profound impact on the other children. They were frightened and stressed. It is essential to provide a safe environment for our children where they feel secure and protected. Addressing this issue promptly and ensuring that appropriate discipline measures are in place is essential to alleviating their fear and restoring their sense of well-being.

Kris's mother was always hard on me, as she criticized me for everything. We did not get along, no matter how hard I tried; it seemed like I was never good enough for her son. When I talked about the reasons why Kris and I were having issues, she did not seem to care. She said, "He can have 10 girlfriends, and you cannot do anything to him." I felt hurt and disappointed, as I thought, being a woman, she would understand.

At this point, arguing with her was pointless. I waited for her departure, and I was eager to drop her off at the airport. I felt that if someone needed something from you, they would treat you with respect, and their demeanor towards you would be good. Once the thing was obtained, it was over, and they dropped you like a sack of potatoes. I felt this was the case here, as I brought her to Canada to help Kris.

I remember, one day, the whole family went to Rocky Point Park, and I thought taking Kris's mother sightseeing would ease some of the tension in the home. The kids enjoyed the park by running around and eating their ice cream. Kris, his mother, and I walked behind them. Kris told his mother and me to catch up to the kids.

Confused, I asked Kris what was going on, to which he simply replied, "Just go." As I turned around, I saw that he was flirting with the two young women who exited the limousine. It was an uncomfortable feeling. The incident with the young women at the park only made our fights worse, and I did not want to deal with Kris anymore. However, his mother kept making excuses for him, telling me that it was normal for men to cheat. I was shocked when she nonchalantly said, "You should just get used to it." I could not fathom what I was hearing. To add insult to injury, she went on to say, "He is a good father to your kids. What more do you need?" I could not bear the thought of living in a world where infidelity is acceptable.

I wanted Kris to leave, but he knew how to manage me, and I always ended up giving him another chance. I blamed myself for being too emotional and not being able to let anyone suffer. The worst part was how it was affecting our kids. They had finally gotten their father back, and I could not kick Kris out, especially if it meant the kids would miss spending time with him. I was at my wit's end, emotionally exhausted and drained by our marriage, which had become a joke.

Our interactions were always about getting back at each other. The saying "what is good for the goose is good for the gander" came to mind. I had been the perfect Indian wife, always faithful and subservient. Never did anything to disrespect him or cheat on him. However, I did not want to be a doormat anymore. So, I began venting my issues to my colleagues at work, and they listened intently. They encouraged me to leave him, but I refused to do so. My kids, my parents, and society's opinions were all important considerations for me. I was more like my father, and his traditions and beliefs were deeply ingrained in me.

The following year, I managed to graduate from my criminology program, and I was relieved that I would finally be able to support my family financially. I realized that I could not depend on Kris anymore, especially if we were living in my parents' basement. Kris refused to contribute to our household expenses, and he often used his paycheck for his enjoyment instead of supporting our family. It was frustrating to live like this, and I knew that I needed to make a change for the sake of myself and my children.

And the time came when our kids grew older, and they began to understand what was happening. Although we tried not to fight in front of them, they could tell from our demeanor that something was wrong. They started to ask us questions about our fights and whether we were getting a divorce. We both told them that we were trying to work it out and that we were not getting divorced. However, I did not think Kris would ever change his ways or even try to make things better. I had lost all trust in him, and I knew that I would never be able to trust him again.

Over time, as the children grew older and more intelligent, a conversation arose about their desire for a closer relationship with their grandparents. Their thoughts unveiled a saddening truth: our religious beliefs and biases had unwittingly created a barrier between them and their grandparents. They even felt as though their grandparents displayed favoritism towards Christian children, leaving them feeling excluded. This realization was a powerful wake-up call that compelled me to reflect deeply on how we could cultivate a more inclusive and accepting environment, promoting stronger bonds between my children and their grandparents, regardless of any perceived differences.

When my daughter was 10 years old, she shared with me the reasons why she did not feel closer to my parents. She explained that my mother, her grandmother, would frequently make negative comments about her weight that made her feel unloved and not good enough to belong in the family. She had many experiences of this nature, which led her to avoid visiting her grandparents. In response, I told her that her grandmother had treated me the same way growing up and that she could not continue treating my daughter this way. I told her that her parents and brothers loved her just the way she was. She did not need to change anything about herself for anyone.

I spoke to my mother about her bias, bringing up the times she had treated me unfairly based on my weight and skin color. I made it clear that I would not permit my daughter to be subjected to such treatment and emphasized that she should not place her expectations on others if they are happy with themselves. After our conversation, my mother tried to refrain from making negative comments and attempted to repair the damage. However, it was a long and difficult journey to repair the damage that was done. The relationship was slowly mending after working hard on it; it was restored before Grandmother passed away.

To move forward from this experience, our family has taken steps to ensure that such situations do not occur again. We have had open communication about the importance of accepting and loving each other regardless of differences in appearance or any other factor. Despite the difficult situation, we have learned from it and grown from it. The realization for me came after my children were excluded from family gatherings while the children of Elizabeth's partner were included. It was a hurtful experience for my children and me, and I believe that other families may have faced similar situations.

I strongly believe that children should not feel neglected or unloved by their families because of their religion or for any other reason. The negative experiences that my children went through will always be with them. Parents must create an environment that is inclusive, loving, and respectful. As a future grandparent, I pledge to love and treat my grandchildren equally, no matter their religion.

While religion and culture are essential parts of our identity, they should not divide families. It is important to encourage children to learn about and appreciate each other's beliefs and cultures. It can help foster a deeper understanding and love between family members. Ultimately, love and support should be the foundation of any relationship. As parents, we must validate our children's feelings, acknowledge their pain, and work towards creating positive family memories that promote inclusivity, love, and respect.

I believe it is essential to have open and honest conversations with family members and acknowledge any mistakes that may have caused hurt. It is also crucial to work towards repairing any damage and moving forward to create a healthier family dynamic. By taking these positive steps, we can build stronger relationships within our family and promote a loving and inclusive environment that benefits everyone. I am also open and respectful towards the beliefs of others, recognizing that we all have our journeys to take.

Ultimately, it is our actions and our treatment of others that speak louder than any religious affiliation. By striving to live a life of kindness, generosity, and empathy, we can make a positive impact on the world, no matter our personal beliefs. I believe in respecting and celebrating the diversity of beliefs that exist in the world, as each one provides a unique perspective and understanding of the divine. At the core of all religions is the call to love and serve one another, which we should try to embody and spread in our communities and the world at large.

Chapter 14

Exploring and Disrespect

O ur first vacation as a family was fascinating for the kids, as they had never been anywhere before. It was just the four of us, as Cole had moved to Alberta. We were going to Cuba for a week. The kids wanted to do everything; however, I just wanted to sit at the beach. Anyhow, being a mom meant making sure that the kids were safe, so I signed up to do things that I never thought I would do in a million years. We arrived in Cuba, and it was just as beautiful and hot as I remembered. I wanted to book some trips for all of us so we could spend time together. The kids went ahead to explore the hotel, beach, and surrounding area.

I feel like I lucked out as a parent because my young adult children did not smoke or drink alcohol. The crazy drinker in our family was Kris; he never knew when to stop. As for me, I was a social drinker. I would drink to forget my problems, but I always made sure to remember where and who I was. As we gathered in the lobby on our first day together in Cuba, I could not help but feel grateful for this chance to spend time with my family in such a beautiful setting. We were all excited for our horse-riding outing, and my kids were a bit nervous as they had never ridden before.

On the other hand, Kris and I were old folks at this sort of thing – we had ridden together on previous trips. The mountains towered above us, the peaks in full view, with no clouds in sight, while the ocean sparkled in the distance. As we set off, the air was filled with the sweet scent of tropical fruits, but as we rode closer to the coast, it gave way to the salty taste of seawater. The sound of waves crashing against the shore was like music to our ears as we galloped along the beach. It was exhilarating - and just what we needed after all our worries and stress back home. As we made our way along a winding path to the top of the mountain, I felt my mind clearing and my heart filling with joy.

The second day, we ended up going cross country in a 4 x 4. The town we went to was flooded by a storm the night before. My son Dev was driving the vehicle, and I was amazed at how he handled it, not knowing where the roads began or ended. As we went through the town, we saw people working together to pump out their flooded homes and businesses. Some were using buckets to carry water, while others had pumps set up to remove the water. Everyone was pulling together, helping each other out in any way they could.

We drove through some deep water. The waves were splashing up against the sides of the vehicle. But my son kept his cool, expertly navigating through the flooded roads. I was worried we might get stuck, but he knew exactly what he was doing, and it was like he had been there before. It was an eye-opening experience to see how people can come together in times of hardship. Despite the devastation, there was a sense of resilience and hope in the air. People were determined to rebuild and move forward. As we drove back to the town, I felt grateful for God's blessings and for the opportunity to witness such strength in the face of adversity. It was a humbling reminder that we are all in this together and that we can overcome anything if we work together.

On the third day of our trip, we decided to go snorkeling in the Atlantic Ocean. It was an unparalleled experience to see different species of fish swimming around us. Being in the ocean made us realize just how vast and magnificent it was, as compared to just looking at it from the shore. My kids and I had been swimming for hours, enjoying the underwater life, until the instructor urgently informed us of an oncoming storm.

As we started to head back, we noticed something lurking in the water. Shocked, the instructor advised everyone that the storm had brought sharks into the water. As we were frantically swimming towards the shore, the instructor helped those who were not strong swimmers, adding to the already tense situation. A mixture of fear and excitement coursed through me as I faced a heart-stopping scenario. I was more concerned about my children than for myself, so I waved to them to continue in front of me. The sharks came into the vicinity, though not directly alongside me. This knowledge left me on edge, with adrenaline pumping through my veins. Looking back at my younger self, I would have adamantly refused to venture into the same waters as these sharks. I would have firmly declared, "Absolutely not, not in a million years."

On the fourth day, all of us went to explore the Crystal Caves in Varadero, Cuba. We were in awe as we descended thousands of feet into the depths of the cave. The sight that greeted us was truly breathtaking. The caves sparkled and shone, with their crystal-clear pools reflecting the dazzling formations that surrounded us. I never thought I would be experiencing something so extraordinary, especially since my prior expectations were limited to sitting on the beach with a beer. As we ventured further into the cave, my kids could not contain their excitement. They could not resist the lure of the inviting hot springs within the Crystal Cave.

The thought of swimming in the warm, therapeutic waters was irresistible to them. With their excited splashes and giggles echoing through the cave, they added an extra layer of joy to our adventure. With each step we took, exploring the intricate beauty of the Crystal Cave, it felt like we had stepped into a magical world. It was a stark contrast to our initial expectations of a typical beach vacation. The Crystal Caves in Varadero, Cuba, had truly exceeded anything we could have imagined. It was an experience that left us in awe of nature's wonders and created lifelong memories for our family.

On the fifth day of our trip to Cuba, all of us went to Varadero town to explore the local market and shops. It was an exciting experience, filled with colorful sights and vibrant energy. However, there was an unfortunate incident that cast a shadow over the day. Kris had consumed too much alcohol; his behavior became inappropriate and disrespectful; he was openly drinking beer from his coffee container and making unwelcome advances toward women. It was disheartening and embarrassing to witness his actions.

As we approached the market where two women were working, Kris took his behavior a step further and began flirting with them openly, completely disregarding my presence as his wife. He even dared to instruct me to wait outside, implying that he would join me when he was "done" with the women. I was filled with anger and disappointment. When my kids noticed the commotion and asked about what was happening, I decided to be honest with them. I explained that 'your father is trying to pick up women.' When I confronted Kris about the incident, he replied, 'I was getting dates for our son.' I honestly did not believe him, as this had happened once too often.

Kris was acting utterly disrespectful, and I could not believe it. I pondered how he would have felt or reacted if I had done something similar. Although both of our children felt ashamed regarding what they had witnessed, they refrained from confronting their father. However, I had to deal with my problems on my own. My solution to the issue was to stop paying for these trips where I was the one getting hurt. My daughter and I sat on the beach, watching the waves break on the coast. The view was so breathtaking that it looked straight out of a movie. That evening, it was tranquil, as if all my problems had disappeared.

Overall, the trip was a fantastic experience. We saw vintage car exhibitions, visited various markets and shops, and enjoyed a jazz concert. It was incredible to see such beautiful sights, and I am grateful for the opportunity to have gone on this adventure. I still have reservations about going on trips and have turned into a homebody. I began removing vacation destinations where they offered unlimited drinks because Kris was not mature enough to handle his alcohol consumption. But when I spoke to him about my decision, he refused to believe that he had a problem.

So, I stopped all our vacations at tropical all-inclusive resorts. Even today, he still asks me why we do not go on vacation. I suppose we will have to wait until he turns 100; perhaps by then, he will be able to handle himself better. He always thinks that I am not aware of his actions. However, this trip reminded me of the importance of exploring new places and experiencing different cultures. It allowed me to step out of my comfort zone and try new things, which ultimately made me feel more confident and adventurous. I learned so much about myself and the rich history and culture of Cuba.

All the little things in life that we do are what count. The Cuban people were incredible and resourceful, and I realized how fortunate I am to live in a country that has the necessities like health care, education, and clean water. The lack of these things in Cuba made me appreciate how much I take for granted. Further, being in a country where internet access is limited made me realize how much time I waste mindlessly scrolling through social media. It made me appreciate the importance of disconnecting and being present in the moment.

Overall, my trip to Cuba opened my eyes to the world and gave me a new perspective on life. It was a humbling experience that taught me to appreciate the little things in life, to step out of my comfort zone, and to embrace new experiences. During the trip, I also learned a valuable lesson: You cannot have complete control over someone, no matter how much you desire it. Sometimes, it is wiser to distance yourself and hope that life surprises you with a better outcome, free from the burden of constantly monitoring someone's behavior.

It was a chilling and eerie night when my boss suggested that I could leave work early at 3 a.m. As I hopped into my car and started driving down the desolate bypass, an unsettling scene unfolded before me. There was not a single soul in sight, not even another car. As I took a turn around the corner, my eyes widened in surprise—four police cars suddenly appeared, two parked on the side in the opposite direction and two more ahead of me in the turning lane. One officer, facing the opposite direction, seemed to be engaged in conversation with the others.

As I cautiously approached the flashing lights, one of the officers aimed his flashlight in my direction, compelling me to slow down and eventually come to a halt. Rolling down my window, I was startled when he bellowed, demanding to know where I was headed. I calmly replied that I was heading home after working a long shift at work. After a cursory glance towards the lights, he continued his conversation with his fellow officers. I sat in my car, waiting for the officer to say something; he did not acknowledge me. Assuming that I was free to go, I began driving again, unaware of the unfolding drama behind me.

Suddenly, four police cars blared their sirens and sped up, closing in on me. Confused, I assumed there was an emergency, and then I realized they were prompting me to stop driving, so I stopped. The police officers got irate. One officer started using the loudspeaker to instruct me to pull over, obliging their orders. I moved to the side of the road, only to find myself encircled by all the officers who had emerged from their vehicles. Two officers approached my car, sternly asking for my license while reminding me to keep my hands visible.

The rookie officer, with a tone of authority, asked if I knew the reason for the stop. I responded, bewildered, that I was not speeding since I was well within the speed limit, nor had I run a red light. I honestly could not fathom the offense I had committed. To my surprise, he informed me that I had driven through a roadblock. I mustered the audacity to question where the gates and cones were, prompting irritation from the senior officer.

After a brief exchange between them, they issued me a ticket for disobeying instructions, cautioning that I was fortunate they chose not to tow my vehicle. I was allowed to proceed home, but a lingering sense of unease followed me. I could not shake the feeling of being pursued by one of the police cars that had suddenly become my unwelcome shadow.

Months later, I appealed the violation ticket and had to attend court. Kris and I went to the courthouse. Kris was extremely nervous and did not know what would happen. He went on, saying I was lucky I only received a ticket. I was not the scared-off type and dealt with things head-on, and I was not going to back off. So here we were to prove my innocence, whether I win or lose.

The courtroom was crowded, and everyone was nervous. You could feel the tension in the air. I spotted the officer's presence, and Kris looked at me and said, "Your goose is cooked." I was not nervous, as I attended court very frequently for cases and to give testimony. The judge entered the courtroom, and everyone stood up. We all sat back down, and the judge called our last name. The judge looked at Kris, asking him to stand up. I got confused as to why he was asking Kris to stand. To our surprise, the judge asked Kris how he pleaded, and Kris looked at me, pointing his finger, and said, "It is her, and she did it."

The judge apologized and asked me, "I said not guilty," and the officer was asked to take the stand. The officer shocked everyone, even the judge when he stated that all the charges were being dropped. The judge said I was free to leave, and as shocked as I was, I could not believe the outcome. In the courtroom, I could not help but notice the envious glances and resentful stares directed my way. The judge's warning about changing the outcome if I stayed only fueled my determination to exit the courthouse with my head held high.

Sharing my experience with others, it became clear that gender dynamics can play a significant role in courtroom interactions. The reaction to the judge's words made me reflect on the assumptions and biases that can influence outcomes in legal settings. Kris, too, grappled with the implications of being perceived a certain way by authority figures and pondered how different the situation might have been if the tables were turned. It highlighted the importance of vigilance and self-awareness in navigating such complex and nuanced environments.

Anyhow, as my health began to decline, work became increasingly overwhelming. The toxic environment at work, combined with my diabetic condition, took a devastating toll on me. I was in the dark about my health at the time, and some days, I could barely muster the energy to drag myself out of bed. Despite my difficulties, I pushed myself to go to work and make it through my shifts. I remember being called to the office and told that my attendance was inadequate. In response, I defended myself by offering a medical note to confirm my health issues. I left the office feeling frustrated and disappointed that they could not see the severity of my illness.

At times, I just wished for God to end my life. I was not a big believer in going to church. I knew that if there were a God, he would hear my thoughts and check in on me. Work was not any easier. I faced harassment from everyone I worked with and trusted. They bullied and picked on me every day, worsening my health problems. I would sit in the parking lot before entering work, too physically and emotionally sick to face another day. This roller coaster went on for months.

The situation continued until I finally decided to seek help from a doctor. The diagnosis was anxiety and depression disorder, and I knew it was going to be a long road to recovery. I hoped that my workplace would show some understanding and compassion towards my situation. After enduring months of challenges at work, I eventually applied for work safe to assist with my situation. Through my journal, I was able to recover the necessary details for the investigation. I obtained medical treatment from work-safe-approved doctors and therapists, yet the investigation of my case took over a year. During this time, lawyers, investigators, and doctors advised me to abandon the case, as I would not receive a positive outcome.

Sharing the reason for my constant sickness with my parents was not an easy task. I expected them to react negatively and discourage me from pursuing anything further. However, to my surprise, my father showed empathy and understood my situation. He was upset about what had been going on and offered words of encouragement not to give up. Drawing from his own experience with his eye injury, he reminded me of the importance of fighting for what is right and that the truth would be discovered. His words emboldened me to keep pushing forward.

Numerous challenges and obstacles have marked my journey as I fought tirelessly for my human rights and work safe cases. From the struggle of proving my rights were violated to deciphering complex workplace regulations, I faced countless challenges. Through unwavering commitment and determination, I ultimately emerged victorious in both cases. When I informed my father of my triumph, he was amazed that I had achieved this without legal assistance or a lawyer. This experience has left me stronger and more confident, equipped to handle any future challenges with perseverance and resolve.

As time passed, the legal battles I have faced strengthened my determination to seek justice and fairness. My commitment to equality reflects my belief in upholding the rights and dignity of all individuals. I recognize the importance of advocating for both me and those who may be marginalized or overlooked. My commitment is to advocate for equality, ensuring that everyone is treated with the respect they deserve. My past experiences and the challenges I have faced have forged me into a resilient, determined individual who is unafraid to fight for what I believe in. I am committed to challenging systemic inequalities and defending human rights. I am a passionate advocate for justice.

As the days and months went by, COVID hit the world. I was worried about my parents, as both were over 70. I went through the months without going outside due to my health issues. I was afraid of catching COVID, so I stayed home every day. I received a frantic call from my mother saying Father had passed away. I felt my whole world shattered, and I could not breathe or think. I was his girl, always by his side, and now he is gone. We were all shattered by the death. Little did I know that would have been the last time I talked to my father. I told him we would celebrate his birthday and go out for dinner. I was not feeling well; my anxiety was so bad I could not leave the house. I was physically sick, vomiting each time I got ready to leave. My father was so understanding, and he would always support me emotionally. He was my rock.

I began a journey of introspection, searching for sources of joy and seeking a deeper sense of purpose in my life. In my quest for answers, I realized that some questions had no immediate answers and that finding peace would take some time. The absence of my father left a profound void, and I understood that nothing could ever truly replace him in my heart. Mother was alone now, and I tried to be there for her. My son or daughter and I would go with my mother to her eye appointments. All this time, I never heard or observed Elizabeth drive my mother or go with her. I guess everyone else was busy living their life.

I do not know when or how I got elected to take care of my parents and do everything for them. I would read their mail, do follow-ups, and reply to them. I would take them to their appointments at government offices or hospitals. I helped them apply for their old-age benefits and do their taxes every year. If they needed my help I was always there at their side. I never moved out of the province. Unlike my siblings, I always stayed close to help them.

Michael loved to travel, so he would always be away, whether it was Mexico, Europe, or Central America. He lived in Mexico for a year and then lived in Vegas as well. Elizabeth was living in another province and did not keep in touch; my parents hardly spoke to her. She was always too busy with her single life. After years of being missing, Rani returned, and it was for Father's funeral. She was only there for a purpose, as she had never spoken to them for over 30 years. Mother called me to say that Rani searched the whole house for Father's will and documents. No one wanted Mother to deal with her, but Mother wanted to give her a chance to change her ways.

I had mixed emotions about inviting Rani for dinner at a Brown's social house, and my husband was unhappy about her presence. At the restaurant, we had a private table. This event led to me feeling a sensation of unease. Rani and I had a strained relationship, and being around her brought back unpleasant memories. I tried to forget the past and try to mend our relationship. I gave her many opportunities to try to change her attitude and behavior. She refused to acknowledge her behavior and did not want to work on the relationship.

I could not help but think back to 1985 when she visited and shared her divorce news. Our father was furious, and he kicked her out of the house. Our mother intervened, asking me to let Rani stay for the night, and I reluctantly agreed, unaware of the shocking events that would unfold. Unbeknownst to Kris and me, Rani undressed and stood in front of us in her birthday suit. I was torn between my morals and my desire to get rid of her. After struggling to find my voice, I finally yelled at her to put her clothes back on. It took her several hours to leave. I was in shock, in disbelief, and appalled that this was my older sister. Rani's disturbing behavior and disregard for rules, values, or even morals were evident in her actions that night. She was the opposite of me in every way.

There was so much one could take from Rani. All of us were uptight as to what drama would unfold with her. She was known as a drama queen in the family. Rani started to get physically aggressive toward me. She started to hit and jab me in the ribs and stomach with her cane, calling me Moti (fatty) like she used to when we were little. We dropped her off at Mother's as fast as we could. Overall, the dinner with her was a tense and uncomfortable experience.

As I continued to reach out to her with kindness, it became increasingly clear that her combative and aggressive behavior was rooted in deeper issues that required attention. While it was challenging to navigate this difficult situation, I could not help but recognize that as adults, we have to take responsibility for our actions – and hers were not just hurtful but also a cry for help.it is possible her behavior was not entirely her fault, and as a result, I tried to approach the situation with empathy.

My husband and I discussed it and decided to try to be more understanding toward her. It would be hard, as she was constantly belittling me, but we did not want to make her condition any worse by mistreating her. We had to be patient and hope she received the help she needed to overcome her problems. Michael's suggestion to treat her with kid gloves was something we both took to heart. We knew it would be a challenge to deal with her mood swings, but we had to remain calm and supportive. It was the only way we could help her. I was still a little skeptical of her, and my husband said we should give her a chance. I said I would keep an open mind.

When Michael called to update me that Rani was returning home and was currently at the airport, it was frantic. She was denied boarding and missed her flight, leading him to buy a new ticket for her. The news that she was finally on her way home brought immense relief to our family. As we said our goodbyes, there was a palpable sense of relief in the air. We all knew that dealing with her behavior had been extremely challenging.

We learned a lot during this experience about empathy and the importance of treating others with kindness and understanding.

We wished Rani all the best and hoped that she could find peace and happiness in her life. It was a difficult journey, but we were grateful for the opportunity to help her and make a positive impact on her life.

I thought I was having a difficult time dealing with my father's death. All of us forgot that Mother was dealing with it as well. She was dealing with depression and anxiety, along with her diabetes. Mother was always sad and seemed lonely. Michael moved back to town and worked locally. He was there for Mother, supporting her. Michael told me not to worry; he would look after her, and then he said to focus on my health issues. Finally, our mother seemed to be getting a little better with Michael at home.

I was grateful for his support and knew that he was the best person for the job. He had always been close to Mother because he was her only son. I knew Michael would do everything in his power to make sure Mother was taken care of and she was getting the help she needed. I was grateful for his help and support throughout this difficult time. He had been there for us when we needed him most, and I knew that we could always count on him to be there for us in the future.

Mother spoke to me about losing Father and how she had to remove her mangal sutra (marriage necklace). She went on to say, "You do not know how much it means to you until you lose your husband." She went on to tell me, "You should wear your mangal sutra as you are married'. I only wore my mangal sutra at family functions or when attending the temple. I did not feel that connection to it as Mother felt to her mangal sutra; I guess it was from years of marriage issues. Also, the other fact is that Kris did not wear a wedding ring, which I kept telling him to start wearing.

I listened to Mother and tried to understand where she was coming from. I could tell how much the loss of Father was affecting her, especially because they had been married for a very long time. I knew wearing a mangal sutra was an important tradition in a Hindu marriage, but I did not feel as attached to it as she did. However, I understood the sentiment and respect behind it. I decided to wear my mangal sutra more often, even if it was just around the house, to show Mother that I understood and was trying to support her in any way I could. I hoped that it would bring some comfort and peace, even if it were a small gesture.

I realized that everyone has their own way of dealing with loss and grief. It was important for me to be there for Mother in any way she needed, even if it meant doing something that I did not necessarily connect with. I said to Mother, "If it makes you content, I am sure Father would not mind you honoring him by still wearing it." Mother smiled softly at me and thanked me for understanding. She went on to say that the mangal sutra was a reminder of the love and commitment shared between her and our father, and wearing it brought her a sense of peace and comfort.

Mother told me that Rani, or Elizabeth, never understood or wanted to talk about anything related to our traditions or cultures. We hugged, and I felt a sense of closeness and understanding between us, something that had been missing for a while. I knew that it was going to be a long journey. It is so important for parents to instill a sense of cultural pride in their children. Often, the desire to assimilate into Western culture causes us to forget or neglect the traditions and beliefs that make us who we are. I agreed with my mother and told her that it is up to us to carry on our cultural traditions and pass them down to future generations. I promised her that I would teach it to my children.

My mother was grateful for my support and said that she felt relieved to know that her traditions would be carried on. It was a heartwarming conversation, and it made me realize the importance of keeping our cultures and traditions alive. I told my mother that I was teaching my daughter and my non-Indian daughter-in-law how to wear sarees and more traditions. It just was not about traditional garments; our talks included my son and my non-Indian son-in-law, and I shared the back story of festivals, events, and culture as well. We talked about the significance of Diwali and Holi and the traditions and customs associated with them. I shared stories about our own experiences growing up and how our family celebrated these events. I realized that sharing our traditions and culture with our children and future generations is essential to keeping our identity and values alive.

Even though we live in a fast-paced, modern world, it is essential to hold onto our traditions and customs. As we finished our conversation, my mother thanked me for carrying forward our family traditions and emphasized the importance of passing them down to the younger generation. Mother further told me that no one wants to follow anything if it is not Western. It was a beautiful moment that I will always cherish, and it reinforced my commitment to preserving our culture and traditions for future generations.

In hindsight, by encouraging Mother to wear her mangal sutra, I was showing respect for her and our father's relationship while also reinforcing the value of our cultural practices. After talking to Mother, I learned that daughters could keep the mangal sutra as a keepsake. It is essential to create a balance between accommodating society and preserving our roots. In Hindu traditions and religion, it was once customary that when a husband died, the mangal sutra, a sacred necklace worn by married Hindu women, was buried with him as a symbol of their eternal bond. Similarly, if the wife passed away, the mangal sutra would be laid to rest alongside her. This practice reflected the belief in the inseparable connection between the spouses, even in the afterlife.

However, as times have evolved, societal norms and personal choices have influenced a change in this tradition. Nowadays, it is more common for the mangal sutra to be passed down as an heirloom within the family or returned to the wife as a cherished memento of her marital commitment. This shift highlights the fluidity and adaptability of cultural practices in the face of changing circumstances and individual preferences.

Going back to marriage, I believe that allowing our children the freedom to choose their partners or spouses enables them to grow, make commitments, and learn responsibility. One of the challenges Kris and I encountered was adapting to the differences. When my children began dating individuals who were non-Indian in high school and were invited over for dinners, Kris and I had to adjust our views and traditions to embrace this new ideology within our family. However, I trusted my children's choices because they would have to live with and commit to their partners, allowing them to decide how they wanted to live their lives.

In a less than ideal scenario, my parents held firm beliefs-that no child or grandchild of theirs should engage in relationships, let alone marry someone outside of our culture. The rigid mindset exposes the biases and discriminatory tendencies that, unfortunately, still prevail. The decision of who to be with should not be left in the hands of parents or grandparents, and it is disheartening to witness such prejudiced behavior. Building and maintaining relationships can be an uphill task, especially when the partners of their children do not adhere to the same cultural background. I put an end to this notion that, as parents we did not demand any such expectations from our children and would not let my parents dictate outdated notions. My parents could not control their younger children, so why would I let them control my children?

I can say that my relationships with my son-in-law and daughter-in-law took time and a lot of effort. Our relationship is good, and we are a close-knit family. We spend every other weekend together, sharing meals and catching up on what is going on in life. I would not trade our family for anything. I believe in giving a person a chance to get to know the family, and you may never know what hidden talents or personalities you get; it could be that hidden gem your children were looking for in their lives.

We have learned to appreciate the time we have together and make the most of every moment. We know that life is unpredictable and that we must cherish the people we hold dear while we still have them. Despite the loss of my father, we are grateful for the time we had with him and will continue to honor his memory.

One day, I went to visit Mother and Michael at their house. As soon as I walked in, I noticed a difference in Mother. She seemed more energetic and happier. Mother had decorated the living room with photos of our father and the family. We all sat down and had a cup of tea. Mother told me that she had been feeling better since Michael moved back. He had been spending more time with her and taking her to all the medical appointments.

We talked about Father and shared some happy memories. It felt good to reminisce and laugh. I realized we were all healing in our way and that we needed each other to heal. As we sat there and talked, Mother shared stories of her and our father's younger days. She talked about how much they loved each other and how much they enjoyed spending time together. Michael chimed in and added some stories of his own about Father. We all laughed and shared our favorite memories.

At that moment, I realized that even though Father was no longer with us, his memory lived on through us. We were keeping his spirit alive by sharing stories and remembering the good times. It felt like he was still with us in some small way. As we finished our tea, I hugged Mother and Michael tightly. It was a comforting feeling to know we loved each other and were there for each other during this difficult time. After we visited Mother's house, I felt a sense of peace. I knew that it would take time to heal from our father's passing fully, but we were all on the right track.

Thinking back on that visit, I realized how important it is to spend time with loved ones during difficult times. That small act of sitting down and sharing tea with Mother and Michael helped lift our spirits and bring us closer together. It was also a reminder that life goes on and that we should cherish the moments we have with those we love. As time passed, we found new ways to honor Father's memory. Looking through the photo album of him and his life. Looking through the pictures with each other brought us comfort and helped us keep his memory alive. In the end, it was the love and support of family and friends that helped me, Mother, and Michael slowly heal. Michael had been a great support system for both Mother and me, and I was grateful for him.

As Kris and I spoke, I thought about how life can sometimes be difficult, but with the right people by your side, you can get through anything. I learned that even in the darkest of times, we could always count on each other and our love for each other. The loss of my father changed my life in profound ways. It made me appreciate the importance of family and how quickly things can change.

As the head of our household, my father's decisions heavily influenced our family dynamics. His rules were to be respected and followed. However, his passing left us struggling to find a new way forward. Without his leadership, things felt uncertain and unfamiliar. It was a challenging and eye-opening experience that showed me the importance of cherishing the time we have with our loved ones. After my father's death, I decided to heed Michael's advice and prioritize my well-being. Understanding the importance of self-care, my husband supported me by driving me to therapy sessions, enabling me to focus on my mental health. Recognizing that I had neglected my emotional well-being for far too long, I knew it was time for a change. With Michael taking care of our mother, I was able to focus on myself, allowing me to embark on a journey of emotional healing.

I decided to keep myself busy by taking improvement courses. I brushed up on report writing, interviewing, and communication. I then thought, why stop here since I was doing so well? I started a private investigator program and was so excited. It felt like a million years since I felt excited about anything in life. I got that warm feeling in the pit of my stomach. I spent every waking moment studying and reading. It gave me a sense of purpose and meaning in my life that I was desperately missing.

It was challenging work, but I felt alive and motivated. My family was proud of me for taking charge of my life and pursuing something that made me happy. I was busy; my time was spent in class and doing homework. It was a good feeling to be busy again. I was proud of myself and my achievements. I had overcome so much, both emotionally and physically. I was on my way to recovering from my traumatic experience. My family was happy for me that I was finally doing something productive.

My mother said, "Your father would be proud of your achievements." I wished he was still around; everything would be okay. He had a way with words, and just his positivity made anyone feel good. But I knew deep down that his spirit was still with me, guiding me every step of the way. I remember as an adult he encouraged me to pursue my dreams and never give up on them. I knew he would be proud of me now.

I felt proud of myself as I sat in my room and looked at the certificates. It was amazing! The dedication, long hours, and hard work had paid off. I knew that my father would be proud of his daughter, he was looking down on me from wherever he was. I promised myself that I would continue performing diligently to bring him pride every single day. I ultimately finished the program course of study and acquired my private investigator license. I experienced a tremendous sense of success and, at last, thought I had discovered my real purpose in life.

My father's words of wisdom and positivity will continue to inspire me, and I will always carry his memory in my heart. Even though he may no longer be physically present, his influence and his love will always be with me, and I will continue to strive for success in his memory. Father's generosity and kindness towards newcomers to Canada are truly inspiring. He understood how difficult it was to start a new life in a foreign land and wanted to make the process as smooth as possible for others. His willingness to welcome strangers into our home and help them integrate into Canadian society showed me the importance of empathy, compassion, and standing up for what is right.

Losing my brother Michael in such a traumatic way has been a devastating blow to our family, especially for my mother. He was helping her heal after my father's passing, and we feel lost without him. It still does not feel real, and I keep expecting him to walk through the door at any moment. My mother got more and more depressed, and she tried everything in her power to pick herself up and get out of the house. But as she aged, her health kept getting worse. Then, losing her husband and her son nine months later was the biggest shock in her life.

Hearing people say that it will get easier with time feels unrealistic, and the grieving process has taken a toll on me physically and emotionally. The ups and downs of emotions are exhausting. Grief is a process that cannot be rushed, and everyone experiences it differently. It is understandable to feel overwhelmed and lost. During this difficult time, it is important to take care of yourself by getting enough rest, eating well, and asking for help when you need it. You should also allow yourself to feel all the different emotions that come with grief—sadness, anger, confusion, and more.

By sharing memories and anecdotes about our brother, we support one another. It will become easier over time to choose positive moments over the grief of losing him. We shall continue to pay tribute to his memory in our unique ways since we realize that he will always be a part of our family's history. It seems strange not to run into him each time I go into town sometimes. I remember my brother's recognizable voice calling out to me. When I was driving on Lougheed Highway, in the adjacent lane, he asked me where I was heading. After Father died, he was constantly concerned about my well-being. Father had urged him to watch out for me.

It does not feel fair that we lost so much, but whoever said life was fair, we all expect some ups and downs in life, but this kind of loss is so close together. It is time to try to pick up the pieces of our lives and heal. It will not be easy, but we will have to learn to live without my brother's presence physically around us. We will miss his jokes, his laughter, and his generosity. We will hold onto the memories we shared with him, and his legacy will continue to live through us. We will honor his memory by being there for each other, just as he was there for us. We will continue his kindness, generosity, and compassion as a way of keeping his spirit alive. We will cherish the times we spent with him and remember the impact he had on our lives.

Looking back on that difficult time in our lives, I realized just how important it is to support each other, even when we are facing struggles. We are a team, and we need to be there for each other no matter what comes our way. I could not help but feel overwhelmed and helpless. The weight of sorrow hung heavy on my shoulders, and it seemed like every day was just another reminder of the pain and loss we felt. Father was already a devastating blow, one that we were trying to come to terms with. Just when we thought we could start healing, tragedy struck again with the loss of my brother Michael.

Michael worked in Alberta, but since Father's passing, he worked locally to be closer to the family, especially for our mother. It was late at night when he decided to go to the bank machine. He told Mother he had work in the morning and needed to get cash. He left and never came back home. It was not like him to not tell her where or when he would be back. So, Mother started to get scared and worried. She called me, panicked and frightened about the situation. Mother had Elizabeth and Brian there already to help her deal with things until I got there.

Mother tried to call Michael, but his phone went to voice mail. She started to get worried and anxious. She called his friends and colleagues, but nobody had heard from him. Mother reported him missing to the police, and they started their investigation. They checked the bank surveillance cameras and found footage of Michael withdrawing money from the ATM. However, the camera did not capture who was with him or where he went after that.

Days passed, but there was no trace of Michael. Mother and the rest of us could not bear the uncertainty and fear of not knowing what happened to him. We prayed and hoped for his safe return, but deep down, we knew something was not right. He was robbed sometime after the bank visit and went missing. No clues were present—no phone calls or anything. It is such a difficult situation when someone you love goes missing with no idea where they went.

Our family searched everywhere for him. Elizabeth and Michael's friends went through the neighborhood, looking through bushes, parks, lakes, and abandoned buildings. There were no signs of where he was or what happened. I sent emails to homeless centers, churches, and government offices, hoping someone would have seen him and have information. The police finally located him and informed the family that he was deceased. It was like a nightmare; I could not believe my ears, and my heart did not want to accept it. I do not know how all of us are going to get through this situation. It was as if we were being continuously punished for something unknown, and it left me feeling an overwhelming sense of despair.

We held a funeral for Michael, and it was a somber affair. Everyone in attendance was drowning in their sorrow, feeling the weight of the loss. It was hard to hear people speak about his amazing qualities, as we all knew that he had been taken away from us too soon. There was so much more that he could have accomplished and so much more life for him to live. I hoped that he knew how much he was loved and appreciated. How much he meant to all of us. After the funeral was completed, the aftermath was the most difficult part.

Life continued, and without him, we all felt lost. My heart ached, and it missed a beat every time I drove or strolled by the bank where he vanished. I had to tell myself that it was not him if I saw someone bald or with a similar build. Anywhere he was spotted was a reminder of him, and that hurt. I began to wonder what else we could have done. Did we overlook anything? Everyone was plagued by these questions. Perhaps disasters such as this could have been avoided if we had been more alert and present.

Amidst all this pain, there was also a sense of community. People came together to mourn, to support each other, and to honor our brother's memory. It was a reminder that even in the darkest of times, we are not alone. And maybe, just maybe, that is enough to keep moving forward. Each passing day brought new challenges, and it felt like we were trapped in a never-ending cycle of misery. Life seemed to be testing us, pushing us to our limits, and I did not know how to fix it. It felt like there was no escape from the darkness that had enveloped our lives. But amidst the despair, I knew I had to find a way to keep going. I had to find strength, not only for myself but for my family. We needed to support each other and find solace in our shared grief. It was not easy, and the wounds of our loss would never fully heal, but we had to find a way to move forward.

I sought comfort in the memories of our loved ones, cherishing the moments we had together and finding solace in the love that remained. It was through this love that I began to realize that life is hard; we were not punished but rather unfortunate circumstances that we had no control over. I had to accept that life dealt us a cruel hand, and it was not our fault. We could not fix everything, but we could choose how we responded to the challenges we faced. I started seeking support from family, friends, and even professional help to navigate through the storm of grief.

Chapter 15

Time, Healing, and Deja Vu

S lowly, as time passed, the wounds began to heal, and the weight of sorrow became a little easier to bear. I learned that it was okay to feel pain and to mourn the losses, but I also had to find the strength to keep moving forward. Life would never be the same, but I could find a way to rebuild and find happiness amidst the grief. So, as I confronted the unfairness of it all, I realized that the true measure of strength lies not in our ability to avoid pain and sorrow but in our resilience to face it head-on and keep going.

While it was a difficult journey, I knew that taking care of myself was important not only for my well-being but also for the well-being of my loved ones. It allowed me to be more present and supportive of them during this difficult time. Though the pain of loss will never completely go away, taking care of my mental health has allowed me to better cope with it and be there for others in the future.

My daughter told me, "You have to get up and be strong." My son was supportive as well, saying, "We love you, and we cannot see you struggling like this alone; we are here for you." My husband held my hand and kept me steady. He reminded me of how strong and stubborn I could be. Their words of encouragement and support gave me the strength to keep fighting. I knew I could not give up and let my grief consume me.

I had to be there for my family and myself. I started getting up earlier in the morning, trying to take care of my physical health as well as my mental health. I made appointments with a therapist and doctor to help me manage my depression and anxiety. Slowly but surely, I started feeling a little better. My family continued to be my rock, always there to lend an ear or a shoulder to cry on. We talked about our loss and shared stories of our loved ones. It helped us heal as a family. We all tried our best to move forward and cherish the memories we had with Michael. We found solace in knowing that he was now at peace and reunited with my father in heaven.

It was a difficult time, but it was also a time of growth and strength for us. We learned to rely on each other and to appreciate the little moments of joy and happiness in our lives. As a family, we also learned to appreciate the beauty and fragility of life and to never take it for granted. Even though we still miss our loved ones, we are now more resilient and better equipped to face future challenges together. It has not been easy, but with the love and support of my family, I have been able to find the strength to keep going. I know that there will still be hard days, but I also know that I am not alone and that I have a strong support system to rely on.

When you think life has given you enough problems, Kris came to me with what looked like tears in his eyes; I felt something was wrong, so I asked him, "Did you lose your job?". He answered, "Yes." How did you know? I felt terrible. As I said, it seems like it from the look on your face. How could I have been so absorbed in my issues that I did not notice the struggles he was going through? We talked for hours that night, and I learned just how stressed and anxious he had been feeling.

As we began to navigate this new challenge together, it struck me just how much Kris had been there for me, even during my worst moments. Through my health struggles, he stood by my side every step of the way, supporting and comforting me even when it felt like the entire world was against us. Throughout this whole process of looking for another job, he was worried that we did not have extended health to cover my medication. I told him we would figure something out.

Now, it was my turn to be there for him. We worked together to find ways to make ends meet, from cutting back on expenses to looking for new job opportunities. There were moments of stress and worry, but through it all, we managed to stay strong for each other. We stayed up at night drafting his new resume and doing cover letters. Eventually, Kris did find a new job, I was proud of him and grateful to have him back in better spirits. I was impressed that he did not sit back and get depressed or change his perspective on work. He was unemployed for a few weeks.

My mother went in for gallbladder surgery. The doctor said she needed another surgery because her bowel was perforated in two places. Later, the doctor informed the family that she needed a blood transfusion to save her life. I recall a previous conversation with Mother: "Do you need to get the surgery? But she said the doctor wants me to get it done." Sometimes, I sit and wonder if we should have waited, but unfortunately, no one knows the future.

Brian was at the hospital when he called me to say Mother was awake, so I spoke to her, telling her to be strong and come home. All I heard after that was, "They are killing me." Mother's voice echoed through the phone, and then Brian told me he had to go. That was the last conversation I had with my mother. After the procedure, Mother did not recover and was placed on a ventilator. She kept getting infections; I believe we were already too late in saving Mother's life. The doctor told us that she needed another surgery to save her life, and we needed to put a tube to help her breathe.

The family saw how weak Mother was, and she was not getting any better. The family decided that we could not see her suffer anymore and decided to stop trying to save her as it was not working. After three weeks of suffering, Mother died, leaving all of us emotionally broken and speechless. Routine surgery ended up costing our family everything; no money in the world could replace what we lost that day. I cannot believe my mother is gone, and everyone is greedy, fighting over money and property. I thought family was more important, but nowadays, some people only care about materialistic things, and it is hard for me to understand why my family could not come together in this time of grief.

Rani's primary focus was on the money, and she made it clear that she wanted to ensure her eleven children and three grandchildren received equal shares of the inheritance. To achieve this, she resorted to manipulation, trying to coerce me into pooling all our inheritances to benefit her children with larger shares. Additionally, she persistently urged me to talk to Elizabeth and convince her to cooperate with her plans. However, I firmly refused to engage in that conversation and instead told her, "It is your plan; you should do what you want."

Amidst the manipulation, Rani's communication turned nasty as she bombarded me with hurtful and unpleasant text messages. Accusing me of greediness and selfishness for not sharing with her children, she placed the responsibility for her children's financial future on my shoulders. Despite her tactics, I firmly maintained that my role in raising her children had been fulfilled, and they were now independent adults.

Recognizing the toxicity of the situation and the unlikelihood of finding a resolution, I made the difficult decision to cut off communication with Rani for the sake of my well-being. Hopes for cooperation were shattered when Elizabeth revealed a similar mentality driven by greed. To achieve her goals, she engaged in deceptive behavior, fabricating a story about being at my mother's lawyer's office while I babysat her child.

However, the truth emerged: Elizabeth had been at her own lawyer's office, attempting to transfer everything under her name. Canadian law prevented her from successfully executing her deceitful plan despite her attempts. Even Brian, who went with Elizabeth and sought legal advice, disclosed the information when he came back that Elizabeth was furious with the lawyer for requiring equal distribution of the inheritance among the three siblings.

In my opinion, when electing an administrator, you need to pick someone who is not the beneficiary. The greed and dishonesty that surface when money is involved turn even families against each other. Upon knowing if you are left out of the will or if there is no will and you have to share the inheritance, no matter how much you think you can trust anyone, there is always an opportunity to be dishonest or cheat. As in our situation, we learned that once you appoint an administrator, it costs a significant amount of money to remove them. If you are experiencing a similar situation, I hope my story sheds light on this topic.

Closing

In closing, as I reflect on my journey, I must admit that I was once a product of my parents' views and the cultural norms of Indian society. At just sixteen years old, I found myself in a forced arranged marriage and without a choice. It was a path my parents enforced due to family traditions, Indian culture, and societal pressures., but I could not alter the past. Instead, I choose to focus on the present with a positive outlook, determined to make things right. From taking on the responsibility of raising my nephews to embracing motherhood with my children, my journey has been filled with challenges and responsibilities.

However, I never lost sight of my desire for education. Despite juggling the act of caregiving, I decided to go back to school and then continue to college, determined to fulfill my educational journey on my terms. Through hard work and perseverance, I managed to strike a balance between my family and my academic pursuits. My story is a testament to my dedication and the importance of personal growth and development.

One thing I hold dear in this life is my son and daughter, precious souls who bring immense joy into my existence. I cherish them deeply, just as I have nurtured my nephews without any expectations or demands. It is with faith that I believe God watches over me, always ensuring fairness in life's trials. Above all else, my children's happiness and well-being take precedence in my life.

Yet, I also derive great joy from pursuing my passion and indulging in hobbies that ignite my soul. I have come to appreciate the beauty of each moment, taking nothing for granted. Life's brevity reminds me of its precious nature, compelling me to make the most of every second. Love, kindness, and gratitude guide me as I aim to lead a life worth living. Amidst the adherence to cultural norms, I made a conscious decision as an adult to break free and discover my independence. It was through pursuing my education and career that I gained not only a sense of self-reliance but also the means to support my family financially. There is one thing that my father said to me that stands out: ***"Learning never stops, and life requires a lot of learning and growing."***

This newfound freedom allowed me to fight for what I believed in, stand up against injustice, and question norms that brought no benefit to anyone. My only regret is that I should have pursued my education sooner in life. Through the years, I have learned invaluable lessons from the choices I made. These experiences have shaped me into the person I am today, and as I forge ahead, I am committed to maintaining a positive outlook in life.

My true aspiration is to be a guiding light for my children, teaching them the importance of authenticity and staying true to their beliefs. I bravely challenge societal norms that hinder progress and invite change. Despite the setbacks and struggles I have faced. Optimism fills my heart as I envision a future where faith, hard work, and positivity make anything possible.

Though my life may have veered from the path I once envisioned as a child, I accept it wholeheartedly, making the best of what I have been given; in my own right, I have carved out a name for myself and found fulfillment in my chosen career and life. Throughout this remarkable journey, I have learned that life is unpredictable, and it is perfectly fine not to have everything figured out. Adaptability is key, embracing the unexpected and remain open to different possibilities.

In the face of challenges and setbacks, my strength and resilience have grown immeasurably throughout my life. In hindsight, I now realize that every experience, whether pleasant or painful, has shaped me. I am immensely grateful for the valuable life lessons and the incredible individuals who have crossed my path. Though I may have lost a part of my identity along the way, I have gained so much more -strength, resilience, and a sense of gratitude. I navigate life with an open mind and open heart, determined to create a better present and future for not only myself but also those I hold dear.

I hope that by sharing my story, I can inspire others who may find themselves in similar situations. It is possible to break free from cultural norms and societal expectations and to live a life that resonates with one's authentic self. Yes, the journey may be arduous, but the rewards are immeasurable. I encourage everyone to believe in themselves and their limitless potential and never to abandon their dreams and aspirations. With determination, hard work, and a positive attitude, anything becomes possible.

In conclusion, my life story embodies a tale filled with obstacles, challenges, and setbacks. But through it all, I found strength, resilience, and faith to overcome. I boldly cast aside cultural norms and societal expectations to create a life that honors my true self. Pursuing my education, career, and passions became my compass, guiding me toward personal fulfillment.

Above all, my family's happiness and well-being remain my greatest priority as I strive to be a positive role model for my children. My life story is a testament to the triumph of the human spirit over adversity. It is a tale of breaking free, of unyielding determination, and the belief that impossible is just a word. I hope that my words will touch the hearts of those who read them, urging them to embrace their journey and craft a life of unapologetic authenticity. I focus on shaping a future brimming with promise and possibilities. I aspire to ignite inspiration within others, encouraging them to embrace their individuality and chase after their dreams with tenacity and positivity.

My love story did not start as romantic as falling in love and the emotions that go with it. Though it did not come from a book or movie has come full circle as now I have come to believe that if you are dedicated and persistent, you can overcome obstacles and find what you have been missing. Trying and sacrificing does not mean you are settling. It means that you are fine and have found your peace and where you want to belong. I am thankful for Kris, who became my rock and now treats me with love and care.

Overall, my family's story is one of resilience, perseverance, and adaptation. From the 1920s to the present day, our family has faced numerous challenges and obstacles but has always emerged stronger and more united. We have learned to adapt to our new culture and social environments, flexing and shifting our beliefs and values as necessary to survive and thrive. As we move into the future, my family's story serves as a reminder of the power of resilience, unity, and the importance of respect and compassion for all individuals, regardless of their background or beliefs.

Our experiences have taught us that we are all more alike than we are different and that the bonds of family and community can help us overcome any obstacle that comes our way. Unfortunately, since the death of my parents, the familial bonds have been strained, as my older sibling and the youngest sibling do not believe in my father's vision of family unity and strength. Love and family are inheritable things that everyone should have in their lives. It helps foster the concepts of empathy and compromise.

Thank you for joining me on my journey of self-discovery. Remember, you are strong, beautiful, and capable of achieving anything you set your mind to. Let us continue to uplift and inspire each other as we navigate through life's challenges. I would love - to connect with you further. Feel free to reach out to me on social media and share your stories of growth and empowerment. Together, we can create a community of support and encouragement. Keep shining brightly, my friends. I will leave you with the life quote that helped me on days when I felt I was drowning: *"We all strive to better ourselves, but sometimes, in the process, we lose ourselves. We need to focus on ourselves first; then we can truly be empowered and fruitful in our lives and help others as well"*.